ANDREWS Gordon BANKS Ian
n BIRCHENALL Jo   e
  Steve CLARIDGE   E
RE Tony COTTEE   S
KOV Dion DUBLIN Matt ELLIOTT
S Matty FRYATT Chris GARLAND
ON Lenny GLOVER Steve GUPPY
on HOLMES Sam HOLMES Steve
MARK Rob KELLY Maxine KERR
ON Craig LEVEIN Gary LINEKER
MARSHALL Ali MAUCHLEN Larry
CARTHY Mark McGHEE Frank
ROSE Gary MILLS Gordon MILNE
David NUGENT Frank O'FARRELL
vin PHILLIPS Matt PIPER David
  Paul RAMSEY Bobby ROBERTS
AMMELS Robbie SAVAGE Alan
  Gerry TAGGART Andrew TAYLOR
mmy WALSH Steve WALSH Arlo
WORTH Tommy WILLIAMS Frank
Tommy WRIGHT Alan YOUNG...

CAN'T BUY THAT FEELING

Simon Kimber & **Gary Silke**

Edited by **Derek Hammond**

CONKER

Conker Editions Ltd
22 Cosby Road
Littlethorpe
Leicester
LE19 2HF
Email: books@conkereditions.co.uk
Website: www.conkereditions.co.uk
First published by Conker Editions Ltd 2018

A CIP catalogue record for this book is available from the British Library.
13-digit ISBN: 978-1-9999008-1-6
Design and typesetting by Gary Silke.
Printed in the UK by Mixam.

"We could start enjoying it after the final whistle.
Knowing that you've won, and going up those stairs...
you can't buy that feeling. Knowing that there are 40,000
Leicester fans there, a lot of them grown men in tears."

Iwan Roberts

CONTENTS

Twenty-nine years ago, *The FOX* landed its first ever interview. It wasn't difficult to arrange, as our inaugural interviewee, Ian Baraclough, was dating assistant editor Matt Francis's sister at the time.

Over the three decades since then, we've racked up 130 interviews with players past and present, with managers, coaches, board members, famous fans, the son of a manager and the daughter of a chairman.

We've travelled the length and breadth of the country in search of our quarry. Muzzy Izzet was to be found just a mile down the road at his football academy in Whetstone, but awaydays have carried us as far afield as Torquay down south (home of former boss Frank O'Farrell) and Chester-le-Street up north (to visit Steve Howard). A prestigious international fixture had to be arranged to take on Paddy Byrne with notebook and pint of Guinness.

We've sat in the manager's office at Belvoir Drive faced with ten different City managers, and have stuck a dictaphone next to many a player having their lunch in the canteen after training.

We've found a quiet corner in a huge variety of locations over the years, from the Filbert Street dugout with Iwan Roberts to Gary Lineker's dressing room at the old BBC TV Centre in White City. A squash club on Frog Island (Paul Ramsey), a Pride Park executive box (Roger Davies), the bench at Burton Albion (Mike Whitlow) and Matt Elliott's open-topped car have all served a purpose.

The more recently retired or those still involved in the game or media tend to prefer to meet in hotels: Gary McAllister,

Steve Claridge, Alan Smith, David Nugent, Ian Marshall. Whereas the older chaps are happy to entertain you at home: Davie Gibson, Bobby Roberts, Jon Sammels, Andy Lochhead, Gordon Milne, Jimmy Walsh.

While all were perfect hosts, Mark Wallington went beyond the call of duty, taking us to his local and *insisting* on buying us dinner. "Your money's no good in Lincolnshire!"

Not surprisingly, the pub can produce a convivial atmosphere for an interview, and we met Carl Muggleton, Steve Walsh and Lenny Glover in the boozer for a pint or two – or, in Len's case, his pre-arranged 'fee' of a bottle of bubbly.

Having finally decided to collect all these interviews together, we read back through what is now a huge body of work and were struck by the way they form a giant tapestry of first-hand experiences of Leicester City over a period spanning 60 years. This is the inside story of the club from the late '50s, when a young Gordon Banks first arrived at Filbert Street, right through to the present day and the Premier League title era.

What also hit us was the poignancy of the passing of time. When we think of our heroes, we imagine them as athletic young men in their prime, in royal blue shirts with the fox on their chests. And yet we were often talking to old boys in their 70s or even 80s, and not always in the best of health. But, irrespective of age, every one of our interviewees was happy to recall stories of their glory days – reliving the whole corresponding range of emotions – and we were thrilled to listen.

As City fans, we've all come to know hundreds of players through their performance on the pitch, through potted biographies and football sticker images. But what about the real characters behind the blue shirts and the back-page reports?

We hope you enjoy this journey through the history of Leicester City in the company of the men who made it.

MiCKY ADAMS

Looking after number two

We went to Belvoir Drive to interview manager Dave Bassett, who proved unavailable. It was beyond the call of duty for his assistant to offer to stand in at no notice, still sweaty from training.

Is there part of you that's enjoying the challenge of this tough season?

"I've questioned my wisdom. I don't want that to sound disrespectful to anybody but for two years I've been used to winning games of football. I'm now working with a squad of players who are used to losing. It can take it out of you. The beauty of football is that you can lose a game on Wednesday but you're soon preparing for Saturday when you get another go. I knew this job was going to be a challenge, though I have been surprised by some things around the football club. I'd rather keep them to myself, though."

What did you find when you arrived?

"I found a group of players who were lacking in confidence, lacking in direction, lacking in motivation, lacking in fitness...

to start from the bottom has been difficult. I'm not having a pop at Peter Taylor. As a manager, you get judged firstly on results, but then also on the people that you bring into the club, staff and players. You have to say that they weren't good enough."

It can't have been an easy decision for you to leave Brighton...

"I could have carried on with a winning team, building my reputation and hopefully getting a job a bit further down the line. I like Harry Bassett, having worked with him before. The club was sold to me. The new stadium. Hopefully in the Premier League. We still cling to that. And the challenge. Perhaps I have a self-destruct button inside me – winning all those games wasn't good for me!"

The long-term plan here at the club involves you becoming manager...

"Well, Dave has got a contract for this year and next year, and I've got one for one year after that. Dave has the option of deciding when he's had enough, basically. In the summer, the option is available to him to take a back seat and let me get on with it."

Do you want the job?

"There would have to be certain things that would make me want the job. Certain things would have to change... I would think there would have to be a massive turnaround of players if we did get relegated. Or even if we managed to stay up. I suppose one of the reasons I got the job here was because I've worked with no money before, twice, and I've got two promotions. I don't know whether that attracted the board of directors to me in the first place."

If we do go down, how difficult would it

be to keep your best players?

"I think it would be nigh on impossible. Firstly, for their own ambitions, and secondly, could we afford to pay them what we're paying them now in the First Division? From a financial point of view it would be a disaster if we went down. There's only one player out of contract this summer; the rest, we're committed to in terms of wages. If we go down then the current squad is good enough to get us promoted, including the strikers, but finances might dictate that we can't keep that squad of players."

Are you surprised at the speed of the club's decline, considering the healthy state it was in 18 months ago?

"No, because it takes years and years to build up a football club. The foundations, the team spirit – it doesn't take a lot to destroy it. If you're playing a certain way and it's successful, then why change?"

Can we ask you about the TV show that covered the game at the Reebok? Did Dave Bassett discuss it with you?

"No, we don't have to discuss things like that. I personally don't like football programmes. They tend to show you in a certain light. Although that programme was about stress, I think most viewers would be a lot more interested in what was going on in the dressing room."

Yes, we were. Like Dave Bassett's heated reference to 'Wisey's poxy square balls...' How do you cope with pressure?

"It's funny, I mean I've been number two before, and I sleep at night. I don't wind myself up as much as I do when I'm a manager, making decisions. At a lower level of football you're the chief scout, a counsellor. You run everything, from top to bottom. Dave wakes up every morning and decides what we're going to do and how we're going to do it. 'Who am I going to talk to today? What meetings have I got? What games am I going to go to?' As a number two, you don't quite get that pressure."

Do you miss that?

"Yes, big time. I want the job if it's right for me. As I said before, I would want my own players in, maybe bring a different coach in. As a number two, sometimes you have to bite your tongue."

> "We share certain beliefs in terms of hard work and organisation, but we're also quite different."

13

Micky ADAMS

Crisis management

Fourteen years after our previous encounter we were invited round to Micky's house in Market Harborough, and found the former City boss in a much more relaxed and reflective mood. He'd only recently finished with Sligo Rovers, his last management job.

Back in 2001/02, you became manager as soon as relegation was confirmed – closely followed by the club entering administration...

"Well it seemed obvious to me and Dave that there could be problems from our first day. We were told we had to raise a million pounds in three months, because the debt was piling up. After relegation that got worse and we started selling people – Matt Piper to Sunderland. We sold Gary Rowett to Charlton with a bad knee – I'm not sure how we managed that, but we did. Robbie Savage went. It was a

case of clearing the decks as best we could. John Elsom, the chairman at the time, told me at four o'clock in the afternoon that we wouldn't go into administration, and by that evening I was in a meeting at the Leicester Hilton being told that we would be going into administration the following morning."

Redundancies, no new signings, and a players' wage deferral. Was it hard to stop the club's problems becoming a distraction on the playing side?

"Well, the beauty of it was that we were winning games. We used it towards a siege mentality rather than an excuse for failure. Yes, we had to eat mince every day, so what? Let's get on with it. No one was coming to help us out, there was no one on a white charger coming over the hill. You want your money back? Then get promoted!"

And when that task was accomplished, you began rebuilding the squad with some very experienced players...

"Yes, not necessarily the players I would have picked, but we had no money for transfers, only wages. This meant we had to go round looking for Premier League 'misfits' who had experience but weren't quite in the prime of their youth. We had Les Ferdinand, Keith Gillespie, Craig Hignett – no spring chickens. I must be one of the unluckiest managers ever, to get promoted to the Premier League and not be able to spend a penny. I look back on that season now and I kick myself for certain situations that occurred, though I was a young manager in the toughest league in the world."

Later that season the players were involved in an incident in La Manga, which can't have helped matters?

"It was a complete set-up. It didn't feel right from the start. The hotel was for sale, the whole complex was for sale, and there was nobody there except for us. As our coach pulled up you could see straight into reception, and the three, shall we say 'scantily-clad' young ladies in there. I stood up at the front and said, 'Your time's your own from now until tomorrow morning, behave yourselves. Have a drink if you want, but I'll be working you hard in training so no excuses in the morning. And by the way, have a look at those girls in reception, please don't fall for that one.'

The next afternoon, after training, there was banging on my bedroom door. I saw the police detective and feared the worst. I thought someone had died, because it felt like one of those knocks on the door. At that point they told me there'd been 'a complaint of rape and sexual misconduct amongst your players.' We went to the police station and, as soon as we were in, an armed policeman popped up by each door. Steffen Freund is the first one called up, and he'd actually admitted that he'd been with one of the girls. Two minutes later he comes back out and says, 'I can go, I'll see you later.' Off he went. Paul Dickov was the next one in. Five minutes later he comes out, but he's handcuffed! And that was it for the rest of them, they were all done the same and led away. I had to go and ring all their wives up. I could enlarge on a few things, but you'll have to wait for my book!"

That's not really in the job description for a football manager?

"I've actually done a few lectures for

"The chairman told me at four o'clock in the afternoon that we wouldn't go into administration..."

the FA on Crisis Management because I've been with three clubs that have gone into administration and had a load of players arrested, so I know all about it."

Who do you think was your best signing?

"Well, I didn't sign many. I suppose one of the best in my time there, though it would go down on Dave's record, would be Paul Dickov. He was a cheap signing, and he did a very good shift at Leicester. There were a few who didn't perform up to their reputations for us. Martin Keown was forever moaning. We played at Millwall in the new all-black kit with the blue sash. Martin was at it: 'Why are we wearing all black, it's red hot?' He never stopped: 'At Arsenal I used to stand here and Thierry Henry used to be behind me.' 'Well, with the greatest of respect, Martin, you're not at f***ing Arsenal any more.' Me and him clashed big time. I think he was touting for my job."

Happy days: sandwiched between administration and ignominy.

Martin ALLEN

Time will tell the wiser

Martin Allen's tenure as manager was only four games long, but he still had time to pack in a huge amount of intrigue and controversy – along with an oddly intense *FOX* interview.

When did you know you were going to be a professional footballer?

"I was a professional footballer when I was eight. I had to practise my ball skills from a young age, and my dad would test me. Off the field, my mum taught me about manners, behaviour, conduct, politeness. On the field, my dad taught me the total opposite. No friends on the field. Competitive. Winner. He was manager of Cheltenham Town, and I used to go training with them when I was 12."

What kind of a player did you become?

"I was a player who could compete. I never liked losing. I used to take it hard when I lost. I think what you could say about me is I made the absolute most

of the ability I had. Hard training, extra training, extra practice. Running long distances."

What were the highlights of your career?

"Scoring a 30-yard belter at Filbert Street in 1986. The ball came forward from our right back. I was out near the touchline. It bounced once and I hit a volley across my shoulder and it flew into the far corner. The ball stuck up in the stanchion. It was magic, an unbelievable feeling. However, I got sent off five minutes later."

You retired early, when you were just 32...

"Yes, it was down to wear and tear on my knees. It's a nightmare scenario when you finish your football career and it dawns on you that you've got to start all over again. During a football career it was like there was a tree down the bottom of the garden that had golden pieces of fruit on it. When your career finishes, you go down there and discover that someone has taken your tree away."

Alan Pardew gave you your first coaching role at Reading, but you really made your name at Brentford...

"On the first day I put up a list of 18 players I'd be training with. I told the star player and crowd favourite that it would be best if he got hooked up with another club – and the same message to another nine players. Everyone said it was a mad, crazy thing to do. We had two magical years. We were hard-working on a low budget. Well organised, disciplined. We could go anywhere and beat clubs that had budgets five times the size of ours. Brentford actually got into the Play-offs with a negative goal difference; but at MK Dons I wanted my sides to be more creative and score more goals. We adapted our aims, and now my challenge here is to keep that going. Keep making progress."

What were your first impressions when you arrived at Leicester City?

"We pulled up outside the main stand and we all just stood there with big smiles on our faces. It was our personal dream, an opportunity like this. After a while, I said, 'Look, we've not come up here to hang around and be happy. We've got to do things our way and make our mark. There's going to be a lot of hard work while we set it up how we want it to be. We haven't come to Leicester to mess about.'"

How does the decision making shake down between you and chairman Milan Mandaric?

"Selling players. Values: my opinion, chairman's opinion. Come to a mutual opinion and do deals. Recruitment of players: I have ideas, the chairman has ideas. Do the research, put everything on the table. We are very, very thorough. We make decisions in the best interest of the football club."

You place real stress on your relationship with the fans...

"Yes, I always have done, really. I know every supporter is a manager. Every supporter comes to the game and questions who is playing. Fact. Every supporter knows who should be taken off and who should come on in his place. When we win, the manager never really gets a mention, because it's just, 'We won!' And when we lose, every supporter says the manager should have done this or that. It's the same all over the country. You want to see your team win, and when they don't win, it hurts. But you still go back because you love them and it's in your blood.

> "We need to improve in certain areas but, of course, I won't say where. That would be disrespectful."

Without being disrespectful to religion, football supporting is a type of religion. It's a homage."

How far do you think can you take this club?

"It's a big job. It's a big club with a very, very ambitious chairman, but also a realistic chairman. Last Saturday, there were times when the atmosphere in the Walkers Stadium made the hair on the back of my neck stand up. It made my spine straighten up a bit and I had to do my big sniff, steel myself and keep concentrating, looking forward, because at times in the second half it was magic. I've got some pieces that still need to go into the jigsaw puzzle, no doubt about that. But I don't want to come here and be a Mid-Table Tommy, hanging about. How far can we go? Only time will tell..."

Martin straightens up his spine and does his big sniff.

Ian ANDREWS

Here comes the weekend

Ian Andrews played in goal for City in the mid '80s, then returned as physio a decade later. That's when we spoke in the boot room at Belvoir Drive.

You made the number 1 shirt your own in 1984, replacing Mark Wallington after a 5-0 defeat at Sheffield Wednesday...

"It was an 11 o'clock kick-off, against Aston Villa. I didn't have any fear of not playing well. I remember John O'Neill saying to me, 'Make sure you come out for the crosses.' And they did put in a few early ones to test me out, I think – and I was coming out and taking everything. I caught one cross and then half-volleyed it as hard as I could, straight down the middle to Lineker, who took on a couple of defenders and scored. That was a fantastic feeling. We went on to win 5-0."

Then came that extraordinary Boxing Day result against Liverpool. Everyone was raving about your performance.

"I remember our coach pulling up outside; the 'This Is Anfield' sign above the tunnel; Bruce Grobbelaar wishing me all the best. All the time, I'm thinking, 'That's brilliant. That's brilliant.' I was totally amazed by Anfield. Early in the game, I remember getting the ball, bouncing it

a few times, looking up and seeing the Kop at the other end, just a huge sea of faces. I thought, 'My God!' My whole body turned to jelly for a few moments and

I bounced the ball a few more times. Some of my team-mates were screaming for the ball by now but I just wanted to savour that moment, so they had to wait..."

The 1986/87 season started well under Bryan Hamilton, and you made the England Under-21s. Did you feel in the spotlight?

"It didn't bother me because for a while I went through a phase where I just knew I was going to play well on a Saturday. I really looked forward to games, and I'd go to bed early in the week just to make the weekend come quicker. I wanted Saturday to come because I was in a real purple patch. My body would reject injuries. I would refuse to let anything stand in the way of my playing. A few weeks into that season we played at QPR and, although we were under a lot of pressure from them, Alan Smith scored a late goal and we won 1-0. When we went into training on Monday morning the manager was having a go at me because of my starting positions. I thought I'd played one of the games of my life. At that point I knew something just wasn't right..."

The whole team's confidence and form suffered a dip which led to relegation...

"I think keepers tend to analyse things and then overanalyse things, because you want to be the very best you can be. Any career is made up of peaks and troughs but when you're a goalie it's just more obvious."

Did Hamilton's departure change things?

"No, I needed a fresh start. David Pleat said, 'Can I have a word with you in my office? There's a guy come down from Celtic to have a chat with you.' Apparently they'd already agreed terms, and it was just up to me whether I fancied the move or not. It didn't take me long to say 'yes.'"

Banks of England

It was a thrill and an honour to meet up with Gordon Banks of Leicester City and England – one of football's greatest ever goalkeepers – near to his home in Stoke.

First things first, could we take you back to 1959, when you first appeared on most football fans' radar?

"I'll try. When you get to my age, your memory's not so clever, and that was over 50 years ago. I'd played professionally for around half a season in the Third Division when the Chesterfield manager had me in and told me they'd had an offer from Leicester, which they'd accepted – and would I be interested in going? I said yes, thank you, straight away. It was a big opportunity to play in the top league."

Were you nervous when you quickly got the chance to step up from the reserves?

"Well, yes. Pre-match nerves were there every time you played. Especially when you're sitting in the dressing room and just about to go out. Even when you're shooting in. But as soon as the whistle went you had to push all that behind you and concentrate on your game."

What was goalkeeper training like back in the early '60s?

"There was none of the specialist goalkeeper training then. I had to do the outfield training, run the laps, do all the exercises, and then we'd finish up with five-a-side. But because we didn't have an actual training ground then, we had to play on the Filbert Street car park. I couldn't dive about on that surface so I didn't go in goal, I played outfield. A few years later, when they got the training ground, that gave me the opportunity to go back in the afternoon. The lads finished training at lunchtime, so I had to get some of the apprentices and reserves to come

back and bang some balls at me."

Your first really big match for Leicester was the FA Cup final of 1961, against Tottenham Hotspur...

"We were playing very well against them and we were actually their bogey team. We'd beaten them at White Hart Lane and I don't think they liked playing against us. We were playing very, very well but then Len Chalmers got injured and we had to play with ten men for a long time. Eventually they got on top and beat us 2-0. But we were really unlucky that day."

When we went down 3-1 in the 1963 Cup final against Manchester United, it was regarded as an upset...

"Yes, we'd had a great season and they'd had a poor one and had been struggling. But, for some reason, we didn't play anything like we'd been playing in the League. There were a lot of big names in the United line-up and we stood off them

and allowed them to knock it about. We had a poor time all round."

After winning the League Cup with City, you got your first England call-up...

"I was down at the ground when I found out about it. Matt Gillies, the manager, came into our snooker room, shook me by the hand and said, 'Congratulations, you're in the England team.' I couldn't quite believe it as the squad hadn't even assembled yet. Obviously, Alf must have said something to him. It was something of a shock and a great delight. I remember feeling very, very proud."

Your international debut was against Scotland at Wembley. A nice easy one to start with?

"Oh crikey, not half! Every single time we played Scotland over the years, no matter whether at Wembley or Hampden, it was a really tough game. About 90 per cent of the Scots played in the English First Division so they were always a match for us. We lost 2-1. They got a penalty past me, and I was feeling quite down, but Alf Ramsey came up to me and said, 'Well played.' That gave me a bit of a lift and I was pleased that he'd seen something in my game."

Do you still get asked about 1966 every day of your life?

"What can you say that would describe how it feels to win the World Cup? It was a fantastic feeling. I

knew I had lots of years left in the game, as I'd trained well and worked hard, so at the time I didn't see it as the pinnacle of my career. I thought that both England and Leicester City would push on from there and get better. Both were good set-ups with players coming to the best part of their careers. I thought really that was just the beginning."

But that season after the World Cup was your last at Leicester...

"I'd seen Peter Shilton occasionally while he was playing for Leicester City Boys and then he got in the England Schoolboys side. I saw him in the gym – two mats down, with trainer George Dewis banging balls at him. I watched him for five minutes and I thought, 'Bloody hell, this lad has got some real technique here!' When he signed as an apprentice, he'd join in on the little goalkeeping sessions that I organised."

How did you feel when you were transfer-listed?

"I was shocked and amazed. I couldn't believe that they'd want to get rid of me. I'd seen this report in the paper where Peter was supposed to have said to the board, 'I either want first-team football, or I want to leave.' When I saw that, I laughed. I thought, 'I've played for England and won a World Cup. Does he honestly think they're going to drop me and put him in?' A couple of weeks later, Matt Gillies came to the training ground, which he never, ever did. We were running around the track, warming up. Before he even said a word, I knew exactly what was going to happen. He told me, 'The board have had a meeting. What would you think about leaving?' Straight away, I knew it was done, so I said, 'Well, if that's all you think about me, then I'll go. It really shook me up – children, friends, social scene – we were really settled."

20

What were your options at that time?

"I'd heard rumours that Liverpool wanted me. Roger Hunt said, 'Don't sign for anyone because Bill Shankly is going to come in for you.' Many years later, he did tell me that he went to his board but they refused him the money. Martin Peters told me that West Ham wanted me, but they signed Bobby Ferguson from Kilmarnock for £57,000 three weeks before I was put on the list. That was a lot of money. Stoke paid £50,000 for me."

What was the peak of your time at City?

"I think that would have to be Liverpool in the semi-final of the FA Cup at Hillsborough in 1963. They were top of the table and a great side, and it was one-way traffic towards my goal. I seemed to be punching, diving, coming out to collect for most of the game, and I think I had the game of my life. Mike Stringfellow scored with a header after about 20 minutes and then they just kept coming at us even more then! There was an incident that

"We didn't have a training ground then, we had to play on the Filbert Street car park."

really hurt me, however. At the final whistle some of the lads were jumping on me to congratulate me. I saw Richie Norman, my best mate, and grinned at him. In between us was Ian St John, who was obviously gutted, walking with his head down and tears in his eyes. Someone took a photo at that moment, but left out Richie – so it was just me and Ian, and it made it look as if I was laughing at him. It sickened me that supporters thought I would behave like that, because I never would."

Do you have any regrets?

"I wish I'd been a better driver! Although my career was cut short by my accident in 1972, I did go on to have a good few more years in the game, coaching at Stoke and playing in the NASL. No, to have a life in professional football was fabulous. Playing in front of thousands of people, enjoying every minute, and travelling all over the world into the bargain. Wearing the England shirt with that badge on it and standing there singing the National Anthem, I can't possibly have any regrets."

Banks blunts the Blades – closely watched by the Birch, when he was just a sapling.

Ian BARACLOUGH

In the beginning

Our first ever *FOX* interview was easy to set up, as City Youth star Bara was a local Narborough lad, and dating our then-assistant editor's sister at the time. Ian went on to play over 700 senior games for the likes of Notts County, QPR and Scunthorpe, and is now Northern Ireland's Under-21s manager.

You've recently signed professional forms; but isn't football a precarious occupation?

"I know sport is usually played for enjoyment, but I can't do much else! I realise it's a very short career, so I've got to make some money out of it. I suppose it's like acting, really. Most entertainment jobs aren't very secure."

Who has been the biggest influence on your career to date?

"I suppose David Pleat has got a lot to do with it. He's really given me a chance this season and has now put me forward for the England Under-18s trip to Moscow. Also Bobby Roberts, our coach who takes the Youth team. He has many ideas that we try and put into our play."

What does a typical day's training entail?

"We get to Belvoir Drive at about 10 o'clock, get changed and have a muck-about in the gym first. Then about 10.45 we start with a jog and stretching exercises. We train 'til about 12.30, perhaps a bit shorter if there's a game at night. Then we have our lunch. We might have an hour in the afternoon, then we just go home!"

What a piece of piss! Who's the fittest player at Leicester thanks to this rigorous training regime?

"Mike Newell, definitely. He's such a skilful player and he always gives 100 per cent. He'll run all day."

What's the main difference between playing in the Youth team and the reserves?

"The Youth side is more enjoyable to play for. We've built up an understanding of each other's play. Lots has been written about it, and we all like that. In the reserves, the blend of Youth players and people in and out of the first team makes it less settled. You're more likely to find yourself up against seasoned pros who are out of favour. It's good for experience but I prefer playing in the Youth side."

Was your appearance in the squad against Crystal Palace a valuable experience or just a long drive down the motorway?

"I don't think there was any danger of me playing, but it was an experience exercise for me and Des Lyttle. It was more nerve-racking being in the squad against Forest because of the injuries to Mauchlen, et cetera. We felt more a part of the squad that night."

Do you see the Youth side graduating into the first team, as at Manchester City or Forest?

"I can do, yes. I hope so. To play together for so long is invaluable. But I'm not sure Leicester can afford to graduate so many together. The boss does give young players a chance. Darren Williams made a few appearances this season, Grant Brown as well. He does experiment with younger players. But, when the time is right, he will know."

Power behind the throne

For 15 years, Alan Bennett made things tick behind the scenes at Filbert Street as club secretary. We met him at Cosby Golf Club when his morning round had been rained off.

You joined Leicester City from Aston Villa back in 1979...

"Yes, at Villa I was club secretary, and the commercial department was completely separate. Leicester wanted me to be general secretary, in charge of both. Basically, I was in charge of everything except the team. If the pitch was suddenly covered in snow, it was my responsibility to get it cleared. But I'd previously been assistant secretary at Chelsea in the '60s, so there weren't too many surprises."

You were dealing with money, transfers, hooligans, ground development...

"I suppose the job title today would be chief executive. When I first arrived, the ground compared fairly well with most clubs. But we were being overtaken in the '80s and early '90s. Our first proposition was to turn the pitch round and use the Double Decker as a full-length stand. Then build a new Main Stand along Filbert Street. Then build two new ends. The Burnmoor Street end would have been tight, but there was plenty of room at the car park end. It would have worked, but it didn't get planning permission. So we pushed through the Carling Stand."

Which of the managers did you best get on with?

"Well, I'd known Brian Little since he was a 15 year old at Villa. In fact, I'll take a bit of the credit for him coming to Leicester. Martin George was pushing to bring John Beck in from Cambridge, and I was quite happy when that fell down. Brian came in like a breath of fresh air.

He was pretty young for a manager and he came with a superb team round him in Allan Evans and John Gregory. John was a very good coach, while Allan was an excellent organiser and administrator. Although those two didn't particularly get on, Brian could sit in the middle and take overall charge. He was good at the PR and talking to the players."

Were you in charge of huge bags of cash on matchdays?

"Most of the turnstiles took cash. Each one had a meter which would be read by the turnstile supervisor before they opened. The turnstile operator just counts his money, bags it and hands it in to the cash office in the Main Stand. We know he should have, say, £500 so when we count it and it's £497 then we say, 'Okay, thanks!' If someone comes in with £450 then he gets sent away to count it again. By about half-time everything would be bagged up along with the programme money and sent off to the bank. It used to be in a taxi but ended up with Securicor. Erm... it got a bit dicey once, I think!"

Alan BIRCHENALL

Meet the Team

With Filbert Street's grand Carling Stand under construction, we met City's long-serving PR man in temporary offices above a car dealer's on Upperton Road.

Back in 1975, you did a 'Meet the Team' feature for *Soccer Star* magazine. Could you go through the team again, just for us?

Peter Shilton: "Shilts was a real loner, he always went his own way. When he went for the manager's job here, he wanted me as his assistant as he said he was a bit dour, and I'd be the bloke to jolly them along. But that side of football doesn't hold much attraction for me. I think back to Jimmy Bloomfield, and I'm sure a big part of the reason for his death was the pressure of football. He kept things bottled up inside him. I remember all the placards draped around Villa Park: 'Bloomfield Out!' I felt so sorry for Jimmy. It's such a stressful job. I think if even one person was saying 'Birchenall Out!', I couldn't stand it."

Steve Whitworth: "Ginger was a good attacking full-back. He could be dumped on his arse but then he'd be back round picking them up again."

Dennis Rofe: "Sid! We called him 'Sid' because he looked just like Sid James, and he's still 'Sid' today. A tenacious little bugger, and a great character to have in your side."

Graham Cross: "Well, he's 'on holiday' at the moment! He was a good player for a long time, probably one step away from an England place because he played

for the Under-23s a few times. Valerie, his missus, used to say to me, 'Why do you call him Fatty?'"

Alan Woollett: "Well, what can you say about the Wool? He was here 30 years and he made 15 appearances. The year we got to the semi-final of the Cup, the directors decided to send us to Barbados as a reward. We had a vote whether or not to take the wives and girlfriends. Me, Frank, Lenny and Sid were looking along the row and we saw Sjoberg and Woollett with their hands about to go up – until we fixed them with the most evil glare, and their hands went back down. We stayed at the Paradise Beach Hotel. We were lying under a palm tree, and all of a sudden we saw the Wool walking with Crossy along the water's edge. As he walked past, a tiny little cloud went over in an otherwise perfect blue sky and dropped a couple of drips of water. The Wool said, 'So much for Barbados, Crossy. I bet it's not f***ing raining in Wigston.' At the first home game of the next season, I went into the players' room and all the wives completely blanked me. And Brigitta blanked Frank, which was unusual because usually they were all over each other. I didn't really know what I'd done. When I got in the car, my missus said, 'It had to be you, didn't it? Leader of the gang. Valerie Cross told us there was a vote at the training ground for us to go to Barbados...' Oh, no. Crossy had dropped us right in it!"

Jon Sammels: "He took a lot of stick, did Sammy, but he would never, ever hide. A great guy, and still as fit today, even though he sits in that car giving lessons all day!"

Keith Weller: "One of the most gifted attacking players that I've ever had the pleasure to play alongside. A real crowd pleaser; but he did cause a certain amount of disharmony. One time, when he wasn't very happy, he kicked a ball into the

"He wanted me as his assistant manager as he was a bit dour. I'd be the bloke to jolly them along."

crowd and hit a kid straight in the mush. Bad news. At half time, Jim had a go at him, and he didn't like it. He slung his shirt off, got in the bath and refused to come out for the second half. The real problem was that the Bolt (Mike Stringfellow) was the sub, and it took about three days to get him warmed up with deep heat, with his creaking joints."

Len Glover: "Len was the biggest moaner and the biggest shit-stirrer in football! He's still a friend of mine, and I can call him that. He was critical of players that he thought weren't up to the standard required. One of the best understandings I've ever seen in football was between Lenny and Frank."

Frank Worthington: "It would take me about a year to tell you all the stories about Elvis. I remember after his first game at City we were in the players' lounge – only a small room, so there were two or three players and their wives standing around. In walks Frank in a cowboy hat with beads round it, a black T-shirt with 'Elvis' on it in sequins, the tightest jeans you've ever seen in your life, and cowboy boots.

And he looked like he's got his lunchbox rammed down the front of his jeans. The following home game, the players' room was rammed with wives and girlfriends, as word had got round about Frank! One day I was driving down Charles Street and there was a huge traffic jam. It took half an hour to get down there – and there's Frank's sponsored car being loaded on to a tow truck. The next day, I asked him if it was his car. He said, 'Yeah, man. I thought it had broke down but apparently it had run out of petrol.' I said, 'Well, what did you do?' He said, 'Well, I just walked off and left it. It's not my car.' He was in a world of his own! The police used to come down every month with a bundle of his parking tickets."

What a team, eh?

"We beat Luton at their place in a Cup match in 1974, and I've never played in a game where everything went so right. After the game, Malcolm Allison dropped by the dressing room and said to us, 'Look lads, I've managed the League champions, but I can tell you that is the finest attacking performance I've ever seen in my life. I'd just like to say that.' Then he turned round and went out of the door."

Birch helpfully points out Mike Stringfellow in a 1931 tream photo.

Alan BIRCHENALL

Bring back the Birch

Birch kindly gave us the grand tour of Belvoir Drive, meeting the laundry ladies and checking out some expensive new training equipment. When we'd arrived, he was looking through a pile of early 1970s *Mercury Sports Finals* that someone had sent him.

"You know, I love getting this stuff. I show it to people round here and they take the mick a bit and regard me as the old dinosaur that I am. But it's funny. I was standing in the tunnel before a game somewhere and a couple of the players waiting to go out said, 'That pitch is really crap Birch, have you seen it?' Well, you couldn't help but laugh at them. You've got grass all year round with synthetic bits woven into it. You're playing on bowling greens, lads! The pitches we played on had grass too – by the corner flags."

Filbert Street was worse than most...

"It looked like a beach most of the year. If I ever do a Q&A I always get asked what is the difference between then and now. Half the professionals of the '60s and '70s wouldn't be playing because you get breathalysed on a Monday morning! Still, what remains the same is that by the

time you're 35 and you've had your 500 games, 95 per cent of our trade is finished. The new diets help you reach the pace of the modern game but they don't extend your career span. All the wonderful diets and heart monitoring and specialist gym equipment here wouldn't have made Keith Weller a more talented player."

For those City fans who never saw you play, what sort of player were you?

"When I first came to Leicester I was still a striker. I teamed up with Rodney Fern, Malcolm Partridge, Ally Brown – and none of them could work with me. So after nine years of playing up front at Sheffield United, Chelsea and Palace, I said to Jim, 'I think I can contribute more to the team from midfield.' I sat back and had Keith Weller on the right and Jon Sammels on the left. Well, you could put a monkey in my position and you'd be all right with those two either side of you. It worked quite well, what I called the 'concertina'. I'd bring the midfield back to ten yards in front of the defence, and it was difficult for teams to get through the two banks of four. We'd ping the ball up to Frank who could hold it up for a fortnight, if required. Then he'd hit it out to Lenny on the left and we'd be threatening their goal. That always used to make Wells a bit fed up after he'd run 50 yards forward to support him. That was part of the friction between them. It was like a competition between them which drove that side on to some of their great performances."

On our day we were one of the most attractive sides in the country...

"That's what enraged Martin O'Neill when he was here: 'Don't talk to me about the '70s, you won f*** all!' I'd say to him, 'But Martin, people used to walk away

from Filbert Street with their sons saying, 'Did you see Shilton palm that one over?' and 'Did you see Weller beat that defender?' and 'Did you see Frank volley that one in?' It used to drive him mad!" My first passport said 'Entertainer' on it, honestly it did. That's how we were looked upon then. I remember once we were coming out of the tunnel at Filbert Street for the second half against Arsenal and it was absolutely tipping down. There was a girl in the crowd next to the tunnel with an umbrella, so I grabbed it as I went past and took it out with me. The ref did his quick check before kick-off and saw me standing there with it. Another time I went and sat on the East Stand wall while someone got treatment. I nicked a lad's bobble hat off him and put that on. Then the geezer in the white coat came round with his tray of pies. I stopped him and gave out about 20 pies to all the fans. The play restarted and I took the throw-in. The ref said, 'Birch get that thing off your head, you t***.' At the end of the game Jimmy was addressing us all, and the dressing room after a game is sacrosanct for all kinds of reasons. There was a loud knock on the door. It was the pieman saying, 'Birch, you owe me £15.' It caused uproar!"

Not a lot of people know that you were the Leicester manager for a while...

"Yes, Brian Little had left to go to Aston Villa and Martin George rang me up and said, 'Birch, I want you to be in charge of the lads for the trip to

"Martin George said, 'Birch, I want you to be in charge of the lads for the trip to Norwich.'"

Norwich on Saturday.' My God, all my dreams had come true! I was still in the footwear trade then. I said, 'I won't be able to get there until 10.30 because I've got an appointment at the British Shoe Corporation.' Well, it was my living! That night I didn't sleep because I was planning everything. Don't forget, I'd had two and a half years at Trowbridge Town! Sure, sooner or later I knew I'd be sacked but until then I was dreaming of winning the FA Cup and taking City into Europe. But when I got to the ground, the coaches Kevin MacDonald and Tony McAndrew were waiting for me. Kev said, 'Birch, you need to call the chairman.' Martin said, 'There's been a bit of a change of plan. We still want you to be involved today, but they're going to pick the team.' Fair enough, I completely understood. Mind you, when we lost 2-1 at Carrow Road I did say, 'Hey! We'd have won that f***ing game using my tactics!'"

Soft soap: Birch introduces two long-serving team members, Sheila and Dill.

27

Jeff BLOCKLEY

Block and tackle

Brought in by Jimmy Bloomfield to stiffen the back line in 1975, we had our own retrospective team talk with Jeff at his local Whetstone Golf Club.

You're a Leicester lad, Jeff. Did you support City?

"Born in New Parks, went to Forest Lodge Primary School. Oh yes, I was a Leicester fan, still am, always have been. I used to go down to Filbert Street with my dad, and we followed them everywhere."

You played for Leicester Schools alongside Peter Shilton and also Romeo Challenger who went on to become a member of Showaddywaddy. Did you ever envy him his career?

"Well, this was the '60s so I suppose we all wanted to be pop stars. But I think the pop stars all wanted to be footballers!"

You signed as an apprentice at Coventry City, and were captain by the age of 20...

"That's right. When I was playing for the England Under-23s at Derby, Brian Clough called me over and started talking to me about Coventry. I didn't realise at the time but he was picking my brains about the club because they'd just sacked Noel

Cantwell and I think he fancied the job. Sir Alf and all the players had gone to get on the bus and I was left with Cloughie still talking to me. I said, 'Sorry Brian, I've got to go, they're waiting for

me.' He said, 'You'll go when I tell you you can go, young man!'"

You were bought by Arsenal in 1972 as a direct replacement for Frank McLintock...

"They bought me for £200,000, which was a lot of money then. The great Double side had peaked and they were in a period of transition. Things didn't really work out for me down there. I was 22 when I signed, with no advisor or agent to help me out. If I'd had a choice between the clubs who put an offer in for me – Man United, among others – I'd probably have gone to Leeds."

What do you remember about winning your England cap?

"It all went by rather quickly. I signed for Arsenal on Thursday, played for them at Sheffield United on Saturday and made my England debut on Wednesday, against Yugoslavia at Wembley. A few years previously I was watching England win the World Cup and then suddenly you're playing alongside Bobby Moore. Sir Alf was incredible. Funny and sharp, and not a bit aloof. He was an absolute national icon, and I was a bit starstruck. I've got Christmas cards from Sir Alf, and you can bet that I've kept them."

The game was a lot more physical then. Did you always give someone an early dig?

"There was usually a bit of 'welcome to the game' early on, but it went both ways. Joe Jordan would always give you an elbow across the face, first challenge, and you had to be aware that it was coming. Andy Lochhead who played for Leicester was such a hard man, and he knew what he was doing. You had to really gee yourself up for them and give it your best. Every team had tough characters for when you had to mix it. Johnny Giles at Leeds was a very talented player and about 5'8" but he was one of the worst. It wasn't about seeing red, it was about being clever."

Leicester were rock bottom of Division One when you moved back here in 1975...

"Jimmy Bloomfield didn't really have to sell it to me, to be honest. I wanted to leave Arsenal and I really wanted to play for my hometown club and I knew a lot of the players here. There was me, Graham Cross, Dennis Rofe and Steve Whitworth, and we blended into a good unit with a system of playing fairly high and tight. We had good communication, and were able to set the offside trap for any strikers trying to get behind us. After sorting the defence out, Jim then brought Chris Garland in. He scored plenty of goals, Frank Worthington started scoring again and the whole side got their confidence back. Jimmy always saw the positives in people rather than the negatives. I was very disappointed when he left. I think there was a lot of politics going on in the boardroom with a new guy in, stirring things up."

We have to ask you about a training ground incident with Chris Garland that left you with a broken jaw...

"We were playing a five-a-side in the hall at Belvoir Drive and we were just messing about, or I thought we were. I went towards him with my arms spread out and he chinned me! I think he thought I was going to thump him and he just swung out. He was a bit frustrated at the time, I think he wanted a move. I don't think it was pre-planned or he had an issue with me. Anyway, he got his move to Bristol City and I got a free holiday!"

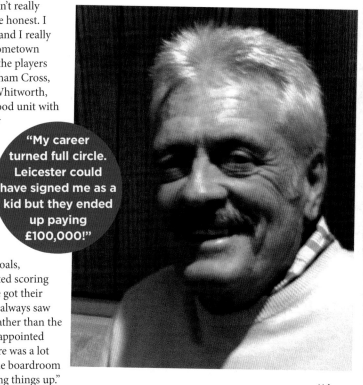

"My career turned full circle. Leicester could have signed me as a kid but they ended up paying £100,000!"

You left for Notts County a year after Jimmy Bloomfield departed for Orient...

"I signed a two-year contract and I was also looking after the reserve team. Then the chairman brought Howard Wilkinson in as a coach. I wasn't that keen on what they were doing so I resigned my post. I was still involved in football, managing Enderby Town and Shepshed. If you think lower-league managers had their problems, you should try managing at that level! When the chairman thinks his son should be playing and is drunk out of his mind shouting at you through a window. Martin O'Neill was my successor at Shepshed but he must have been a lot smarter than me, because it only took him two months to work them out and leave!"

Do you know? Who graffitied over Filbert Street's 'BLOCK E' sign to read 'BLOCKLEY'.

David BLOOMFIELD

Son of my father

What better way to get an insight into the heart of Leicester City in the '70s than to speak to someone who was there behind the scenes alongside manager Jimmy Bloomfield? When we met at the Traveller's Rest in Harrow, David Bloomfield was media officer at Barnet, then in 91st place in the Football League.

At what age did you move to Leicester?

"I was about 13. My dad was manager at Orient and we lived in Epping. He'd established them as a level-two club, having won Division Three the year before. Then Leicester came in, and they had to pay Orient a compensation fee of £10,000. I was keen to go because I thought that, with Leicester being in the top flight, I'd be able to augment my autograph book."

Did you become a Leicester fan?

"Yes, I followed them everywhere. I used to go on Kinch's Casual Coaches, and the first time I went on there they weren't sure whether to charge me or not – so they eventually did."

Jimmy's Leicester side were maybe just a couple of players away from silverware...

"Two players that Dad had really earmarked were David Mills and David Armstrong at Middlesbrough. They were both available for £200,000 each, but the directors didn't stump that money up. I think Mills went for over £500,000 a couple of years later, which was a British transfer record fee at the time. Then, when Frank

McLintock came in, they spent money like water for a while."

Wasn't John Toshack all but signed up?

"Oh, he was done and dusted. There's quite a nice reference in *Gosh It's Tosh*, Toshack's book of poems. There's a photo of my dad going to Lytham St Annes, where you had to physically hand in the transfer registration form in those days. It was a big disappointment when that didn't happen. After the medical exam, the conclusion was reached that he wouldn't last the rigours of a full season. He seemed to do fairly well at Liverpool after that, forming a great partnership with Kevin Keegan. Worthington and Toshack might have been an interesting combination."

It must have been a blow for your father when Peter Shilton left in 1974?

"Well, Peter Shilton had wanted to leave almost right from the very beginning. It's odd in a way that he went to Stoke, although I think they were top of the table when he joined them. He should have gone to Manchester United or Leeds, really. I remember Brian Clough saying to my dad, 'Don't let him go to Leeds!' Cloughie was a big fan of Shilton and thought he might make them unbeatable."

Do you remember your father being away a lot, scouting?

"Well, he'd go and see a game or two a week, and I'd often go with him. I remember one scouting trip to see Frank Worthington play for Huddersfield reserves. All four of us went up there: brother, mum and dad, one Wednesday night, pre-season. We paid to get in and sat at the back of the stand. I remember Worthington doing a spectacular overhead kick. My dad used to give me a nudge if he saw something he liked on the field, and he gave me a few that night."

Did a maverick player like Frank ever test your dad as a manager?

"Yes, but the main thing with Frank was that he really admired his ability. Someone who's that good at football might not be perfect at everything else, so you just had to manage that. There were times when we would babysit for Frank Junior, who would materialise at the front door, while Frank and Brigitta went off to rekindle their relationship!"

Can we ask you about an incident that happened while your dad was in charge...

"'You can't fall in love with a footballer,' Dad said. 'They'll either want to leave or let you down.'"

"Yes, I bet you mean Keith Weller at half-time?! Weller refused to go out for the second half of a game against Ipswich. I think the root of it was quite a lot of jealousy and animosity between Keith Weller and Frank Worthington at the time. On reflection, my dad managed it quite interestingly because Keith played in the very next game. If you're watching an old City game, I always look to see, if Keith scores, does Frank go up to him, and if Frank scores does Keith go up?"

What were Jimmy's proudest moments as Leicester City manager?

"A lot of the accolades that the team got at the time were very pleasing to him. He did believe that football was an art form, something you could express yourself in. Even as a young player he wanted a team to play in his image – making him sound a bit like God there! – but when you're a manager you're able to do that. An occasional passing movement would cause him a joyful moment of reflection. I think one of dad's achievements at Leicester was building a side that could go anywhere – Liverpool, Manchester United, wherever – and be able to think, we might win this. On our day, we always had a chance of getting a result. It was a nice feeling."

Green meets sparkling blue

Paddy BYRNE

For our only overseas interview, the former winger picked up Simon at Dublin Airport and drove to sunny Skerries on the coast. The Blue Bar proved the perfect spot for memories, lunch and a Guinness.

How did you come to move from Bohemians to Philadelphia Fury?

"I was actually supposed to sign for Fulham but they went into receivership! The same scout that Fulham were using was also signing players for the NASL. I played with Alan Ball and Johnny Giles, so I couldn't have asked for better tuition as a youngster. It was a bit like fantasy football at times, there was so much razzamatazz before each game. We were owned by the Rolling Stones and Peter Frampton; it was another world! Then Jock Wallace asked who was free and available through Martin Henderson, and so that's how I was approached by Leicester. Jock had seen me play against him previously when he was at Rangers."

Do you remember much about your early games at Leicester?

"I remember the crowd at Leicester was very passionate. Jesus! They were really close to you, and I was playing as a winger which meant they were on top of you. I would have preferred to play inside, but of course you had Eddie Kelly and Andy Peake in there so I played wide right."

Jock had some great young players in his side...

"Yes, but it's as much about belief as it is ability. Gary Lineker is a prime example of this. When I first went to Leicester there were young lads like Mark Goodwin and Andy Peake and they had a lovely touch, natural ball players. Then you had Gary. He had a poor touch, but his speed got him noticed and it would help him when he miscontrolled it because he could outpace any defender to pick up a loose ball. When he came into the side he did incredibly well through self-belief, and he excelled at one thing – he was great in the box. He wasn't a great natural striker of the ball but, Jesus, when you gave him the ball six yards out, it was going in! My only regret is that the fans at Leicester didn't see the best of me. I was a bit young and maybe not strong-willed enough. That was down to nobody but myself, it was my own self-belief that was maybe lacking."

How did the Second Division title compare to other career achievements?

"Nothing compared to that! An Irishman in England winning a league – it was something I'd dreamed of as a kid. But the following season we didn't have the money to bring in the type of experienced player that we needed, and maybe Jock struggled at times as well because motivation can only get you so far, and tactically he wasn't strong. He was learning just as much as we were, and maybe he didn't realise how difficult it was going to be. You'd never see any flaws or doubts in Jock because he had such belief in himself. He'd set his stall out at the beginning of the season and decided that this bunch of players was good enough; he didn't want to admit to anyone that, actually, they weren't. He believed in everybody, and I wish we'd stayed up for his sake. Actually, I wish we'd stayed up because then I might have got another contract!"

You went on a bit of run after a famous win at Liverpool but there wasn't quite the momentum to stay up...

"The goal I scored was one of those that you catch just right. Even though I was a way out, the ball came across and I hit it first time. If I hadn't got it right, it would have killed a few seagulls on its way out of the ground! But what a feeling to see the ball in the net at the Kop end; that's why you play football, for moments like that. Even now, people still want to talk about it, which I find incredible."

When did you know you were leaving Leicester?

"Jock called me in and said that there wasn't enough money to offer me a new contract, that they'd had an offer from Hearts. It took me a long time to get over that. It broke my heart. I loved Leicester, the city, the people, where I lived. Going in to Filbert Street every day was heaven for me."

Back at Shamrock Rovers you were capped for the Republic of Ireland, and then went on to manage Shelbourne very successfully...

"I think being picked for my country was amazing but I would have to say that the experience at Leicester was very special. I remember the celebration at The Holiday Inn after we won the Second

"I loved Leicester, the city, the people, where I lived. Going in to Filbert Street every day was heaven for me."

Division title. It was a great night, but Jock included everyone in the celebrations. At the top table, Jock had put people like the laundry lady, girls from the ticket office, the groundsman, the tea lady and other people from behind the scenes. When he made his speech, Jock said that we couldn't have achieved our success without these people at the top table, the most important people in the club. He didn't mention the players at all, which was brilliant. His view was that players came and went but the backroom staff were the heart of the club. That was Jock Wallace all over – no superstars, and everybody has to graft and play their part."

The Day the Earth Stood Still

Steve CLARIDGE

It's hard to believe 'Super Steve' was only at Leicester for two years, during which tumultuous time he secured a special place in fans' hearts. The indelible image of Claridge charging about with his socks round his ankles proved unexpectedly relevant on the day we met him at a hotel near Portsmouth. Steve was an hour late due to car trouble. But no worries, he ran the last mile.

When Martin O'Neill first brought you to Leicester, you weren't in the best form...

"It was strange how that happened. I basically got quite ill. I'd gone something like 11 or 12 games without a goal and I couldn't work out why. I knew I felt a bit odd and a bit listless, something was missing. I went another six or so games at Leicester without scoring. Then I went to hospital for a blood test and they said, 'You're very low on thyroxine, you're very ill.' If I'd been an office worker, I'd have been sent home to bed but I was going out and playing professional football. They gave me thyroid tablets and I immediately began to feel better."

What were your first impressions of your new boss?

"When he bought players you sensed that he was always thinking ahead. It was always a case of 'I know what needs to be done, and that player can fill that void.' Whenever anyone came in, they always brought something better. Brought a little bit more than we already had. Apart from Graham Fenton!"

He was allowed one!

"It didn't take long for people to realise what Martin was doing. He got rid of a few, like Steve Corica, who was good on his day. He paid for myself, Muzzy Izzet and Neil Lennon by getting rid of two or three players."

Iwan Roberts left at the end of that 1995/96 season...

"Yes, there's an interesting thing about Iwan. A couple of the players were trying to work a bit of a scam on throw-ins straight after kick-offs. They'd bet on a throw-in in the first minute. A certain player aimed the ball out for a throw but Iwan went up to head it, got clattered by a defender and broke a rib. He missed the Play-offs. Iwan was out there trying to make it look real, somebody under-hit the ball instead of over-hitting it and poor old Iwan was out for the rest of the season."

What were you thinking during those first few weeks at Leicester when things weren't going very well?

> **"You can see that I hit it beautifully. That's typical of me: say something stupid and play it down."**

Super Stevie Claridge catches it just right.

"Well, I was thinking, 'I'm ill!' I remember running out for a game against Millwall and by the time I'd run out of the tunnel and out on to the pitch, I was knackered! I think Martin took me off after something like 15 minutes. He said to me: 'Your first touch is f***ing shit!' I said, "Gaffer, I can't even feel the ball!' I had raging pins and needles in my legs and my feet were completely numb."

There came a huge turning point in that season – starting with a terrible game at home to Sheffield United, where fans were calling for Martin O'Neill's head...

"We had to go out the back entrance that day. We couldn't get out the front because of the protest. Martin never, ever forgot that."

"A few days later, you travelled to Charlton and it all seemed to click together. How close were you to being left out of the side for that game?

"Very close. I pleaded with him not to leave me out. After three days on the tablets I was feeling much better. Not properly right, but much better. I went in and made a special case to play. 'Just play me, please. I'm not a bad player overnight. Play me and I'll show you.'"

It must have been a huge relief when you scored that night?

"Yes, I can't tell you. It was important for Leicester, but for me and for my career it was massive. I needed that goal. I needed to be on the inside with a chance to show

what I could do."

Between that goal at Charlton and going up via the Play-offs, the side only lost one more match. You started off that run in ninth place. When did you begin to think, 'We can do this'?

"Straight away. As soon as Lennon and Izzet came in, we knew. You know when you're in a good side. With the ball and without the ball. The balance was right."

If we can take you back to that Play-off final at Wembley. It's 1-1 and there are seconds to go until a penalty shoot-out. City have a free-kick on the halfway line, and Martin O'Neill brings 'Spider' Kalac on for Kevin Poole...

"Garry Parker knew it was almost time and so he took the free-kick too quickly, and I hadn't made my way into my normal spot. I was the one who was fouled for the free-kick. I said to Parks, 'Hang on a minute, let me get into the box.' But he's scared the ref's going to blow the whistle, so he delivers it before I get there. It's headed into my path – and the rest is history."

35

crowd are halfway out of their seats with their arms in the air, second guessing it, but this time nobody moves."

And it caught the commentator out, Alan Parry...

"Yes, he doesn't commentate on the goal. He says something like, 'Could this be the winner for Claridge?' And stops. And then: 'It is!' The world stopped."

There were many remarkable moments in that first Premier League season. But scoring in the replay against Middlesbrough and winning the League Cup – was that as good as it gets?

"No, the Play-off was. A million times better."

But the League Cup is a major honour and a passport to Europe...

"No, you're joking? Would you have swapped the Coca-Cola Cup for a place in the Premiership?"

From our point of view, City have gone up and down between the first and second tiers for years. A trophy and Europe was something different for us...

"Well, yes. But what if you never got back up again? I mean, that goal against Palace meant that everything was elevated. The likes of Matty Elliott, Muzzy Izzet, Robbie Savage... it was the difference between five grand a week and 25 grand a week. That one goal that took us into the Premiership changed people's lives. I treasure that medal more than I do my League Cup medal. I've been beaten in the semi-final of the Play-offs, twice, and I know what that feels like, too."

At the final whistle, Gary Newbon shoved a microphone under your nose and you told him you'd shinned it in; but you didn't, did you?

"No, it was a stupid thing to say and I don't know why I said it. You can see that I hit it beautifully. When Nigel Martyn saw it, it was already too late to dive. It was on the rise as well. That's typical of me: say something stupid and play it down."

Can you describe to us what that felt like at that moment?

"No, I can't. You haven't had it. It's why I played football for another ten years. For a moment like that. That's why the game is so hard to give up and why people struggle when their playing career is over. Because that takes you somewhere you will never go again."

Were you aware of that strange delay between the ball hitting the net and the roar of the crowd?

"Yes, absolutely. It seemed to take a second to sink in. If you watch it on TV, you see it hit the net and normally the

Lost City

Greg Clarke started out as a Kopite and became City chairman during the club's darkest days. His corporate experience helped City out of administration, and then helped him land the role of Football League chairman. Greg welcomed us into his HQ by Hyde Park.

You were chairman of Leicester City during an extremely rocky period...

"I took over as chairman to try and save the club. The problem was that we made a number of decisions that didn't turn out to be very good ones. Some of them we had to make. For example: Filbert Street was condemned. We got this surveyor's report that said there was concrete cancer in the Double Decker; that was falling down, this was falling down, no women's toilets on the Pop Side. We had to build a new ground – and we finally managed to get our arms round the old gasworks site. When you build a new ground, you're making a bet that you won't go down..."

And that was when the manager quit?

"Peter Taylor did his best, but he wasn't Martin O'Neill and we went down. We were moving to a new ground in the middle of a recession where nobody was buying players, ITV Digital fell apart and then we got relegated. Everything that could go wrong, did go wrong. We were suddenly on the hook for £35 million. The football board said we can't sell any players. So we were in a right state. I took over as chairman at that point to try to renegotiate over the terms with the stadium guys and

Teachers, but never could I get all four big creditors nailed down. We went into administration as soon as we could to leave the administrator enough money to run the club without sacking everybody. We then put together a consortium as a backstop just in case no one else turned up to buy the club: I knew how to deal with international bond and distressed debt teams; James Johnson is a leading banking partner at Clifford Chance; Jon Holmes is big in media and football. We had a very credible bunch of people to try and raise some money and get the club back trading again. And we just got enough money to save the club. *Just.* We raised enough to keep it afloat until Milan Mandaric came along and bought the club. And then we went down! It's ironic isn't it? I remember Jon and I telling Gary Lineker that we didn't think we were going to make it and he was nearly in tears. He said, 'We can't lose the City?' God, was it stressful. The thought of Leicester people saying: 'Remember when we had a football club that's now a block of flats? Well one of them was *him!*' That's nearly as bad as taking penalties at the Euros..."

Stephen CLEMENCE

Seriously, skipper?

Former Tottenham Hotspur and Birmingham City midfielder Stephen Clemence was with City for three seasons, but his 34 games for the club were sadly all behind him when we met our injured captain at Belvoir Drive. He later joined Steve Bruce's coaching staff at Sunderland, and has since followed him to Hull and Villa.

Last summer, with Birmingham promoted back into the Premier League, you took the surprising decision to leave...

"I knew Steve Bruce would be looking to bring in some new players and I went to see him in pre-season. He said, 'Why would I want to sell last year's Player of the Season?' I'd done well for him for four or five years, but he wouldn't stand in my way if an offer came along that was good for me. I thought I could help Leicester get to where we all want to be – in the Premiership. Unfortunately, it hasn't panned out that way so far."

Martin Allen was manager when you arrived. Was he as 'off the wall' as the media like to portray him?

"Well, before I came to meet him I'd heard the stories about him jumping in lakes and all that sort of thing, but there was nothing like that going on. Obviously, he wasn't here all that long, but he was very serious about his football and he wanted to take the club forward. We went up to Scotland for a week pre-season and there was a lot of team-building going on. Football is quite ruthless and people come and go quite quickly in this game. If you want to be successful then you can't sit around and mope about it."

So Gary Megson became the boss, presumably with a contrasting style?

"Very different. Gary was very serious about his football and when you were on the training pitch there wasn't so much laughing and joking. It was more like we were at work."

And Ian Holloway is different again?

"Yes, he is. The lads all love him. He's very serious about his football, there's no mucking about there but he does love a laugh and a joke as well. He wants the team spirit to be good. As he says himself, 'You won't meet a more enthusiastic person than me.' When he first came here he was telling us about the three Es. Enjoyment, encouragement and... what was the other one, I'd better remember it... and enthusiasm. That's the way he tries to go about his everyday work."

What would you class as your stand-out career goals?

"I think the first goal for your club is always a special moment. My first goal for Tottenham was in the Cup at White Hart Lane, against Fulham. It was something I'd dreamed about as a boy. My first for Leicester was the last-minute winner at Forest, after starting a goal down. As I ran back towards the fans I could see them all jumping up and down all over each other. We hadn't beaten Forest away since 1972!"

38

Wanted man

Stan Collymore was only a Leicester City player for nine months, but he was seldom out of the headlines during that memorable time. We chatted on the phone while Stan was at his gym.

What were your first impressions of City?

"I imagine a lot of the players had thought, 'What's he gonna be like? Is he gonna be a bit 'big time?' But I knew Robbie Savage from his Crewe days, so I didn't feel like a complete stranger. My first training session was on a Friday morning and Steve Walford came out with a bag of balls and said, 'Right, f***ing hurry up lads, you can have a five-a-side and then I want to get down the pub!' At Liverpool and Villa, training was very regimented but this was unbelievable, everybody was laughing and it really was fun. Don't get me wrong, it was organised and hard work but I started looking forward to training."

Your home debut was the 5-2 win over Sunderland – a classic City performance...

"Martin has gone on record saying that that Leicester side was as good a team as he's managed, which is praise indeed. Of course, Emile went on to Liverpool after that game. Personally, I was disappointed that I didn't play with him for longer because we could have had a really good partnership. From a professional footballer's perspective, Emile is one of the most underrated strikers that there's been in the British game. Then I was in New York when I heard that Martin was talking to Celtic and I thought, 'Oh, here we go again.' I've had a few months under a manager that I totally respected and now I was about to lose him. I was devastated, to be honest. Sometimes all you need is to feel wanted and to feel a part of what's happening, and I have to say that the Leicester team spirit was the best that I'd ever experienced in my professional career. Proper men, I would say. People that would look after you on and off the pitch. People that had a sense of humour and a proper sense of camaraderie. Once the initial few days were out of the way – and I think La Manga helped me in a way – I think the lads got to know me and realised that I was one of them."

What was your relationship like with your new manager, Peter Taylor?

"When you actually get to work with somebody then you see the difference between somebody being a nice fella and being a good coach. He had a lot of self-belief when he was appointed to Leicester and he brought a coach with him called Steve Butler, who had only just retired from playing for Gillingham. I've got to be honest, they didn't have a clue! Peter bought sub-standard players like Ade Akinbiyi and Trevor Benjamin into a system that we'd got used to under Martin. He just didn't understand that Martin had taken a long time to build what we had at Leicester and all he had to do was make minor changes. And I know that a lot of the senior pros agreed with me."

David COATES

City's secrets of the '70s

Former Mansfield Town wing-half David Coates became City's coach under Frank O'Farrell in 1968, thanks to a timely introduction from his old Players' Union friend and new City assistant boss, Malcolm Musgrove. Over 40 years later, we met David at his house in Oadby.

What type of boss was Frank O'Farrell?

"Well, if he didn't like you, he had a way of letting you know. I found it quite amusing. Somebody said how fantastic Rodrigues was running down the right and outpacing everybody, and Frank said, 'Yes, he is... and when he gets ready to centre the ball the crowd in the Double Decker get ready to duck.' It was a humorous aside, but it also happened to be true, and it wasn't long before Frank put Steve Whitworth in the side, from my reserves. He was quick, and although he was quiet I thought he had the bottle. He couldn't kick a ball long but I used to make him practise kicking the ball along the ground up to Frank Worthington up the inside-right channel. The normal thing was for a right-back to clip it long for the forward to chase after the ball, but Frank Worthington didn't chase after the ball. If anyone kicked the ball past him he'd stand and point to his feet. He didn't like running, and he would tell you that. But he loved playing with the ball. Some of his colleagues didn't like him because he didn't run, but he didn't care because he didn't rate them as players. He didn't really recognise defenders because they couldn't play like he could play."

So were there divisions within the side?

"There was a bit of rivalry and jealousy

> **"The Wool was so hopeless at shooting, I said, 'Alan, just go into the woods and stay there.'"**

between Frank and Keith Weller as to who was the 'top man', that was the phrase that was used. Keith Weller was a phenomenal player. At one stage there was a huge fall-out of a domestic matter which led to several members of the team trying to freeze Keith out of the club by not passing the ball to him. Things had gone badly wrong, and I told Jim, 'There's going to be an explosion in this football club.' Then came the infamous match at home to Ipswich – the Big Freeze. Keith came in at half-time, threw his gear on the floor and headed for the bath. 'F*** this for a game of soldiers. If they're not giving me the ball, I'm not going out.'"

How was it all resolved?

"Keith lost the captaincy over that, and some of the lads still didn't know what the hell was going on. They had a team meeting to sort it all out, but we had to make sure Peter Shilton spoke last because he always plunged meetings into chaos. Peter would stand up, quickly becoming the best goalkeeper in the country, and say: 'The problem is we're just not f***ing good enough!' Which translated as 'you lot aren't good enough'. But I was proud to be a part of his progress. I admired and liked Peter Shilton. A lot of people admired him, but not many liked him!"

He was at the heart of City's fantastic defensive record, most notably back in the 1970/71 promotion season...

"Yes, but we had Colin Mackleworth in goal in January. We lost at Middlesbrough and then conceded four goals at home to Birmingham. Pete had decided that he wanted more money. He said to Frank

O'Farrell, 'I'm not playing, I'm fed up.' This never came out in the press, they made up some excuse. After we'd lost to Birmingham, I was outside the referee's room and overheard Frank O'Farrell say to Malcolm Musgrove, "I don't care what f***ing happens, Peter Shilton plays on Wednesday!" And he never swore. The board met with Peter Shilton, and everything was sweetness and light. The headlines read: 'Shilton Signs New Contract!' but they didn't say what sort of money had changed hands. Not only did we not lose another match that season, he only conceded about five goals in all that time. But Alan Woollett, who wasn't a very good player, said to me, 'You've trained every day with him for two years but you still don't know him.' Wool had a way of looking at you that indicated that you were out of your mind. 'Peter Shilton is for Peter Shilton,' he said. 'The next time he wants more money, he'll do the same again.' And, bugger me, the Wool was right. But, the next time, he left."

Does any one training day stand out in your memory?

"I remember we went on a trip to Sweden, a place called Hindasgarden with a lake next to it, which was like heaven. As we were flying out there, Dennis Rofe got drunk on the plane – in fine buoyant form. We had a training session as soon as we landed; but we had directors Mr Sharp and Mr Needham with us. The only trouble was Dennis was pissed and couldn't move his

legs properly. In the end I had to say to him, 'Dennis, at shooting practice, I want you to shoot the ball way beyond the goal,

go and fetch it, but don't come back. Do you get my meaning?' So he toddled off and stayed amongst the trees! The Wool was so hopeless at shooting, I said, 'Alan, just go into the woods and stay there.' That shooting practice went down in the annals of club history."

Tony COTTEE

Malaysian malaise erased

We caught up with City's veteran striker at the Belvoir Drive canteen, at a time when his career was in the midst of unexpected Indian summer.

Your move to Malaysia didn't work out quite as planned. What was wrong with the football out there?

"The football was disappointing and my wife was pregnant, so there were two very good reasons to come back as soon as possible. After 15 years in the top flight of English football, it was just nothing like what I was used to. The weather was unbelievable, it was about 92 degrees, plus the humidity. It was a great leveller, I suppose that was the best way to describe it. I felt like a non-League player at times. I was the record signing, so all the defenders wanted to kick the shit out of me, basically. The refereeing was dubious, the pitches dreadful, the stadiums average..."

Apart from that, though?

"I mentioned the corruption problem to the owner before I actually went there, and he said that it had all been sorted out. But there were possible goings-on when we were playing the bottom team in the league. We were 2-0 up at half-time and within ten minutes of the second half we were 3-2 down. Some of the goals were the worst I've ever seen, so I thought, 'Hmmm... I'm not so sure about this one!' I always knew I'd

come back to English football but I didn't ever expect it to be a Premiership club. I just thought, you know, Second or First Division, at best."

Did going on loan help you get back to Premier League fitness?

"The club started last season so well, I was getting frustrated playing reserve-team football all the time. I was playing at 50 per cent and still scoring goals, and it was too easy, really. At Birmingham City, it was first-team football. The competitiveness of the First Division helped me. I think me and the manager didn't have a fantastic relationship at the time because I wasn't one of his first-choice players. I was about to get on the bus to Notts County for a reserve team game. He called me into his office and said there was somebody injured, probably Marshy... 'If you do well tonight, there's a good chance you'll be involved on Saturday.' That was the first time he'd given me something to go for. I scored the goal in a 1-0 win at Notts County, and then I scored the winner at Old Trafford on the Saturday! It restarted my career. You miss the interviews and talking for the cameras, but above all you miss playing and the buzz of scoring. If you aren't doing well, then it's a tough life."

How did you deal with Muzzy Izzet having you as a childhood hero when he used to follow West Ham?

"As soon as I arrived, the lads were telling me about Muzzy. I find it hard to come to terms with any adulation from anyone, really, because I think of myself as a normal bloke. It's difficult to realise you've become the player. I think of myself when I looked up to 'Pop' Robson the same way. Muzzy grew up watching me from the terraces and is now playing alongside me –

or am I playing alongside him?!"

When you started out, was it only ever going to be West Ham for you?

"Yes. I trained with Arsenal, I played a good game for them and scored a hat-trick. I could have signed for them, they were very keen. Terry Neill was the manager at the time. Crystal Palace were also interested. Terry Venables was their manager then. But as a West Ham supporter I became aware that they wanted me and signed straight away. Associate schoolboys at 13 and and apprentice at 15. There was only ever one club for me."

You must have found yourself landed among your heroes, at the time?

"Trevor Brooking, Billy Bonds and Frank Lampard were the older players, and Alan Devonshire was good to me. He looked after me. Two years previously, I was watching them from the terraces and then I was playing alongside them. But I got to a frustrating stage in my West Ham career. We finished third in 1985/86, but then the next two seasons we almost got relegated. I didn't want to be fighting relegation at that stage of my career, I wanted to be fighting for trophies and earning a bit more money. It might sound a bit hypocritical, but I wanted to better myself at the time."

You've played alongside a lot of striking partners. How do you rate Emile Heskey?

"He can be as good as he wants to be, really. I don't need to tell you that he's a tremendous player. He's got everything you need in the modern-day footballer,

"You miss the interviews and the cameras, but above all you miss playing and the buzz of scoring."

and he's still only 21 years old. If he can progress, he'll be a regular England international. The great thing about Emile is that he's so down to earth. He wants to learn. I've enjoyed a good partnership with him this season. I'd like to think I've helped him and I certainly know that he's helped my game."

Where do you see your career going, looking forward?

"Well, I'd like to keep playing for as long as I can, even if it means going down the leagues like Peter Beardsley. Ultimately, I'd like to remain in the game as a manager, perhaps at one of my former clubs. West Ham, Everton... or maybe Leicester!"

Happy Hammers: Master and apprentice united at City.

Roger DAVIES

Roger the Dodger

In a Pride Park executive box we got together with Leicester's record £250,000 signing of 1977. Roger was disarmingly frank about his disappointing time at Filbert Street.

How did Brian Clough and Peter Taylor come to sign you from the non-League?

"I'd only played about ten games for Worcester, but there was a little bit of paper talk when I got seven goals in three games. It was Peter who had watched me play, so I went to Derby on his judgement. Brian was the one who used to lift me to an unbelievable extent. We played Bolton in the Central League during my first season there and I scored one, chipping the keeper from just inside our own half. Cloughie said to me, 'I dreamt that I scored a goal like that once.' I still remember it now! He was so good at delivering one-liners to people, whether it was praise or a bollocking. He knew exactly what buttons to press."

There's famous documentary footage of a training session with Cloughie, which was reconstructed in *The Damned United*...

ROGER DAVIES

LEICESTER

"Yes, I think it was Barry Butlin who took a corner because he was shouting at him, and I scored a great volley from that corner from outside the box – and it was only a five-a-side sized goal. But you don't see that, you just see him shouting: '*Baz!* You're a bloody disgrace.' The film has a bit of director's licence, but it's okay. The book was a truer reflection of the time."

Did you identify anyone playing you?

"I think it was George Clooney! I told Archie Gemmill that they'd got little Jackie Wright, the bald man in *The Benny Hill Show*, to play him."

You were Belgian Player of the Year at Bruges in 1977, then left to join Leicester in the middle of an appalling season...

"Frank McLintock didn't have to sell Leicester too hard. I was looking at the calibre of players. Keith Weller was still there. Steve Kember. They brought Geoff Salmons in. David Webb, Jeff Blockley, Dennis Rofe – these were all good players. Eddie Kelly, Billy Hughes, Steve Sims. Why did we lose so many games? Even with an inexperienced manager, we should have done a lot better. I think I had a decent start and got Man of the Match my first game against Derby, then played well the second game; but after that it was completely gone. Somebody said to me afterwards, it was like putting a spoonful of hot water into a bucket of cold. We all lost confidence and just couldn't turn it around. Having come in as a record signing, I have to admit it was the worst spell of my career. The ball was coming to you and you weren't just trusting yourself to do what came naturally. You were thinking, 'Do I really want this?' or 'Don't make a mistake'. I was pretty successful everywhere else, for Derby and Bruges and in the States. But I'm sorry, Leicester fans, I didn't do it on purpose."

Frank McLintock talked about the team looking good in training. It was just Saturday afternoons when we fell to bits...

"I think there came a point where Frank was trying to change everything, change, change, change, instead of sticking with a tried-and-trusted plan. Clutching at straws, a bit. One game, near the end of the season, I remember Steve Earle going down the left and me thinking, 'I hope his cross doesn't reach me.' What a state to get yourself in."

Meanwhile, you had a day off to get married while City were playing at Old Trafford. How did you manage that?

"I know, it wouldn't happen now! It was part of the contract, the whole wedding had already been arranged when I signed for Leicester. It was all booked for the 27th December. Perhaps if I'd been banging the goals in, they might have thought differently and changed their minds."

What were your first impressions of Jock Wallace, back in the summer of '78?

"Big. Loud. Quite strict. Once you got to know him, he was great. I had an injury problem dating back to the Belgian Cup final, a slipped disc, so I'd been playing with pain in my back and down my legs. I had to have surgery that summer, and Jock told me he admired the way I'd battled through all that. I think I was his sort of player, one who put the effort in, and he was really great with me. I think everyone loved him; maybe not quite so much when they were running up and down those sandhills. Eddie Kelly was trying to put a brave face on it. He said, 'Sandhills? I've been in bigger bunkers!' I played a few games that season, got a couple of goals, but it was clear, really, that it wasn't going to work out for me at Leicester. As soon as I moved out to Tulsa, it all came back. I started to play well again. You were playing in warm weather in your trainers and I was back on form. We played a game at Fort Lauderdale and Jock was there because he was on holiday. I met him afterwards and the first thing he said to me was, 'Why the f*** didn't you play like that for me?!'"

> "I remember thinking, 'I hope his cross doesn't reach me.' What a state to get yourself in."

Tim DAVIES

Staring into the void

Leicester City had just come out of administration when we first met the club's Chief Operating Officer in his Walkers Stadium office overlooking the River Soar.

Why did you want to take on the rather thankless role of a football Chief Exec?

"If, like me, you love football, you love Leicester City and you have the right qualifications to do the job, then it's a great job to have; although, you are the person who gets shouted at the most. I'm a custodian looking after the future of this club, and it isn't totally thankless. What attracted me to the job was being a Leicester fan since the age of three or four. I was also involved in sport quite a lot in my career. When the club got into trouble, I thought I'd like to try and

help to save them. I joined the Gary Lineker consortium as one of the four key members."

A lot of fans might not realise how close the club came to going out of business...

"There were a couple of times when the club went within half an hour to an hour of completely going out of existence. There was one particular time when everyone else had given up on Teachers trying to negotiate a figure. I remember calling them at one or two o'clock in the morning to have one last go, and they gave in. There was another time, the day we came out of administration, and the Football League changed the terms and conditions that afternoon. We almost had to pull out then because of what we'd told our potential investors. There was another time when the administrators ran out of money, so five of us had to put in £50,000 each to keep the club running."

Do you think the Football League were giving us a fair crack of the whip?

"Well, I thought the goalposts were being moved all the time. We were very, very unpopular with the Football League, and a majority of clubs hated us for doing what we did. But we were a completely new set of people, and it wasn't our fault that the club had gone into administration."

What about the previous regime?

"I don't want to get into a blame culture, but if the club were ever to get relegated then this situation was waiting to happen. Then there was the collapse of the ITV Digital deal and the collapse of the transfer market. Previously, people had thought they could trade out of trouble by selling a few players. This was suddenly not possible because players wouldn't move because of their high wages, and there were no transfer fees. It's easy now to question certain signings and the annual wage bills. Hindsight is a wonderful thing."

Tim DAVIES

Foxes v Tigers

A year later, we spoke to Tim on a variety of pressing issues, from the mooted groundshare to players' wages and the controversial new one-year kit cycle.

What was it that finally put paid to the idea of a groundshare with the Tigers?

"It was the issue of Primacy of Tenure. If rugby and football clash, then football has precedence. The Tigers didn't want to be in a position where they'd have to move their fixtures. In reality we're not allowed to play at the same time anyway by the police, so it may not have been an issue. In a way, it's good we now know our future. We're on our own, and a lot of people will be pleased about that. But commercially and financially it's not so good. Had the Tigers deal gone ahead, then we would have been able to put a significant amount straight to our bottom line which would have gone to the playing side, and made it easier for us to compete at a higher level."

How much smaller is the players' wage bill compared to last season?

"If you include everything like transfers in and agents' fees, then it's gone from about £12 million to £7 million. Having said that, we had a few players last year, who weren't necessarily in the team, from the pre-administration era – Trevor Benjamin, Matt Elliott, James Scowcroft and Ian Walker – who were on very large wages. So it isn't quite a true comparison. Wages have gone down across the board so it doesn't reflect the quality of the players we have now. We still have one of the largest wage bills in the division."

Season tickets offer good value at around £12 a game; but isn't £34 a bit steep for a single ticket in the West Stand?

"Firstly, you could become a season ticket holder. Secondly, match ticket prices will be a lot cheaper if you're a member."

Compared with the first season at Filbert Way crowds are still 12,000 down...

"Well, they weren't charging enough for ticket prices, and we went bust."

But you're still left with a stadium that's one-third empty on match days...

"Yes, but look at football grounds in general this season and they're emptier, Premiership and our division. If attendances are all about prices, then why are we 2,000 season-ticket holders down on last season?"

Because last season was pretty dire?

"If I reduce the prices, as I tried to do last year, I then get lots of letters from season-ticket holders complaining that I've reduced the value of their tickets. I get more complaints that way than I do about matchday ticket prices. I certainly don't want to upset all my loyal customers. And last year, when we charged £15 for some games,

> **"Season tickets are among the cheapest, rewarding the loyal fans, the majority of our fanbase."**

we didn't really see any bigger numbers. I wouldn't argue that price is an issue, but there are lots of other issues as well!"

Paul DICKOV

The Pest takes control

Paul 'The Pest' Dickov joined City in tough times, suffering relegation and administration in short order. But when we spoke at Belvoir Drive he was in the midst of a personal-best 20-goal season, which helped City bounce straight back.

After seven and a half years on the fringes at Arsenal, you really made a name for yourself at Manchester City...

"Yes, the two promotions were both very special but, from a personal point of view, scoring a goal in the 95th minute of a Wembley Play-off final is something you dream about. At Man City the players wanted to do it for the fans because there were 30,000-plus turning out for Second Division games. The same's true here at Leicester, with 30,000-plus crowds turning out after a relegation season. It's unthinkable, really. It does create a real bond between

"We can help people get their jobs back if we get promoted. It's given us a siege mentality."

the players and the fans."

Is Micky Adams' style a contrast to how we were playing under Dave Bassett?

"Not really, because when Harry was manager, Micky took most of the training. The Gaffer, I mean. You can get fined for that. The Gaffer took most of the training. Harry was more direct. I mean, the Gaffer likes us to get the ball forward quickly but he does like us to play football as well. He's great, especially with all the well-documented problems going on at the club. It's hard for him, but he does his best to keep it all away from us. He's created a fantastic spirit among the lads, which is important after getting relegated. It would be easy to start the next season a bit down and sorry for yourself."

Do you really get fined for not calling Micky the Gaffer?

"Well, we did do when he first took over. It was a fun thing. He likes to have a laugh and a joke with the players. I think Frank Sinclair pays out a bit for being late. Jordan Stewart is always in there. I've had a few myself. It is easy to pick up a fine. You can get one for picking your nose. It's all a laugh, and it all goes to a good cause."

Just before the club went into administration the players agreed on a wage deferral. How did you feel about that?

"The players always wanted to do it. The way it came out, it made us look as if we were all money grabbers. That was disappointing. At the time it was all happening, we were having meetings every other day. And each meeting we were getting told a different story. We always wanted to help the club in any way we could. You have a squad of players here who all want to do their best for this club, and I think that shows on a Saturday. The club and the PFA told us the situation the club was in, and we were told what percentage wage deferral would help the club carry on. We wanted to know if the story was going to change again before we agreed to anything."

What effect do all the cuts and redundancies have on the squad?

"They have a big effect. One of the main reasons we agreed to the wage deferral was that we wanted everyone involved with the club to keep their jobs. Especially the ones who work down at the training ground that we see every day, that have worked here for years and are Leicester City fans through and through. It was very sad. The best way we can help people get their jobs back is to get promoted – and that's helped give us a siege mentality."

It's great that the goals are really flowing for you now – and the yellow cards, too...

"I've been a bit disappointed with some of them, myself. At Bradford, I was thinking, 'Well, their centre-back's been kicking the shit out of me all game and nothing happened to him.' I won't change the way I play. I'll chase every ball and I'll give 110 per cent, but it's always at the back of your mind that if you mistime a

tackle or someone goes down, the yellow card's going to come out. Then you get a bit of a reputation. I'm going to have to be a bit more careful and try and channel my aggression better. It's just my commitment. I don't think you should be punished for being committed to your club."

What's your verdict on the new stadium?

"We're loving it. The atmosphere really gives you a buzz, especially when it's full. It's incredible that there are 10,000 more supporters turning out than there were at Filbert Street last season. Just because you get a new stadium doesn't mean it will automatically get filled."

Do you remember? Dickov returned to City for a second spell when we were in the third tier.

Homes under the hammer

Dion DUBLIN

As one of Leicester's most successful footballers of recent times, it seemed only fitting when Micky Adams rescued Dion Dublin from a career in exile at clubs such as Coventry City and Aston Villa. We met Dion at Belvoir Drive.

You were raised on Burnmoor Street, right next to the ground...

"Yes, we were straight out of the front door on to the pavement. After a game, the road would be filled to the brim with supporters. If there'd been a bad result, then they'd take it out on our windows. My sister used to take me to City all the time. It was £3 then to sit in the orange seats, up the Wing Stand. I would have been about eight or nine. I used to watch Steve Whitworth, Frank Worthington, Keith Weller, Dennis Rofe, Larry May. Some of the best players the club has ever had."

But you weren't primarily a City fan...

"No, I was a West Brom fan. I liked Cyrille Regis a lot, so I followed his career. The 'Three Degrees,' as they were known,

were together at West Brom. We were very much in a minority in the game back then, so I thought I'd better support the boys."

You somehow slipped through the net at Leicester, and ended up at Cambridge...

"We had some really, really good times at Cambridge. A couple of FA Cup quarter-finals, one at Arsenal and one at home to Crystal Palace. We had some good players then. They weren't really given the freedom to elaborate on their skills because John Beck wanted us to play in a certain way. It may have been ugly to watch but it certainly worked. Nobody liked coming to the Abbey Stadium, it was a horrible place to visit. Put the ball in the corners, cross it and then fight tooth and nail to get it into the back of the net. It worked. But it all came to a head at Leicester."

That 5-0 play-off game is still a great memory for Leicester fans...

"Well, we just felt the opposite, obviously. I remember Colin Bailie, a senior pro, saying to me, 'These are going to be some of the best times of your life. Cambridge United aren't going to have times like these again.' We had some really good players..."

City signed Lee Philpott, and Steve Claridge a bit later. It took you longer to come full circle back to Leicester...

"There are a lot of factors you have to take into consideration when you play for your home town. In a way, Leicester weren't just signing me, they were signing my family, too. When my brother goes into work, they all know he's my brother, and it's all about Leicester City there. I've got three brothers and a sister and my parents all in Leicester, so I had to

consider how they'd feel about me coming back. And if things didn't go that well, how they would react. I spoke to them about it and they were desperate for me to come back. I said to them, 'Okay, as long as you know it won't all be plain sailing.' It's been okay so far!"

When Micky Adams left, were you surprised, disappointed?

"A bit of both, really. Very surprised, because he'd brought about 12 players in, and I don't think people gave him enough time to turn things round. He's a very strong, honest, opinionated manager."

How is Craig Levein different?

"Craig is a thinker. He thinks before he talks. He delivers good motivational team talks. They make you sit up. Whatever he does, you know he's thought about it before he's done it. I think he's made a massive difference. He's brought calm, he's brought a lot of belief. The staff he's brought in are good. Training's good. Rob Kelly is superb. I think it's only going to get better with time, too. This season has been poor for the players and the club and the fans. But we have enough here in this squad to do well in this division."

"Up front, I'm doing what I do best. At centre-half, I'm destroying. I prefer to create things."

You made it on to the *120 Greatest Leicester City Goals* DVD...

"Yes, I did. Away at Rotherham. Very rare for me to score from outside the box. I think it was Martin Keown who played it forward, David Connolly nodded it down... I knew I was a long way out but the keeper had been trying to read my flick-ons to David and was out of his goal a bit. I managed to loop it over the keeper. One of my better ones, with a bit of centre-forward's instinct about it."

Another real highlight of the season was the winner at Charlton in the FA Cup...

"The nicest thing about that was the timing of the goal. If we'd scored with 25 minutes to go then it wouldn't have been as satisfying. Charlton had no time to regroup. A lot of joy came out in my celebration in front of our fans. It gave them something back for travelling all that way and giving us such great backing."

Did you know? Dion is the inventor of a percussion box called the Dube.

51

Matt ELLIOTT

Getting out from under

From Charlton reserves and Torquay via Scunthorpe and Oxford, it took a while for Matt Elliott to get his big chance at Leicester City. We talked about his career trajectory in the glam setting of Matt's car in the Belvoir Drive car park.

Realistically, had you given up on playing in the top flight?

"I hadn't given up, but not far off. I remember saying to some of the Scunthorpe lads that when you hit the 25-year mark, you're on the way down; you're no longer a prospect. But then I moved to Oxford and got the chance to play in the First Division, although we got relegated. I kept hearing that clubs were interested, then suddenly it came to a head. When Leicester found out that Graeme Souness was interested at Southampton, I think that kick-started Martin O'Neill into making a move. Martin impressed me a lot, and when he came to see me, John Robertson, Steve Walford and the chairman all turned up as well, which suggested they were keen to sign me. It's nice to feel welcome."

What were your personal highlights of your first season at Filbert Street?

"My home debut, and just playing

against the top sides week after week. Obviously, I'd played a few big sides in the cup competitions but week after week is something different. Also the game against Sheffield Wednesday when we became safe and I managed to score the goal. It saved a lot of panicking and worrying in that last week. Steve Walford stayed on 20 fags a day instead of the 40 he would have been on. The whole season was good, but we were letting things slip and it was dragging on with us short of the survival target, so it was a relief."

Having come to the top flight late in your career, are you still a bit like a kid in a sweetshop?

"I've probably acclimatised a little bit more now, but it's still nice. I've got a collection of tops from the players I've played against. I've got near enough all the ones I want. Some of the lads find it a bit strange – 'What do you want his top for?' – and I say that I might not get the chance to play against them again. They think that I should consider myself on a par with them. I've got Shearer, Wright, Ginola, Mark Hughes... I have a quick word after the game and if they say no, they say no. But nine times out of ten they're all right. I'm still after Bergkamp's, though. I got Vieri's when we played Madrid. It's a good collection now."

The City defence is currently third best in the Premiership for goals conceded. That must be a source of real satisfaction to you?

"We work well as a side. I mean, Neil and Muzzy work feverishly in front of us, tracking the runners brilliantly. Robbie Savage has come in and done really well. Steve Guppy was bought really as an out-and-out winger. I don't think he could see himself in the wing-back role – it isn't his natural game, but he's done really well. Having Kasey, who's a top-quality keeper, behind us helps as well. The side is a unit, so the whole team takes credit for the Goals Against column. I think that people are coming to realise we're a half-decent side. Other teams know they're going to have their hands full against us. I mean, we're a hard-working side, we try and keep up a high tempo, and it seems to work. I don't think anyone can doubt the ability of the side."

What have been the highlights for you this season?

"Our good start to the season, particularly beating Liverpool at Anfield, which we thoroughly deserved. Our European adventure, and playing a side like Atletico Madrid. I think their front five are as good as any side's anywhere, especially when Juninho was playing. And Leicester playing Manchester

lapse in concentration to let Bergkamp in. Although it was a brilliant piece of skill, I perhaps could have done a touch better. Then Walshy came along and saved the day for us. It was a great finish to what hadn't been a particularly brilliant game

> **"At Torquay, I came back from close season a stone overweight. It took half a season to get rid of it."**

United. That was the first time I'd ever been to Old Trafford – never mind playing there, or winning there! Also the Arsenal game at home. They're a really strong side, and we all thought they were going to win the League at that stage of the season. Although they dipped a bit, I think we've now been proven right. Bergkamp is a class act. He's got the lot, really. It was a strange game and, when I scored, everyone was delighted at scraping a point off them. But then we had perhaps a little

up until then."

Now you're playing for Scotland and looking forward to this summer's World Cup in America. Were you tempted to wait for an England call-up at all?

"People were talking about it after I'd played about eight or nine games for Leicester but I didn't really think I'd ever be playing international football. When Craig Brown phoned up and asked me, well, you don't hang about when you get asked something like that..."

Dennis who? Matt steals the limelight in *that* Arsenal game. Temporarily.

53

A difficult proposition

Matt ELLIOTT

Meeting Matt again, we looked back on the events of the past 18 years over lunch at Poacher's Brasserie in Thurlaston.

You ended up with 18 Scotland caps, but they all fell either side of France '98...

"It was a bit frustrating. I roomed with my fellow adopted Scot, the goalkeeper Neil Sullivan. We were actually mates growing up and played for the same team in south-west London. It was quite bizarre to find ourselves, 15 years later, rooming together at a World Cup. Especially as we were playing for Scotland!"

Your first Wembley trip was against Spurs, when Frank Sinclair was dropped...

"Yes, it was another exciting season for us with our Cup exploits. But the final was a non-event of a game. Although they had players like David Ginola, Les Ferdinand and Sol Campbell, we felt that we were a better team than them during that period. So it was very frustrating to lose that one. Before a Wembley game, Martin would take us out to a show in the West End. I think it was *Saturday Night Fever* that year, which was good fun with all the lads bopping about in the aisles. Most of them were totally against the idea at first, but were then all up and jigging about by the end. We had a meal, and after that there was a team meeting, but Frank had gone off to see a mate that lived nearby. His punishment was to be left out of the starting line-up. It probably proved quite costly, you can't say for sure."

Spurs even went down to ten men...

"Yes, Robbie Savage, up to his antics! I thought, 'Well, surely we can do it now, even though we aren't performing well.' But they got a late winner. I think we let the supporters down a bit that day. Wembley isn't a good place to lose. We beat them at White Hart Lane soon after that, which proved that we had the upper hand over them most of the time. Not long after that game, Tottenham came in for me. Martin called me into the office after training. This was a bit out of the ordinary. He said, 'George Graham has put in a £5 million bid for you.' I said, 'You're joking? I can't believe that!' And Martin said, 'No, neither can I!' He said, 'If you want to go, then go. But I'm not saying I want you to go.' I'm thinking, 'What's going on here? Is it mind games?' I went back in to see him the next day and I told him, 'I'd like to stay. I think we've got more going on than Tottenham at the moment.' He said, 'That's what I wanted to hear. Good lad. I'll have a new contract ready for you tomorrow.' I said, 'Oh, okay!'"

The following season, you started playing

up front as an emergency striker...

"Yes, it was quite exciting, really. Not much pressure on me, if I made a mistake it wasn't going to cost us a goal! For the first game, John Robertson said, 'Don't worry, it's only Desailly and Leboeuf!' They'd won the World Cup about two months before. Robbo said to me, 'Just go up there and cause havoc, son.' I think we got a draw that day. I had a bit of a set-to with Roberto Di Matteo and Gus Poyet, who weren't too happy with the physical aspect of my game. We had a few words going down the tunnel and they ended up locking themselves in the away dressing rooms. I chased them in there and they shut the door on me! Luckily, the officials didn't see that one."

You scored the only goal in the League Cup semi against Villa... so back to Wembley!

"Two goals and going up the steps to lift the trophy – that had to be the best day of my professional life. It was like a boyhood dream. Two goals, Man of the Match, lifting the trophy – and my son was due to be born that day, so I had that added concern that he might arrive on time! Thankfully, he held out for another three days so I could enjoy the celebrations. And my dad, who is sadly no longer with us, had £20 on me as first and last goalscorer,

"I chased them down the tunnel and they ended up locking themselves in the away dressing rooms."

so he won £600 – happy days all round!"

Who would you say were your best defensive partners over your time at City?

"I was lucky to play alongside a few very solid centre-halves. More often than not it was a three, either Steve Walsh, Gerry Taggart, Frank Sinclair, they all had their different strengths. And Spencer Prior and Julian Watts before that. I think I had a very good understanding with Walshy and Taggs, and we're still good friends today. We'd have words with each other on the pitch frequently, especially me and Gerry, though fortunately I couldn't understand anything he was saying. The opposition forwards would look at us screaming and bawling at each other, and then be surprised to see us best mates in the players' bar after the game. Walshy didn't shout so much, he'd just have a quiet word. I think when the three of us were together and fully fit we were quite a difficult proposition. Not blessed with much pace, but we got by."

Sven Goran ERIKSSON

The Zen of Sven

Germany 1-5 England. Beating Argentina in Japan. Seven titles in three years at Lazio. And now Sven was at Leicester to add to his list of career highs – just as soon as our calm, rather avuncular leader had run his masterplan past us, in his office at Belvoir Drive.

How would you describe your personal footballing philosophy?

"Well, I like my teams to be very aggressive, to press on to the opposition. I like my players to be technically good, playing the ball as much as possible. I try to be a little bit organised when we are attacking. I want players to know what they have to do to give the man with the ball options. I don't believe in handing them the ball and wishing them good luck."

And how close is this Leicester side to your ideal model?

"Of course, you are always looking for better quality. In training we are playing as much football as possible, we are not running very much. We are playing, playing, playing... because that gives you quality. One of the best expressions I ever heard was from Mourinho. Someone asked him, 'Why are you never running in training, you are always playing

football?' He said, 'If I want to be good at playing the piano, you don't run round the piano, you sit and play it.'"

Fitness, technique and ability are important, but how much of football is in the player's mind?

"That depends on how you are coaching them. If you keep saying to players, 'You have to do this, you have to do that,' then they might not find it that interesting. We like to encourage feedback. We invite them to have opinions. Is this right, or should we try something different? If they don't believe, then they will never do it 100 per cent, and that is the same in every job."

How did you first find out that Leicester City were interested in approaching you?

"I got a phone call from an agent, and he was really offering me another job. I met up with him in London and we were talking about an international post, not in Europe; but he started to talk about Leicester. I was not convinced when I went into the meeting with Leicester's owners, but leaving the meeting I was rather convinced, yes."

What changed your mind?

"Nice people, first of all, but you don't take the job because of nice people. Mainly the project. And the fact that they have high ambitions. At the time I met them, Leicester were bottom of the league, but their ambition wasn't just to stay in the league. They weren't coming to me saying, 'Save us!' They were still aiming to get to the Premier League as quick as possible. They haven't said it is a must this year, but they want it. Everything is here to be in the Premier League, it is only that we are not."

Which performances this season have pleased you the most?

"I was perhaps most pleased last Tuesday. It was an awful football game. Just fighting, fighting. But we did it and we took three points. I'm sure a couple of months ago we would have lost that game. But now we can do it. There is no doubt we can play football but on a night like that, when the pitch made it impossible, we still stood up and won. That makes our belief even bigger. We tried to pass the ball and it was bumping all over the place."

Is that why you asked for the pitch at the Walkers to be relaid?

"Absolutely. After the Manchester City game the pitch was very bad. And the groundsman said to me, 'Sven, it's going to be like that until May.' So I went to the owners and said, 'We need to be able to play football, can we get a new pitch?' 'If you think so, then do it,' they said. Thank you. And the day after, they started on it. It shows what the owners are here for."

After all the preparation, once a game has started how much influence can a coach or manager have from the sidelines?

"My father was very calm, he never shouted at me. Maybe he should have done sometimes."

Use your Swede: Sven reveals his revolutionary 4-1-2 formation.

"Less than you might think. You can only really give instructions when someone is injured and you have the chance to call players over. Shouting, most of the players can't hear because you are too far away and the crowd noise. That's why I think you should have the chance to take time off for 30 seconds in the middle of each half. Half time, of course, is your only real chance to make changes."

Towards the end of your time as England manager the press were giving you a hard time. How did that affect you?

"It didn't really affect me personally. You have to phone your parents and children and explain to them what is going on, but that's not a problem. But I have said this many times, the English people are not a mirror of the English press. English people are educated. Everywhere I have been since I first came to this country it has always been, 'Well done!' or 'Unlucky... lost on penalties again.' Even today. The press is not really what English people are about. I never heard a bad word from the people."

Tim FLOWERS

England's number one

Tim Flowers was a brilliant signing by Martin O'Neill, who pounced when the England keeper was temporarily out of Blackburn's first team. In the noisy Belvoir Drive canteen, we talked winning the League with a real goalkeeping great.

We haven't been able to find out, are you related to Ron Flowers, the Wolves player?

"No, I'm often asked if he's my father, what with the name and the fact that I started at Wolves. I know Ron. He owns a sports shop in Wolverhampton. When I was at Wolves they were so broke that they used to give me a chitty to go and buy some new gloves. So I used to walk up to Ron's shop and he'd write a chitty out for £20 for two pairs of £15 gloves and give me a fiver. I was only a 17-year-old apprentice, but they had to put me in the first team because they couldn't afford to buy another goalkeeper. The apprentices would have to clean the bogs, paint the ground, everything."

Who were your role models as a keeper?

"Well, there were two. It was when Revie was alternating Clemence and Shilton for England games. I thought they were both great keepers. When I signed for Wolves,

TIM FLOWERS

John Burridge was the one that really helped me. I had no money and he used to give me gloves or a pair of tracksuit bottoms, and I used to think it was Christmas. When I went

to Southampton as a 19 year old, Peter Shilton was the number one there and I learnt a lot off him as well. When Shilton went to Derby, Southampton actually bought Budgie back to haunt me!"

Coming up to date, what was said between you and Frank Sinclair after the Arsenal and Chelsea own-goals?

"Well, no one means to score an own-goal, so there was no question of me going up to Frank and saying, 'You t***!' We were all spewing. Arsenal had pounded us a bit but it looked as though we were going to nick a point, which would have been a big result for us and a great start to the season. The Chelsea one was going in anyway. I wasn't going to get it, for sure. Frank had been playing well in both games, I just told him not to worry about it. I told him hundreds of centre-halves have scored own-goals past me, and it hadn't even been a good one!"

"You've already picked up a couple of serious injuries this season. As a goalie, is it possible to be too brave?

"That's a difficult one. I was unlucky up at Middlesbrough because I honestly didn't think Robbie Mustoe was going to dive in. I saw him coming but I thought, 'That's mine.' I couldn't understand why he did it. With the Bradbury one at Crystal Palace, it was a simple case of, if I don't dive in then he's definitely going to score. So then you have the question: do I stand there and shit my pants or do I dive in? I'd rather take a knock and keep the ball out of the net. Nine times out of ten, he'd have booted me and after a bit I would have been okay, but on this occasion I was wide open. I couldn't get my knees up for protection and he just went straight through me."

Your top didn't quite fit Theo Zagorakis...

You've won 11 England caps and made the squad for two major tournaments...

"My first appearance was against Brazil under Graham Taylor. We had a team talk and he said, 'Oh, they've got one lad who likes to shoot direct from corners.' I thought, 'I'll get me coat!' But we got a draw and restored a little bit of pride after losing to the USA. I swapped shirts with their goalie, Taffarel. I had to give him my nice yellow England one and unfortunately got this minging pink one off him! Beating Italy in the French Tournoi stands out, too, because it was Italy and it was 2-0."

Euro '96 was a highlight, too?

"It was fantastic. It was great when the whole thing took off all over the country. After we played a Hong Kong Select XI, the idea was we should all get together for a bit of bonding and building up the spirit in the squad for Euro '96. Me and Alan

"It isn't just about transfer fees. You've got to want it in here. It's got to be burning inside you."

"Theo looked like a schoolboy! I think it was a case of everyone else taking a step back and Theo being left there. He's played in goal in the gym and they all thought he was good, but that was in the six-a-side goals. I mean, he hasn't organised a wall before, so he didn't know you can't take that long over it!"

As a recent arrival, how highly do you rate this Leicester City side?

"I think if it wasn't Leicester City then there'd be a couple more players with international recognition. It was the same at Southampton – Matt Le Tissier didn't get picked for ages. Muzzy Izzet, for me, is sensational. He must be knocking on the door. If Guppy or Heskey were playing for a bigger team, they'd both have a dozen caps by now. I think we're actually as good as our League place now – seventh."

Shearer walked into this club and there was Gazza running up to people and tearing their T-shirts up the middle. The place was heaving. We looked at each other and said, 'This really stinks, we're going to get done.' So we got out of there. I couldn't see the dentist's chair, I only read about that. The photos got in the paper and, the next thing you know, we're all villains and every player in the squad is a dick. Well, they weren't dicks when they got into the semi-finals – I think some of them were up for a knighthood, then. And if we'd have got knocked out in the group stage, they'd have wanted to hang us."

Matty FRYATT

I predict a riot...

Super Matty Fryatt! We met up with our popular former striker at St George's Park, the FA training centre. Sadly, it was on the very day that Matt announced his retirement from the game.

Craig Levein lasted just three matches after he signed you up for City in 2006...

"I think some of the players found Craig a bit on the strict side. Then Rob came in and gave them a bit more freedom to play. Generally, you can be a top-class coach, but maybe lack that ruthlessness that can give you a fear factor. I'm not saying you need to be a bully but, after you've had that initial good response, you need something a bit harder to keep it going. Perhaps an assistant that will dish out the tellings-off, which Rob didn't really have."

How did you get on with Martin Allen?

"I got on okay with him, but he didn't want to know me as a player. I was completely cast aside. He was constantly trying to sell me to raise funds for new players. He turned down a bid for me from Wolves, then the next minute he was asking me to leave the club! I ended up training with the kids. He was an

interesting one. At the Walkers Stadium there was this gym room with some physio beds near the changing rooms, and he changed it into a cinema room. There was a big sofa and famous movie scenes on boards on the walls. Like Arnie Schwarzenegger with his big gun. It was supposed to be a chillout zone after the game. When Gary Megson replaced Martin he went in there and said, 'F***ing chill room? You can forget that, get all that shit out of there. We want it hot, we don't want anyone f***ing chilling!' Martin also had all the flowerbeds changed to blue, white and yellow. I did remember thinking at the time that out of all the things that needed doing at a football club – signing new players, working out how you wanted them to play – perhaps the colour of the flowers wasn't one of the first priorities."

Did things get better under Ian Holloway?

"Well, at that point we had Steve Howard, Barry Hayles, Iain Hume, myself and DJ Campbell. He knew that we all effectively had goals in us, but you can't play five forwards. Sometimes he'd put Iain on the right wing, me on the left wing, Steve and DJ in the middle and perhaps Barry in the hole. It was never settled and it was a bit lopsided. I wasn't blessed with electric pace, so I couldn't beat a full-back and get a cross over. You'd play one game and then not be seen for the next three. Then you'd be back in at right wing, or up front, or in the hole. It really was all over the shop. When you look at that team that went down, it was a disgrace. I know we had a record number of points for going down, but it shouldn't have happened. And I was absolutely diabolical that season, I couldn't finish a chance to save my life. But there was so much chopping and changing, even after we'd won a game."

The last game, at Stoke, saw City drop into the third tier for the first time ever...

"I think, deep down, we were relegated before the game, although it wasn't a bad performance on the day. I think the game before, losing 3-1 to Sheffield Wednesday at home, was the one that did it. After that, the feeling was that we were down. That's how I felt anyway. It was just awful."

You hit a rich vein of goals under Nigel Pearson, with 20 before Christmas...

"Fortunately, it just kicked off from the opening game when I got two goals against MK Dons. My confidence was back and from then on my thinking was, 'How many will I score today?' That season, everything I tried seemed to work for me. Partly about confidence, and also feeling really fit. And having a manager that believed in you. Steve Howard did all the donkey work, and I'd finish off his knock-downs. I've never really played with a target man since then. There aren't many left now."

Was Pearson's success down to a solid team spirit in the dressing room?

"Right from the start, his pre-season was spot-on, and he knew exactly what he wanted. A solid team at the back, but with enough about them to go and get a goal. Even on an off day, we could grind out a win. If he didn't like you as a player then you knew about it, but at least you knew where you stood. We were well drilled, and when you're winning a lot of games you want to be part of that. It was very clear what he wanted from everyone. You could fit in with that, or be out of the door."

Nigel Pearson departed, to be replaced

> "I remember thinking at the time, perhaps the colour of the flowers wasn't one of the first priorities."

by Paulo Sousa – if only for nine games...

"Paulo wanted us to play it out from the back, and I'm not sure we were suited to that. And the players he brought in weren't really an improvement on what we had. It was a very solid team, and he should probably have tried to tinker with it rather than change things so much straight away. That was his downfall. Sven brought in a few name players, but I don't think he really knew what Championship football was all about. Looking back, I probably threw my toys out of the pram and didn't fight for my place. I was soon on my way up to Hull, and I was happy to join up with Nigel Pearson again. It all happened very quickly."

Matt on his broken jaw: "I lost about three stone and grew a beard. I looked like Tom Hanks in *Castaway*."

Blue Is the Colour

Chris GARLAND

Chris Garland was a striker in Jimmy Bloomfield's '70s side. A brave Bristolian in a team crammed with Cockneys, he scored 19 goals in 60 games before heading back to his beloved Bristol City. By the time we met up at Chris's house in Newport, over the Bristol Channel, he had already been fighting Parkinson's Disease for some 16 years.

Snapped up by Chelsea for £100,000 in 1971, how did a young West Country lad deal with the bright lights of London?

"It was difficult. Dave Sexton said to me straight away, 'You're going to have to grow up quick here. Cockney lads are a bit different, and if you aren't careful they'll get to you. You've got to give as good as you get.' They'd leave potatoes and cabbages by my peg in the changing rooms. Lettuces in the summer when they were in season. There was also a big drinking culture at Stamford Bridge at that time. One day we were at the BBC to do 'Blue Is the Colour' for *Top of the Pops*. After rehearsing all day there were several players who simply couldn't stand up, they'd had so much to drink. We had to draft in some passers-by just to make up the numbers!"

You moved from Chelsea to Leicester in March 1975...

"Yes, I had a choice of Leicester or Everton at that time. I spoke to Jimmy and he struck me as a nice,

genuine guy. Leicester reminded me of Bristol City as it was a friendly club and the Leicester people were nice and friendly. They were warm and kind, not so severe as your Cockneys. Mind you, there were six or seven Cockneys in the Leicester team at the time, and Jimmy was a Londoner."

You once said that one of your regrets was not talking to Everton?

"Well, it's just that I was always so naïve. I liked what I saw at Leicester, so I didn't talk to Everton. When I went from Bristol to Chelsea I signed a blank contract and said to Dave Sexton, 'You sort it out.' I was happy enough when my pay went up from £50 to £80 – until I found out that Peter Osgood was on over £200 a week! At Leicester I was on £125 a week, and I was still on that when I returned to Bristol – and I never got any of my signing-on fees. I always took it gratefully because I loved playing the game, but I was done, really."

When you arrived at Leicester we were deep in the relegation zone...

"Yes, I think we drew the first couple of games against Coventry and Liverpool and then we beat Wolves 3-2 at home, and I got a hat-trick. Getting that win then really lifted everything and there was just a different atmosphere about the place. Anyway, I got eight goals in ten games and we ended up getting clear of trouble."

You also scored a hat-trick for City against Sheffield United in the FA Cup the following season...

"Yes, I'm one of very few players to have scored a hat-trick in the League, the FA Cup and League Cup, and I did mine within 12 months. I know my hit rate wasn't that great, but hat-tricks in three different competitions, I'll settle for that."

Who did you most enjoy playing

alongside in your time with Leicester City?

"Steve Kember arrived not long after me. We'd been team-mates at Chelsea so it was good to play alongside Gyppo again. Frank Worthington was a great player to watch, with fantastic skills. I'm not sure we worked that well together, he was difficult to read. Keith Weller was fantastic, probably the best player I've ever seen with the ball at his feet. He provided great crosses, and he was just a natural."

Wasn't there an incident with Jeff Blockley during your spell here?

"Well, at the end of training we'd have a five-a-side game for half an hour, and Jimmy would put a few apprentices into the game to bring them on a bit. I thought Jeff was a bit over-aggressive with some of the young lads. After a bit of this, I stayed near to Jeff – I was on his team, actually – in case anything untoward happened. Then he did it again, so I went for him. It was a lucky punch. I felt pretty bad about breaking his cheekbone. It was a good job for me I put him down with that one punch because if I'd have missed, he would've killed me!"

You were diagnosed with Parkinson's Disease when you were 39. When did you know something was wrong?

"I had a bad neck for two or three years, I thought it was from heading the ball too much. I was only in the doctor's office

for 15 minutes before he said, 'You've got Parkinson's Disease.' I didn't even know what it was. They told me I'd be mumbling and shuffling along and probably in a wheelchair in ten years' time. But thanks to the PFA I now have a stimulator in my chest [Chris taps it and

"Jimmy Bloomfield was a good judge of a player. He signed me, didn't he?"

produces a knocking sound], I have wires going up my neck under the skin which are connected to a probe in my brain. I'm more in control now. I don't fall asleep when I'm driving down the motorway, which is a relief for my wife."

Photo: Neville Chadwick Photography.

63

Love thy neighbour

Phil GEE

Phil Gee had only just joined Brian Little's Leicester City from Derby County when we met him (and his wife, Anita) at their house in Derbyshire.

When did you first hear about the deal involving you and Ian Ormondroyd in exchange for Paul Kitson?

"I'd just been to McDonald's for my dinner after training, and the missus said that Roy McFarland had been on the phone. I thought he was going to say we had extra training! I went down to see Arthur Cox but he never told me it was a swap deal with Sticks. I turned up at the hotel to meet John Gregory and he said, 'Where's Ian?' and I said, 'He's not my agent.' It was nice to have someone going with you to a new club, though I haven't really played with Ormondroyd. I knew John Gregory from his Derby days,

and I used to play with Bobby Davidson a lot. The City squad do make you very welcome, though. I was very nervous. I'm quite shy, really. I got to know them all on the players' holiday to Ibiza. Got to know how much they could drink, anyway."

Is it good to have a young training staff?

"Yes, they join in with everything – five-a-sides, though you can never split them up. They vary it. At Derby, we always knew what we were going to be doing every day of the week. I could still tell you what they're doing now. Last Friday we had a shooting competition, playing one-twos with the Gaffer and then shooting first time. There were chocolates for the winners. Me, Bobby and Ian were one team and we came bottom of the table. No chocolates for us!"

How do you feel about the relative scoring records of you and Paul Kitson, given the difference in valuation?

"Well, he's playing for a struggling team, isn't he? I'm not bothered about anybody else's performance, just my own... but you have to smile, like."

Have you had any bad feeling, still living among Derby fans?

"Er, a bit. I went down to the live game against Bristol City and a few choice comments came in my direction. Witty things like, 'You w****r.' I watched the second half from the players' lounge. I've only been out twice round here since we beat Derby. The Saturday after, I went out to this bar and this geezer said, 'You're bloody brave, aren't you?' I said, 'Why?' He said, 'If I were you, I'd f*** off home.'

Anita: "And he did! He was home by 10.30!"

How did it feel to score twice against your old team when we beat them?

"Marvellous. Micky Forsyth is my best mate, but he said 'no friends' on the pitch and in the first challenge he nutted me one in the back of the head, so I swapped sides and played against Kavanagh. He can't remember doing it, but we both had lumps on our heads. Coxy wouldn't play me unless there was nobody else – y'know, tea-lady injured – and he kept me there in the reserves for three years, so it was quite nice. They've spent all this money but there's no experience. He likes to buy 'clean-living young men.' That's why he got rid of me."

You and Ian didn't hit it off at first...

"No, I was getting a bit worried after five games, but then I got a good one against Tranmere and Sticks managed to put one in off the post from a couple of inches out. He lost his rag on Sunday, though, didn't he? Pointing at that poor Wolves player, poking him in the eye with his nose. He's a good lad and a trier. We slaughter him and he doesn't mind. We've called him 'Bambi' ever since his debut when he was running down the wing and tripped himself up. You don't usually laugh until you get into the dressing room, but I was pissing myself. He got two goals disallowed that day. I think his nose was offside."

What are your thoughts on the new backpass rule?

"I'm just waiting for one of the goalies to miskick it. Up to now, they've all wellied it away. Muggs likes to dribble it around, he thinks he can play a bit. Russell Hoult did well last Sunday; he dropped his shoulder and sent the bloke the wrong way. Never mind 'The Hot-Dog Kid,' I think it was the fourth pint in the players' lounge that helped."

What do you think of Sky and the Premier League?

"I have got a dish. It's a bit Mickey Mouse, the way they present it.

"Does the new rule tire me out by the end of the game? I'm tired at half time!"

Did you know? Phil has got a Sonic the Hedgehog tattoo. Do you know where?

Adverts here, there and everywhere, fireworks at the end and singers at half-time. The Premier League? Well, it would have been all right if we'd made it. It doesn't seem to be very well organised. I don't think it will last beyond ten or 12 years, not a hundred years like the Football League. It's getting a bit expensive for the fans. This bloke was on Radio Derby the other day and he said that it cost him £36 for him and his two lads..."

Our day at Wembley

Colin GIBSON

Colin Gibson's on-trend kitchen quite befits a man who enjoyed a distinguished career with Aston Villa, Manchester United and City – and who now works in financial services. Gibson was left-back in Ron Saunders' title-winning side, and unlucky to be sub for Villa's European Cup final triumph. More importantly, records-wise, he was City's first sub to be subbed, and our first sub to be sent off.

After hitting the heights with Villa, it must have been a wrench to leave the club?

"I didn't want to leave Aston Villa. They made a big mistake by bringing Doug Ellis in, which was the worst thing that could have happened. Because he hadn't been chairman when we won the European Cup, he dismantled that side. I got pushed out of the door. I went up to Old Trafford where Ron Atkinson signed

me, but it wasn't a great time. I was told I'd torn a cartilage, and I played one game in two years. It turned out I'd snapped my cruciate, which is a little bit different to a torn cartilage. I ended up having ten operations on my left knee and lost a yard and a half of pace. Not being disrespectful, but that's how I ended up at Leicester in the second tier. I was still good enough technically to do a decent job in midfield so I came to Leicester and had a ball; absolutely had a brilliant time."

You were originally signed by David Pleat, but it was under Brian Little that we began to turn things around...

"He organised us. Made us hard to beat. There was no point scoring four goals up the other end and letting five in. We had a decent side. There was Gary Mills, who had been brought up well under Brian Clough, and Steve Walsh who absolutely hated losing but had to be more disciplined. Tommy Wright was a pain in the backside but he was very good. He'd say to me, 'Gibbo, you haven't got the legs any more, get the ball off them and give it to me.' We all knew what we had to do and we did it with confidence, although we didn't quite have the legs to get over the finish line in the Play-off final. I missed that one against Blackburn, was sub for the second one and played in the one against Derby. I'll leave you to draw your own conclusions why we won that one."

We got off to a cracking start in 1991/92, and you scored three goals. But then you got injured in November and were out for the season. How did you cope with that?

"It was that cruciate injury again. I'd been playing with my knee flopping about all over the place. My problem was that I was on a very low basic wage with very decent appearance money, so I was okay as long as I was playing. I think I made more money that season than I ever earned at Villa or Manchester United, about £70,000. It was good money, then. I got £1,500 for winning the European Cup with Villa. I was pleased with that."

In the 1994 Play-off final we played a Derby 'Dream Team' that maybe looked better than us. What was Brian's plan?

"We played Tranmere in the semi-finals and there were a few regulars out, so me and Mark Blake played in the middle of midfield. Neither of us were expecting to play at Wembley because we had the likes of Steve Agnew and Colin Hill to come in. We had this meeting where Brian said, 'I'm going to go with the same team.' Maybe it was because Derby were such a good footballing side that he wanted us to do that spoiling job, and we certainly did that. I remember standing in the tunnel and Gordon Cowans, who was a very good friend of mine, saying, 'You all right, Gibbo?' and I completely blanked him. We were all totally focused on winning that game, while Derby were a bit like we'd been against Blackburn, enjoying the day. We weren't there for a day out at Wembley, we were there to get promoted.

The fans had had enough of losing there, we needed to give them something. That previous year against Swindon, I never thought we were really in charge of the game, but this time I had the feeling that things were going for us. At one stage I remember slipping over and letting John Harkes in, but he hit it wide. You start to think this might be our day. This is meant to happen. We had some big lads in that side – Iwan, Walshy, Gary Coatsworth – and in the end we got that grinding result."

"At least I'm in Leicester's record books – like Chris Nicholl and his four goals in a game!"

The playmaker

Davie GIBSON

Signed from Hibs in 1962, David Gibson was a left-sided playmaker with a touch of pure class. Still full of vigour and enthusiasm in his sunny Dorset conservatory, the former Scottish international filled up a whole C-90 cassette tape with pin-sharp memories, followed by an hour-long C-60.

Did you have any youthful heroes?

"I had a bit of an inferiority complex as a kid, in and out of the Hibs team. During National Service, I played for the Army with Jim Baxter, and a little bit of his arrogance rubbed off on me. I thought, 'Hang on a minute, I *can* play a bit.'"

How did it feel to sign for Leicester City?

"I remember the excitement of it. I came down to Leicester on a Friday night and met the directors and Stringy, and then got on the bus to see them play at Everton. I sat in the dugout and I couldn't believe it, there were about 35,000 there. I thought to myself, 'Christ, this is what it's all about.' England was the place to be. After the match I got a night train back to Edinburgh with wee Bobby Collins of

Everton. We called in to a pub on the way back, Bobby wanted 'a couple of pints to unwind'. He says, 'I think you'll do all right there, they seem like a good club. But I'll give you a bit of advice, when you're playing

well, keep the gun at their f***ing head – because the minute you're no good to a club they'll blow you out the door."

You formed a famous understanding with Mike Stringfellow on the left...

"It happened from day one. I'd feed Stringy and he'd go flying down the wing. There was almost a mental telepathy between us. He made my passes good passes. He scored some goals as well, for a winger."

In 1962/63, it seemed the Double was on for the team they called the 'Ice Kings'...

"Perhaps that backfired on us in the end. They put a certain special soil mixed with this chemical over the frost that kept it playable. We might have beaten those teams anyway, whether it was on grass or on sand. We just lost form, basically, being left with four away games, and it carried on to the FA Cup final. I've still got the tape of that game and I hate to look at it, because I think it was the worst game I played for the club. I don't think I passed the ball to Stringy twice."

Did you find Matt Gillies aloof as a boss?

"I remember one Thursday lunchtime over a pint, Frank McLintock talked me into a game of golf, even though it was against club rules in the days leading up to a game. We were striding down the long 15th at Rothley Park when we caught sight of Matt Gillies. We both dived into the bushes on the railway embankment and were covered in scratches from the brambles. We laid low for a while until he was out of sight. 'Do you think he saw us?' I asked Frank. 'He'll go mad if he catches us.' We sweated it out for a couple of days, and nothing was said in training. We played at Anfield on the Saturday and we were both in the team – a good sign. We

beat Liverpool and Matt went round every player, saying 'well played.' Then he came to us two and said, 'And you pair were fantastic... perhaps you should play golf every Thursday.'"

The 1968/69 season was to prove his last at Leicester...

"Managers didn't get the sack too often back then. Not like now – the last Leicester manager lasted nine games! We went to Everton without Matt and got hammered 7-1. It was an emotional day. Matt cried the day he left, and when we got relegated at Manchester United on the last day of the season I broke down and cried in the dressing room. I felt as though we'd let everybody down. It hit me. It had never happened to me before."

But maybe not every player was so committed?

"We reached the FA Cup final that year, and organised a players' pool. Get your team photo taken and the *Daily Mail* will give you 50 quid. But Allan Clarke didn't want into the pool, so that he could make whatever money for himself from interviews. After the final, we got a letter from Leeds – Allan wanting to know what his share of the pool was! We wrote him a letter back saying: 'Dear Allan, f*** all.'"

How did you get on with Frank O'Farrell when he took over the reins?

"I loved playing under the Filbert Street floodlights, feeling like an actor on a stage."

"Okay until the end of my Leicester career, in 1970. I think the game of football can turn a manager into a Jekyll and Hyde. Frank said at the end of the season, 'Come and see me and I'll maybe get you a free transfer'. I had one last favour to ask: 'Would it be all right if I still come and train for a few weeks?' Believe me, his very words were, 'When you go out that door, don't come f***ing back. I've had enough of you causing trouble.' I said, 'Excuse me, are you talking to the right guy? Davie Gibson sitting here.' Wee Bobby Collins got that right. All the years I'd enjoyed at Leicester, and that's how it ended."

The Leicester Diet: "They used to give me sherry and eggs to try and build me up."

Len GLOVER

Winging it

We were all set to meet our wing legend in a lovely seaside pub in Whitstable. But then Lenny sent a text to say he couldn't make it – and promptly walked in the door, to catch our reaction. His 'fee'? One bottle of champagne.

How did you come to move to Leicester?

"I'd put in for a transfer, but Leicester was the last club on my mind. One Saturday, Charlton went up to play Bolton, but the pitch was waterlogged and it was off, so we went to see Manchester City v Leicester. Now, Leicester had just got rid of Gordon Banks in favour of a very young Peter Shilton, and they lost 6-0 at Maine Road. Shilts had a nightmare! We were sat there in the stand saying, 'Wait a minute... they got rid of the best goalkeeper in the world for this young boy?' On the following Monday I walked into Charlton and Eddie Firmani said,

'There's a club coming to see you.' I said, 'Who is it?' expecting him to say either Chelsea or Tottenham. He said, 'It's Leicester...' and I laughed. I went to meet them with no intention of signing. But I think there was some agreement between our chairman and Len Shipman as they were on an FA Committee together. I caved in. I signed. I don't regret it for a moment because I had ten absolutely fantastic years at Leicester."

You didn't have the best of starts under Matt Gillies...

"My heart was still in London. Because I wasn't happy, I'm afraid I never really performed for him, to be honest. Then Frank O'Farrell arrived. After about four or five games he got me into his office and he said, 'Hello Len, when are you going to start playing for Leicester?' I didn't really know what to say to that. He said, 'I know you're getting the train back to London and that's where you want to be. But let's give it six months. You stay in this hotel. If things aren't better by then you can have your move, I'll put you on the train myself.' As soon as I moved into that flat, I started to find my form."

You managed to get to an FA Cup final in a relegation season...

"We got Liverpool at home in the fifth round and drew 0-0 with them. We went up there for the replay and, in the hotel before the game, there was the *Liverpool Echo* with the headline: 'A Mere Formality'. But quite early on I got the ball, went past Chris Lawler and crossed it for Andy Lochhead. Bang, what a header! Then they got a penalty, Tommy Smith stepped up and Shilts saved it. As soon as that happened, I knew we were going to beat them. We ran all over the park and they played right into our hands, boshing this ball up the middle, and it was easy for John Sjoberg, who was great in the air. I thought, 'Yes, keep doing this.' We beat them 1-0 and I think it was the most exciting game I've ever played in."

There was a contrasting style when Jimmy Bloomfield arrived...

"Jimmy had been a good player himself and knew one when he saw one. He brought in Keith Weller, Jon Sammels, Dennis Rofe... players who could play. Except for Birch. Of course, he couldn't play. And then Frank Worthington arrived... what a player and what a character he was. He was so good for the club. One time, Frank arrived for a home match at twenty to three – two hours late. He walks into the dressing room dressed in all his Elvis gear and goes, 'Uh-huh-huh,' doing the Elvis shrug. If it had been anyone else, Jim would have read the riot act to them, but Jim loved Frank and he just smiled and shook his head."

That team reached its peak in 1973/74...

"Well, it had all fitted together, we all knew what we were going to do. Right from kick-off we knew that Steve Earle would give it to Elvis, who would lay it back to The Claw (Birch) who would then launch it out left to Fido (me). Birch would say, 'Fido, shut your eyes, head for the

corner flag, and it'll be there.' It never was once, not in five years. We were at Arsenal once and big Bob Lee got knocked out. George Preston ran on and was treating him while we all stood around. He was cradling his head and said, 'He doesn't know where he is, or who is is.' Birch said, 'Tell him he's George Best!' Then, on the last day of the season, Wool wasn't there to get the bus up to Anfield. Jimmy says to me, 'Don't say a word to anyone, Len, but Alan isn't coming today. His dog's died and he's too upset to play.' I went straight over to Birch and said, 'Birch, guess what? Wool isn't coming today because his dog has died...' It wasn't a secret for long!"

How did you come to leave Leicester?

"I was looking for a loan move to Tampa Bay Rowdies, to play for Eddie Firmani again. But it turned out to be permanent, which wasn't what I wanted. I'd been there nine and a half years so I didn't quite qualify for a testimonial. Ha ha – Wool had one! [Len gets out an envelope full of photos]. There's me and Pele, look. The two greatest players in the world, captains of the Tampa Bay Rowdies and New York Cosmos. 'To my friend Lenny Glover' – that's something to be proud of."

1969 FA Cup final: "Frank decided I could still do something even if I wasn't fully fit, and I had six injections in my groin."

71

Steve GUPPY

Whip it in the mixer

Many fans might not remember Steve Guppy's second spell with City, in the Premier League relegation year under Micky Adams – which provided us with a chance to look back on happier times.

You started your career at Wycombe, where you played under Martin O'Neill...

"I wouldn't say he's changed a great deal. Even back then his passion for wanting to win was evident. He pretty much dragged us from mid-table obscurity to winning the League and going full-time."

It must have seemed a great move when Kevin Keegan took you to Newcastle?

"To be honest, I left Wycombe under a little bit of a cloud with Martin. He wouldn't talk to me for a year. The reality was, I'd had a year in the Third Division and the team coming in for me were top of the Premiership. Looking back now, it

was just too big a jump for me. It was a culture shock going to Port Vale, where the training ground was in the middle of an industrial estate. Most mornings, there was a strong smell of glue floating around. You always came out feeling a bit light-headed, whether you'd run hard or not!"

Then Martin came in again for you...

"The funny thing was, he didn't mention that he wanted me as a wing-back. I'd never done it before. My strengths are going forward. But it all turned out okay!"

You scored ten goals in your first spell – many a cracker from outside the box...

"The goal at Chelsea stands out, with them being such a big club and with it being live on Sky. I was living off it for two years afterwards! When I first came to Leicester I was just obsessed with getting in as many crosses as I could. After a while you have to mix it up a little bit, once the full-backs get wise to you and realise that you want to get to the by-line and whip a cross in. They started to show me the inside a lot, so I used to practise putting it into the top right-hand corner."

Do your two League Cup finals feature among your career highlights?

"Tranmere had a great year and knocked some good teams out, but that's one we were expected to win. The one against Tottenham was disappointing. Under George Graham the team, though they were good, were spoilers. To lose a goal in the last minute of a Wembley final was something you don't want to happen too often. A couple of weeks later we played them again. They were re-showing the game on TV and we knew their fans were gearing up to give us a really hard time. So Martin made us line up and clap them out on to the pitch. The Tottenham fans didn't

know what to make of it – whether we were being gracious in defeat or taking the mickey. To be honest, I think it was just an idea to defuse the situation. It worked really well. Tony Cottee got his 200th goal that day. It was good, but the League Cup final defeat hurt for a long time."

The team never won much media credit...

"We picked up this nickname of the 'Grinders.' Especially towards the end of Martin O'Neill's time, when Stan Collymore was up front with Emile for just a couple of games, we came close to having a very good side, in my opinion. And I know Martin feels the same. One or two players away from a real golden era. But it wasn't to be."

How did you get on after Martin left for Celtic?

"Well, Peter Taylor's a nice bloke, in all honesty. But there was just the fact that he had this horrible habit of not playing me. The first game of the season I wasn't even sub. That was a big shock for me, having played every game for about four years. So I was waiting for him Monday morning in his office, at about half eight. It was quite funny, really. I asked him, 'Why are you not playing me?' He had this magnetic football board on the wall and he said, 'Well, it's like this, Steve...' – he was umming and ahhing for a bit – 'We look a better team... when you're not in it.' This was after one game. I felt a bit like, 'Don't bother opening the door for me, I'll crawl under it!'"

And it got worse. Losing to Wycombe in the FA Cup must have been very painful?

"I had quite a few good friends still in the Wycombe side. I hadn't played a great deal leading up to that game and, just my luck, he played me that day. We went 1-0 down and got back to 1-1 and it looked like there was only going to be one winner. We were really on the charge.

> "I felt a bit like, 'Don't bother opening the door for me, I'll just crawl under it!'"

And then it just sort of fell apart. Essendoh got that late goal – some bloke they'd got off the internet! It was a big opportunity missed, an FA Cup semi-final. And I'd arranged a night out with the Wycombe lads..."

In the end, were you glad to leave City?

"Well, I was excited to be joining up with Martin O'Neill again, and at such a big club. I was all set to sign for Coventry, and it was even announced on the radio. I listened to that on the way to the airport, flying up to Glasgow. When you've spent so many years at a club it's always a wrench, but at the same time I knew I'd made the right decision."

Four Lions: Only Steve has played for England, England B, England C and the England Under-21s.

The best by a million miles

Bryan HAMILTON

On the outskirts of Ipswich, in his splendid garden sloping down to a river, Bryan Hamilton took stock of his spell as Leicester City manager while his wife kept us topped up with cakes.

Football was a simpler game back in the day when you were a player...

"All the sports science has made it a very different game. We used to be tucking into steaks at twelve o'clock on a match day! And clubs have a huge number of staff now. When I was at Leicester there was myself, Dave Richardson and John McVey. That was it. John was the physio. Dave did the Youth team and we shared reserve-team duties. And at one stage, when we went to QPR and beat them 1-0, we were sixth in the top flight! *Sixth!*"

You came to Leicester from Wigan in 1986 in a dual role with Gordon Milne...

"Gordon is one of the best men I've met in the game and I think the world of him. He'd being doing a very good job at Leicester but I don't think he was sure what he was doing next. He was perhaps thinking about a Chief Executive's role, like an early Director of Football. One of the biggest mistakes I made was in not encouraging Gordon to stay at Leicester. I was a young manager in my first big job and wanted to make all the decisions. I

LEICESTER CITY
BRYAN HAMILTON

didn't realise the opportunity I had, and he could have helped me a lot. I was changing the shape of the side because I didn't think we had enough width. Trying to build everything round Gary McAllister because he looked to be such a huge talent. I saw Mark Bright alongside Alan Smith as a potentially great combination. But there were things going on, like we couldn't afford the second instalment on Bright, so I was told to go easy on his appearances. I should have said, 'No, I like Mark Bright, he's playing,' and been a bit stronger."

You had very little money to work with...

"Well, there was no money. I had to sell Alan Smith to Arsenal, but managed to get a deal where we could retain him until the end of the season. I didn't want to lose him but I had to recognise where we were financially. I remember at one board meeting I was faced with a choice. I had £20,000. Now, did I want to put it towards a player, or use it to move the laundry from Filbert Street to Belvoir Drive?"

One of your legacies at Leicester City was the signing of Steve Walsh...

"Walshy was a great lad, terrific for me at Wigan and great at Leicester. I even signed him for Norwich after doing a deal with Peter Taylor for him and Tony Cottee, although that didn't really work out. At Wigan I was always very strong with him, but at Leicester I didn't want to take too much passion and aggression out of him because it might have reduced him as a player. So Walshy had his flaws, but I was glad to have him."

Your first season started brilliantly, beating Liverpool and Forest, drawing with Man United and winning at QPR...

"I was very enthusiastic about the job but there was such a lot to do. I kept a suit carrier and passport in my car in case I had to go away and look at a player. I was trying to buy a house in Leicester and move the family down. So many things that were distracting from the main job. This is why I should have done everything to keep Gordon Milne alongside me."

For the 1987/88 season you signed the giant Finn, Jari Rantanen...

"What a character, I loved Jari! I was desperate to sign a centre-forward and I had no money. He was playing for Gothenburg and I got a phone call to say come and see him. They were playing some team in rural Sweden and I had to fly up

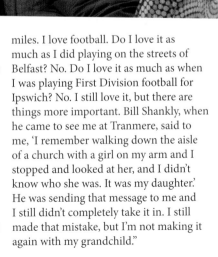

"I was a young manager in my first big job and wanted to make all the decisions."

there after taking training. I arrive up there with my suitcase, and the first flight back booked so I can take training the next day... and he wasn't playing. He was injured. He wasn't even in Sweden! I'd gone all the way up to the Arctic Circle for nothing. He was an unbelievable character and quite a decent player. He was 6'4" and we had to make special kit for him, but I think he had a good effect on the side."

We had some great wins after Newell and Rantanen arrived, but it all went downhill

once Ian Wilson left for Everton...

"I gave it everything. If it had been about hard work then we'd have been top of the league; but there's more to it than that. My daughter can't remember me ever in the house at Leicester. I was out watching games until after they were in bed and out of the house before they got up."

What do you miss most about football?

"Playing, that was the best by a million miles. I love football. Do I love it as much as I did playing on the streets of Belfast? No. Do I love it as much as when I was playing First Division football for Ipswich? No. I still love it, but there are things more important. Bill Shankly, when he came to see me at Tranmere, said to me, 'I remember walking down the aisle of a church with a girl on my arm and I stopped and looked at her, and I didn't know who she was. It was my daughter.' He was sending that message to me and I still didn't completely take it in. I still made that mistake, but I'm not making it again with my grandchild."

"I was very proud to represent Northern Ireland 50 times and be captain and then manager."

Ian HOLLOWAY

It's all in the mind, you know

City were heading down towards the Second Division drop zone when we met Ian Holloway. The former Bristol Rovers, QPR and Plymouth boss was our third manager of the season so far – full of enthusiasm, and happy to pose outside at Belvoir Drive for our photographer.

What were your first impressions when you arrived in Leicester?

"Well, I've bummed around on all sorts of parks pitches and the immediate thing you see here is, this set-up is Premiership. It really is. Unfortunately the stuff on the grass isn't. I've never had the facilities or the budget I have here, and I feel that I'm now in a different role. I've always been an underdog. But it wouldn't feel right sitting here if I hadn't had all those experiences I've had. I've stood at QPR and lost to Vauxhall Motors in an FA Cup match in a replay on penalties. I've had things thrown at me. This is my 12th season as a manager. I've been in nearly every division, I've been in administration, been under five different boards at QPR and kept it solid. I want to bring in the values I've learned during all that."

How big a mess is the club in right now?

"I thanked Milan for giving me the job and I'm glad it's in such a goddamned mess because if it wasn't, I wouldn't be sitting here now. What I want to try and do is be calm and be calculated. We're working on what positions need to be strengthened in January, and we're working towards improving that appalling home form and giving the fans an entertaining environment to come and watch their football in. But I need some support at the moment for all these players, whether they'll be here long term or not. I need them to feel like I'm loving them up, cherishing them and trying to help them, until that window opens. We haven't got any wide players, and no centre-forwards can score without wide men getting that ball into the box. Ninety per cent of the goals come from Alan Sheehan's left foot. And that's gone off the boil because he's a little bit nervous."

We're currently in 17th place in the Championship table...

"And I've got eight or nine players who know that they're the team that got us 17th. It's a mess, but it's one that I can quickly sweep around and tidy up. Over the last couple of games I've gone back to people just so that I can see them play for myself. I never discard anybody unless I've judged them myself. It's a bit like someone coming out of prison. I would give them a job. You might know why they were put in prison, I don't. But I'd give them a chance to do that job. If they can't do it, then I'd get rid of them. But Rome wasn't built in a day. I'm going to be a father to all of these lot. For me, I wanted to give Carl Cort an

ice-cream. He got up off the treatment table and had enough balls to say, 'I want to play for you.' Would I have signed him? With his knee? I'll be honest with you, I doubt it. But now I'm here and he's here and he's got caught up in the atmosphere. I think that some of our senior players are letting the younger ones down, big time. So I've asked them to step up to the plate."

What's the hardest part of managing for you?

"Having to rely on other people for your livelihood is the worst thing. But it's also exciting and a challenge. So the very thing I don't like about management probably keeps me alive. That little bit of adrenaline."

You were famously shown going into meltdown in a TV documentary. How do you handle the pressure now?

"Pressure is man-made. It's about your thoughts and your perceptions. I had a deep underlying anger when things weren't fair, and it was based in the fact that I didn't think I was good enough. Like as a young player, when I was worried that I was too small. This anger-management fella made me realise that basically I wasn't dealing with situations. It was daft things like, if I had a lot on my mind, I'd put my keys down or my mobile and not be able to remember where they were. Then it'd be destructive and I'd get angry and upset everyone else around me. But with some structure and focus I could say, 'There are my keys, I'm in control.'

> "I take full responsibility for making sure you get entertained. I'm in the entertainment business."

"My wife is quite well read and she got me this tremendous book with the most important nine words you'll ever read in it... 'Your life is what your thoughts make of it.' How profound is that? That's what I want to share with Leicester City fans. We're a good club. We may be 17th at the moment but help me help these players. I'll be encouraging them to within an inch of my life, because every human being deserves that."

Jon HOLMES

Agent of change

Pioneering football agent, former City chairman and dyed-in-the-wool fan – we went to Jon Holmes's Southwell home, and he took us up to his man cave.

How did you start out as a football agent?

"My dad bought me a book on Arnold Palmer when I was at university. It was written by Mark McCormack, Palmer's agent, and they were breaking new ground with their partnership. I thought that sounded good, better than working. I joined the *Leicester Mercury*, but didn't enjoy writing about football as much as I thought I would. There weren't really any agents in football at the time, and everyone told me I was crackers and wouldn't make any money out of it. But we had some good players at Leicester – Shilton, Worthington, Weller, Birch – and I started doing bits and bobs for them. A lot of it, I did for nothing. Anyway, I signed up Shilts to the agency and then I got in with all the Forest players..."

Straight away, you were dealing with

some very colourful managers...

"Jimmy Bloomfield was a nice man and a great coach, but hopeless at man-management. He didn't seem to trust anyone; never kept a coach, tried to do it all himself. Jock Wallace was the opposite of Jimmy. Man-management really second-to-none, but coaching hopeless. The thing I've learnt about good managers – Cloughie, Terry Venables, Howard Kendall – they keep their players interested. Thirty or 40 weeks a year they're training, and it's essentially the same thing week in, week out. It could be pretty boring. Shilts used to tell me that Clough would arrive and they had no idea what he was going to say. He might say, 'Go home and pack your bags, we're going to Majorca.' Or Skegness! He always kept them on their toes and interested. Martin O'Neill learnt a hell of a lot from Clough – that you had to have some distance. He never took training, Robbo and Walford did all that. Martin would sit in his office and watch through the window, then go out and have a rant."

Were you conflicted as a fan and as an agent when Gary Lineker left Leicester?

"Oh yes, and it was the same with Shilts. But I just had to face up to the fact that he was bound to go. Liverpool were interested because Ian Rush was on his way to Juventus, but they were hanging on, hoping to get him cheaper out of contract. As it turned out, Liverpool's bid came in one hour after Everton's. Gary scored a lot of goals, had a great World Cup and became a world-famous name. So, yes, it is tough as a fan."

You were heavily involved with pulling Leicester out of financial meltdown in 2002. How did things get so bad?

"Well, they made a bad appointment in Peter Taylor. That was crucial. His signings were terrible. Akinbiyi and Benjamin couldn't see, they both had eyesight problems which weren't checked at the medical. Then they had the chance to get rid of Peter in the summer and actually get paid compensation for him, and they didn't. I think Micky and Dave did a good job, actually. They couldn't stop us going down because we were buggered. The club had committed to moving to the new stadium, and ITV Digital went down. They were stuffed from all sides. If Teachers had played ball, then Greg Clarke could have done a reconstruction job, but they forced them into administration."

Wasn't Eric Hall also involved?

"My first act as new chairman was to throw him out of the directors' lounge. He waltzed in, so I marched straight up to him and said, 'You're not coming in here.' 'Who are you, then?' 'The chairman of this football club.' 'How long have you been chairman?' 'One day. Now get out!' He was issuing us winding-up orders and thought he could wander around where he liked."

City did get promotion that season...

"But when we didn't stay up, Micky lost it a bit. That shambles in La Manga didn't help matters. Micky rang me up and offered his resignation over that. He said, 'It was my fault I didn't put them on a curfew. I trusted them to be grown up.' Craig Levein might have done okay here, but I did warn them not to let him bring down too many players from Scotland – and that's exactly what he did. When they did sign someone from England, it was the wrong player! That Gilbert from Plymouth? They heard he was a long throw-in specialist, but they bought the wrong full-back! After Levein, the money was all gone and we were confronted with Mandaric. He promised to take us up to the Premier League but instead we ended up in the worst position the club had ever been. Fortunately, he made a good move in getting Nigel in then, who did very well for two seasons – and then he got rid of him! Pearson has always been good at signing the right player for the club at the time, though I do think he should have brought in more Premier League experience during the summer. You've got to get through that first season, it's such a big step up."

> "Sousa was a ridiculous appointment. Sven was terrible, too. He spent money like water."

Favourite player? "Davie Gibson. 'Whisper his name and people go quiet,' as it said in the Express."

Sam HOLMES

Play up the Knuts

We visited one of Leicester City's oldest fans in his terraced house in the Woodgate area. Sadly, Sam passed away in 2012, making his memories of going to pre-war games all the more precious.

It was a while ago, but what can you remember about your first game?

"It was in 1931 and we played Brighton in the FA Cup. I'm afraid we lost 2-1. From that day on, it's always been Leicester City for me. In the early years I used to stand at the Filbert Street end, just behind the goal. I used to pay sixpence to go in the Boys' Entrance. That went on until one day the turnstile bloke said, 'You're a bloody old 14! About time you went next door.' From then on I had to pay a shilling, but I'd had a good run!"

What did Filbert Street look like then?

"The Double Decker had been built. The biggest difference would be no roof on the Pop Side. After a few years we moved to the Kop. Every home game you'd be stood in the same spot with your matchday pals. Then I'd have to nip out a minute early to

go and collect my bike. It cost a couple of pennies to park it in someone's alley."

What did people wear in those days?

"Well, I've never worn a City shirt, but you did used to wear a scarf. Especially for the FA Cup. They were the special games, when you'd wear your rosette. I remember before one Cup game this fellow lent me his blue and white umbrella with 'Play Up the Knuts' on it. That was City's nickname for a while. He told me the last time it had been to a game we played Cardiff, and they won the FA Cup later that year, 1927."

You went to every one of City's FA Cup finals in 1949, '61, '63 and '69...

"The Cup wasn't just about the finals. We had some marvellous times in the semis and the earlier rounds. In 1949 we played at Luton in the fifth round. We were losing 5-4 right near the end. We got a corner and Jack Lee scored in the very last second, then we beat them 5-3 in the replay. The only time I've ever lost my voice was at the 1949 semi-final when we beat Portsmouth 3-1 at Highbury. I remember sitting on the steps round Eros in Piccadilly Circus and there were lots of City fans all with sheer delight on their faces."

What were the queues like back then?

"You did have to get down there early if it was a big team visiting. Sometimes the turnstiles would be shut at around half-past one for a three o'clock kick-off with a full house inside. I remember one time we played Everton on Boxing Day, a crowd put their shoulders to the gate and everyone got in for nowt!"

Who was the best player you ever saw?

"Well, Sep Smith has got to be one of them. You've got to have a favourite. Keith Weller was another one, he was a good player. And Davie Gibson."

The target man

Up in Chester-le-Street, we met Steve at his property investment business, based in a converted safari park. From the shape of the building, we suspect it used to be the giraffe house.

Do you think the 'Vardy route' – YTS, proper job, lower divisions – is better for a young player than the Academy system?

"Well, for me personally, I'd say it definitely was. It hardens you and gives you more desire to succeed. I remember when I was at Sunderland there was a lot of respect – you had to knock on the first-team door before you went in. And I remember thinking, 'I really want to get into that room.' When I was released, I was getting £650 a week digging the roads. When I signed for Hartlepool I was on £120 a week, plus £20 appearance money! I remember looking at my first payslip and thinking, 'Oh, God! What have I done here?' But I wanted to be a footballer, so that was that."

Sold without consultation by Premier League Derby, what were your first impressions of Leicester?

"I found the mentality and team spirit to be a bit weak, after what I'd just come from. There were a lot of young players in there. Matt Oakley also came from Derby around that time and we realised that, as more seasoned pros, we had to get something going, because we were struggling. We'd come from one team that was getting beat to another, but the mentality at Derby was better. There were a few players in that dressing room who were dead and buried already.

And perhaps Ian Holloway was a bit lost, too. One night before we played Cardiff in Wales he wanted everyone at the squash courts at 8.30. We went in and there's Ian in his pants, with a bandage wrapped round his head, holding a football. He said, 'Dodgeball! Split yourselves into teams of four.' I think he lost the plot and didn't know what was needed to stay in that league. We were devastated when we were relegated. Lower than a snake's belly. But I think it was actually the best thing that could have happened. We needed to go down, regroup and come back better."

Did your experience at League One level stand you in good stead?

"Matty was the captain that season, and was good at it. I also tried to play a leading role on the pitch and in the dressing room. I'd say to the lads, 'Look, it's one season, that's all it is. Let's get out of this league.' Eighteen lads are trying to get changed in this cupboard at Southend. And I was saying, 'Just get on with it.' It was a great

season. We did what was expected of us." Nigel Pearson led City through that season, what did he bring to the club?

"Structure. Discipline. Ollie tried to be your mate, whereas Nigel was friendly

"There's Ian in his pants, with a bandage wrapped round his head, holding a football..."

but he was your boss. He saw things in black and white. I personally thought he was fantastic. He'd say, 'You're not playing today because you did that.' No sugar coating; no, 'I'm going to rest you today.' I respected that. That's not to say we didn't have some huge ding-dongs. Because he was a big lad and could be pretty blunt, I think a few of the lads were a bit scared of him. But I didn't think he was a bully,

he was a man's man. He wouldn't stab anyone in the back, he'd say it to their face. Every Monday morning he'd get me, Matty Oakley, Jack Hobbs, Andy King together and say, 'Right, any problems?' It could be anything. One of the workout machines is broken. Right. It'd be fixed by the next day. Someone's missus had just had a baby and he'd have to leave training early. Right, that's fine. It was called The Committee. Maybe someone had been sent off, and he'd say, 'Does he get a fine?' It was all part of building a team. We'd report back to the rest of the lads. That was where that very strong dressing room all started from. I think Nigel played a big part in the title win. Obviously, Claudio Ranieri did too, but he had to tweak things rather than make any big changes. Not many managers inherit a winning team. It was mainly the team Nigel built, and I think he'll be devastated at what they achieved without him. But his position was untenable by the end of that season. He had to go."

What do you get up to these days, here at Platinum Capital Investments?

"Well, we got a huge bonus when Derby got promoted, and I bought six houses with it. Whereas Seth Johnson flew his missus to Dubai and stayed at the Burj, got a helicopter in and a helicopter out, and then soon after they split up. Ha'way man! I used to tell the lads, try not spending any money for two months, because that's what your retirement will be like. Lloyd Dyer tried it and only managed a couple of weeks! One minute you're driving a Range Rover and the next you're in a Fiesta. When you're used to the lifestyle, your savings are soon gone."

Izzet a Fox

MUZZY IZZET

Two and a half years into his influential tenure in City's midfield, Muzzy met us at Belvoir Drive with a wave of a brown envelope – containing a new contract.

What do you remember about your debut against Sheffield United?

"I didn't know much about the Leicester team or the number of games they'd gone without a win. I was sub and I can remember the pitch, it was in a terrible state. The crowd were booing, and then on comes this new bloke from reserve-team football they'd probably never heard of. It was a bit intimidating, but I had nothing to lose. I was just on loan. There was no pressure on me. The team took a lot of stick and Martin took a lot of stick, but it all turned round. After that, we won at Charlton and Crystal Palace and went on a little run. Then we went to Watford for the last game of the season. We must have had 6,000 supporters behind that goal, and I got the winner at that end. A Watford player headed the ball straight out at me, so I headed it back towards goal and it went in. I think that was the first time I felt like a Leicester player."

Of course, that goal opened the way to the Play-offs. Was the final against Palace the first time you'd played at Wembley?

"Yes, it was. I didn't really know what to expect. I mean, I'd been to Wembley loads of times to see England, and once to see West Ham, but to actually be out on that pitch playing, it's something that's difficult to capture. I can't really remember much about that game, or the League Cup final. Perhaps you have to play there five or six times before you can really appreciate it."

Was the Coca-Cola replay any different, being at Hillsborough?

"I felt that was a better atmosphere. There were 40,000 there, and it was more compact. It felt more like a midweek Cup game – except with the reward of a trophy and a place in Europe. That has to be one of the highlights since I came here."

You've just committed to Leicester for a little bit longer. How far do you think you can go with this club?

"I honestly think that if we improve the squad by another two or three players then we could definitely finish in the top six and get into Europe. You saw on Saturday – and this is no disrespect to the lads who came on, because they're still learning the game – but when you look at Liverpool's bench and Chelsea's bench and even at teams like West Ham, they've got experienced guys like Moncur, Hartson. We need to get two or three more established players to get up into that top six. And I believe that Martin thinks that as well, otherwise he wouldn't have stayed."

83

Muzzy Izzet

Home from home

It was our shortest ever trip for an interview – just a mile to Whetstone, and the Advanced Football Development Academy which was then run by Muzzy and Steve Walsh.

You hadn't played a first-team game for Chelsea when Leicester picked you up...

"No, I'd been in the squad a number of times and on the bench a few times. I was playing at Kingstonian every Monday night for Chelsea reserves in front of one man and his dog. Four months later, I'm at Wembley playing in front of nearly 80,000. It was crazy. Wicked."

What was the key to Martin O'Neill's success at Leicester?

"I think he knew what to do with what he had. He looked at our three giant centre-backs, none of whom could run, but were very strong in the air and would get you goals from set-pieces. So we played 3-5-2. To compensate for having

no pace in defence, he then had three midfielders who had a lot of running in them who could operate from box to box. We could get back, get forward, close down. Even Neil, who was the holding midfielder, would get forward, and Sav was everywhere. We rotated and complemented each other's roles."

That side was renowned for its team spirit. How does that come about?

"We were a group of working-class lads who had found it difficult to get where we'd got to in the game. We'd all had our ups and downs, had mostly started out at smaller clubs, so we could all relate to each other. It was a special feeling, knowing that on our day we could beat anyone. As soon as Martin left, I never felt like that again. Martin encouraged us to go out and socialise together. After a win, he'd buy the crate of beers for on the way home. Some of the lads even used to smoke on

the back of the bus. Matty liked a fag, Taggs, Frank Sinclair. Ian Walker. But it wasn't a problem – anything that helped you unwind. No one took the piss, though. If we'd lost the game there'd be no one smoking, and there wouldn't be a drink. But if we'd won, then the bus would stop off on the way home and Martin would be out saying, 'Right, what do you want?' He always said before Cup finals, 'Have a beer if you want.' No one really did, although a couple of beers aren't going to hurt when you're as fit as we were."

Martin's first big-name signing was Stan Collymore. How did he fit in?

"Very well. There was a lot of stories surrounding him, so one of the first things he did was just come straight out with the fact that he'd suffered from depression. It was the first time he'd been happy in his football for a long time. Martin understood him and he loved Martin. We now had two players up front who could cause real problems for the opposition defence, and score goals. I thought then, 'Blimey, if we can keep this team together, what will next season be like?' But it wasn't to be."

Peter Taylor came in and things changed. In hindsight, what did he do wrong?

"He shouldn't have got rid of the senior players. Walshy and Tony Cottee were straight out of the door, Garry Parker retired and Neil Lennon was suffering from depression at that time. Matty stayed and Taggs stayed but it just seemed like the soul of our team had been taken away. He wanted us to drop off and sit deep and play counter-attacking football, but you need more pace for that game, and we didn't have it. I started to get my mojo back when Dave took over. Micky Adams was a great first-team coach."

You had a few chances to leave the club over several seasons, but you stayed...

"The first club after me was Chelsea, before they signed Frank Lampard. It was fantastic money, telephone-number

figures, but when I was at Chelsea I couldn't get out of there quick enough. Leicester renegotiated my contract and I thought, 'Do you know what? I owe this to Leicester.' I went up to Middlesbrough and spoke to Steve McClaren, but as I was driving up there I could feel it getting colder! I walked into a boardroom and there was the teamsheet pinned up with my name on it alongside Paul Ince.

"We took a 25 per cent wage deferral to guarantee we wouldn't go into administration..."

A bit of mind games there! Leeds were lining up an £8 million deal until there was that stabbing of their fans in Turkey, and then it was dropped without a word. Everton, Blackburn, Villa... there were quite a few offers going on behind the scenes but at that time great things were going on at Leicester. We were a top-ten team, playing at Wembley just about every year. I sat back and thought, well, if it isn't a top four team then none of these teams are achieving what we are. I was happy at Leicester, what's the point of moving?"

Action replay: the Great Escape

Tony JAMES

City's young centre-half was recovering from a broken leg when we met him at home in Sheffield. Apparently destined for great things, our hero of the Great Escape of '91 never did truly recapture the power and poise that had recently made him our Player of the Year.

Have you seen a video of the incident? We didn't know whether to bring it or not, because it's quite horrific...

"I've not seen it, you should have brought it along. I've heard that it was reported as being Steve Bull but I'm sure it was Paskin. I saw Paskin's face coming towards me as I went in for the challenge."

Everybody seemed to know it was a serious injury straight away...

"Yes, Ali jumped on me and wouldn't let

me look down – you really want to look and see for yourself. Steve Walsh told me it was my shinpad that had snapped, to try and calm me down. It's easy to slip into shock. Really, I knew right away that it was broken, although it's never happened before. The pain was unbearable. The thing that gets me mad is that it was always my ball – he caught me on the follow-through. If we'd been going for a 50-50 ball, I would have been okay. It was a bit sick – 3-0 up, and the ball wasn't even in a dangerous position. If it had been 0-0 and the incident had been a tackle to save a goal, it may have made more sense. The worst part was being stretchered off the field. Every bounce was agony. I remember grabbing Taff Davies, the kit manager's, leg and I wouldn't let go. He thought he was going to get a broken leg as well."

An injury like this must make you take stock of your career?

"Well, until this happened things were going really well. Coming to Leicester was brilliant for me, personally; most of my family are from Leicester. Mum and dad, cousins. Everybody, really. I certainly didn't expect to be in the first team so quickly. I looked at Allan Evans playing in my position and thought about how much more experience he had than me. The last four years have been absolutely fantastic."

Did you realise the historical importance of your goal against Oxford United on the 'Great Escape' day?

"It didn't really hit me at first. We were just looking upon it as

a game we had to win. But what a feeling when we did! After the game there was the Supporters' Club Player of the Season do and when I was given the trophy it was too much. I got home at four in the morning but couldn't sleep. At 6.30 I was down the paper shop, making sure it hadn't been a dream. When the fans came on the pitch I could feel the tears starting. The whole terrible, frustrating season rested on that 90 minutes. I just yelled when the ball hit the roof of the net. David Kelly tried to lay claim to it, but I knew it was mine. He would have to have been a contortionist to get it in from where he was. I think he kicked my foot. All we were really bothered about was winning and cancelling out that season. There was a huge amount of pressure on us during that last week, and I know the supporters were really nervous as well. I know how much they would have hated seeing their team go down to the Third for the first time ever. We didn't appreciate the map of the Third Division in the *Mercury* that week, either. You don't need things like that when you're already a bag of nerves. You need to be told that the fans are right behind you, which of course they were. There was a queue for the toilets in our changing room, I can tell you!"

How did you feel when you won Player of the Year?

"When you look at some of the names on the trophy [in pride of place by mum and dad's TV] – Peter Shilton, Gary Lineker and the rest – it's an honour just to have it in my house."

> **"You fight harder for your best mates than for a stranger. You can rely on them to back you up."**

What are your long-term goals now?

"I'd love to play in the First Division, the Premier League, with Leicester City. Then I'd like to play for England. That's the sort of goal you should set yourself. When I was playing on the parks, I didn't think that one day I'd be playing in the Second Division, so who knows? I'm very happy at Leicester,

"James is Evil!" went the song, but he was actually really nice.

I love the place. It's a First Division set-up with great lads, great supporters and better facilities than a lot of First Division clubs."

Except for the toilets in the changing rooms...

"Yes, they've probably got more toilets than we have. Maybe they should have a Portaloo for important games."

Pontus KAAMARK

Abba, Pontus, Ikea, Volvo...

Pontus Kaamark was a Rolls-Royce of a right-back. That much was clear in his first game and a half for City – before disaster struck. One year on, we spoke to Pontus after his long-awaited comeback.

You were injured in your second game for City. Do you remember the incident?

"Yes, I remember everything about it. It was against Bolton, and I was playing against Thompson. I was chasing him and my kick missed but my body movement continued and my studs were stuck in the grass. It was a straight knee because I was stretching out, so there was no muscle to keep it from... [makes snapping cruciate noise]. When I think about that moment, it takes me about a week to get over it. I've been trying to do some psychological work on that as well, because it's a barrier in your mind that can make you scared. But in my first game back I didn't have any doubts about going into tackles at all."

Were you into English football as a kid?

"I have never been a fan of football ever, really. I have always enjoyed playing, but almost never watched. Partly

it was because I don't drink and they show the games in bars and have a bet and a drink."

You're not a typical footballer, are you?

"No, I don't think so! Back home they call me 'The Professor'. That is not to say that I am very smart, just that I like studying things like languages and science. I enjoy doing it. It is partly because you don't make so much money in Swedish football – just like a normal job, say £2,500 a month – so many players take advantage of their time on their hands to study."

It's said that City have great team spirit...

"It is important in a team game to have eleven players with good motivation, who want to help each other, no matter what. That is why Gothenburg were so successful. We played against all the big sides in Europe. They didn't like to come and play against us. Everybody worked very hard. We played against players like Romario and Stoichkov, but they didn't work. If you look at every single player, then they are a better team than we were, but we kept winning because we worked hard while not all the opposition did. I think we have that spirit at this club now."

You've already been called a 'one-and-a-half-game legend'...

"I appreciate that the people here believe in me, after the club paid a lot of money for me and looked after me. But you haven't seen me, really. I'm sure I can do better. The Swedish papers want to know how I am doing with my recovery, but I think it is easier to get into the Swedish team than the Leicester side at the moment!"

I believe I can fly

Former City player and coach, current City manager. Temporarily. But when we met Rob Kelly in his Belvoir Drive office, 21 points out of 30 had just steered City clear of the relegation zone.

How did you deal with early retirement?

"I was 22 when they told me I wouldn't play again. But it wasn't like I was playing one day and then something horrific happened. I wasn't unintelligent, and had time to gradually come to terms with it, though it was still frightening. I decided to train as a journalist, but I was still coaching – at Villa and West Brom part-time, then at Wolves full-time."

Which managers or coaches have most influenced you?

"While I was here, Gordon Milne was a real, thinking football man. Gordon never lost his temper, always thought things through. You always felt like he was in control. At Wolves, Graham Taylor was very well organised and open-minded, with a great football brain. Mark McGhee was like an old-style football person – good with the players, he'd run more on intuition, sensing situations. Then I went to Blackburn with Roy Hodgson, who had just come from Inter. He was terrific, probably the best technical coach I've ever seen. He had more of the foreign method, concentrating on the first team. That's when I realised it was too big a job to run the whole club."

Do you prefer coaching or management?

"I have more direct contact with the players now and, selfishly, that's the best part of the job. Doing the warm up, doing the shooting and crossing and the team play, doing the video work. The way the game is now, I think the distinction has become rather blurred. I mean, what is Aidy Boothroyd? I know he's a coach because I go way back with him. But he's also the manager. What was Roy Hodgson? He was a coach. I think the game has changed and there are less of the old-style managers around, though some are very good at it. Wheeler-dealer types. Graeme Souness was definitely a manager, but does that mean he isn't a coach? I don't think the two are mutually exclusive now. I just do what I do, really, and I'm not egotistical about what they call me. Call me Robert... it's my name."

"There wasn't a lot wrong under Craig Levein. But I'm using square pegs in square holes."

Rob KELLY

Maxine KERR

Dynasty

A unique insight into City behind the scenes, from a fan whose father and grandfather were both City chairmen. We visited Maxine Kerr – *née* Shipman – at home in the Rutland countryside.

How old were you when you first became aware of your dad's involvement at City?

"I was seven when I went down to my first game. I'm 57 now. Mum was going out and said to Dad, 'You'll have to take Max down to the game, I've got no one else to look after her.' He picked me up from Brownies, so I was sat there in my uniform while he talked with friends over my head. I didn't say a word. Afterwards he said to me, 'Max, I bet you absolutely hated that, didn't you?' I said, 'Dad, I absolutely *loved* it!' I was hooked. He took me down to lots of games after that, and

when he joined the board I went to away games, too. We went everywhere."

Do you think the Leicester public ever knew your dad was such a fan of the club?

"No, not really. I don't know how much it bothered him – Mum and I were probably more the emotional ones. I remember we came out of Filbert Street once and they were all shouting, 'Shipman out!' and then they sang a song about my mum. It all got a bit personal. One time, as we walked through the old Filbert Street car park, someone said, 'Look, there's Shipman's family. They're the ones with their hands in the till.' That just finished me, and I turned round and said, 'Who said that?' They all looked at their shoes and I said, 'You really have absolutely no idea what goes on in there.' In the end we stood there for about 45 minutes talking to these fans and trying to explain how it was. Back in those days it really was all personal money. Only in his later years did Dad actually admit to Mum that he'd put our house up as collateral for the football club! Dad had a family business, which was a haulage firm. It wasn't exactly King Power!"

Were there any clubs you didn't like visiting?

"Some of the London clubs weren't too friendly. Once at Tottenham we were announced to Alan Sugar: 'The Leicester directors are here.' And he said, 'It's only Leicester, I don't want to see them. Pass them on to someone else.' At Upton Park I went to get my mum from the ladies' room – women weren't allowed in the directors' lounge – and I overheard the hostess and the West Ham chairman's wife: 'We've run out of Chablis...' 'Oh, it's only Leicester, get the Liebfraumilch out.' Chelsea, I really don't like. We were there that famous night we got cheated out of the FA Cup. We were in the players' lounge after the game with Martin O'Neill. Frank Leboeuf came in with a cigar on and really crowing about beating us. Martin completely lost it and charged across the room at him. He was absolutely furious and it took three people to haul him away. John Robertson was really upset because he'd been caught up in it and spilled some of his whisky."

Was your dad close to the managers?

"A lot of them were proper friends. Him and Jock Wallace were very close, although he could never understand what he was saying. Dad really loved Jock, they went everywhere together. I don't know how his liver could withstand it. Gordon Milne came to Dad's funeral, they were very good friends, too. They went to Heysel together and Dad never, ever spoke about it to the day he died."

What would you say was the hardest part of being chairman for your dad?

"He wanted to see them right up there doing well in the top division, but got very frustrated. I think he found it very hard when Gary Lineker left for Everton. And when he had to dismiss David Pleat."

There's a photo from the day when David was sacked and Terry resigned, and they both look quite haunted...

"Yes, Dad found that very hard. He seemed to go from 6'3" to 5'10" overnight. He really didn't want to resign but as he'd backed David and it hadn't worked out, he thought it was right to fall on his sword.

Dad was always so funny – a big, quite clumsy man, like Tommy Cooper. He was always first on our dinner-party list, not because he was family, but because he was such good company. He'd throw his arms about telling his stories and knock glasses of red wine over. His end of the table

> **"The plane's banner became a family joke whenever it was time to leave: 'Come on... Shipman, out!'"**

would look like a war zone. He wasn't too impressed when I put his wine in a Tommee Tippee drinks bottle once!"

How devoted to the club was your dad?

"Well, he took us all to Kenya for two weeks once, but it had to be cut to ten days because we were playing West Brom. My sister wasn't allowed to get married in the football season. On the day he died, he was in hospital and the nurses were about to change him into these blue and white pyjamas. He said, 'Oh, my favourites, they're my Leicester City ones.' And then he died. They were the last words he ever spoke. After this great season we've just had, I know he would have been thrilled to see us back in the Premier League."

"Cut him in half and he was blue and white all the way through."

Andy KING

The Good and Faithful Servant

When we met Andy King, City were between managers, having sacked Sven Goran Eriksson, while Hull were still proving stubborn over sanctioning Nigel Pearson's return. The interview was held in the players' lounge at Belvoir Drive – a forest of leather sofas, with a pool table and recent action shots on the wall. At one point Sean St Ledger burst in like an excited young labrador, beside himself at the very idea that anyone would want to interview Kingy – the future recipient of a Premier League winners' medal.

How old were you when you realised that you might be good enough to earn a

living from playing football?

"I think I knew by the age of 13 or 14. I probably got a bit carried away at Chelsea, thinking I had half a chance of making it into their first team when they started putting me in age groups above me. It was halfway through my Under-16 season, around Christmas time, they told me they were going to let me go. I didn't take it badly or anything, I was just desperate to move on and get a new club."

You were only 18 when Gary Megson gave you your City debut, in the season that ended with relegation to the Third Division. You then became a fixture in the side that bounced straight back thanks to Nigel Pearson...

"I think the way Nigel managed players in general was outstanding. He always appeared to be fairly relaxed, I think what he did was heap some of the pressure on himself and shield us from it. Whether it was just me being a young player who was delighted to be in the first team, I don't know, but I certainly didn't feel any pressure going to these away grounds where they were really keen to get a result against Leicester."

He wasn't a very media-friendly or public figure...

"No, he liked to keep things in the training ground and within the camp. He didn't like players going off and spouting on Twitter and stuff like that. Players have a job to do out there on a Saturday and they have to get that right first."

The Championship season

under Nigel Pearson went really well up until the penalty shoot-out in Cardiff. Were you surprised when he then left for Hull City?

"It was a shock. No one really knew what had gone on, and he'd been on a good run at that time. Shocks happen in football, I've been around long enough to know that. We just had to try and get on with it under Paulo Sousa, a new manager with new ideas. We had to learn, and to try and play his way, and unfortunately for him and for us that didn't really work out. There's no doubt that he's a good coach and he was a great player. It's hard to put your finger on why it works or doesn't work. A lot of good coaches get sacked or resign."

Then there was another surprise when Sven, an internationally renowned manager, came in to replace Sousa...

"It was a massive surprise to find out that one of the world's best managers would be taking us for coaching day in and day out. We were really looking forward to it. You've only got to spend some time with him to find out what a great man he is. The way he's so polite to everyone, and the way he carries himself. One of his strong points was the way he spoke to players as people. He's seen the best players in the world play and it makes you want to get as close to that stuff as you can."

"You hear of clubs with bad eggs in the changing room and it can have a big effect."

He introduced a passing game, but there's a theory that you can't pass your way out of the Championship...

"There were times when we passed teams off the park and there were times we didn't. We were good in bursts. I don't feel like we overplayed it. We had a few decisions go against us when he was in

charge and things didn't really seem to go in his favour. Still, with the money we've spent we know we should be higher in the league than we are. We know that as players, there's no getting away from it. It's the manager who gets sacked but ultimately it's up to the players to perform out there on the pitch and determine how the results go."

You're still very young, just turned 23. What ambitions do you have?

"I want to play for Leicester in the Premier League. They're my club now, my family supports them. I've been here so long now that people in town know me, and people in shops – I almost feel like I was born here. Although I'm 23, I think I'm the club's longest-serving player."

Andy was the first player ever to win the League One, Championship and Premier League titles.

93

Neil LENNON

Unfinished business

Over an excellent pasta meal at the Belvoir Drive canteen, City's ginger general reflected with characteristic passion on a season that had seen defeat in a cup final and a tenth-place finish.

Last October, speculation was rife about Martin O'Neill's future at the club. Did that affect the players?

"Oh, sure it did, yeah. After the Leeds game, everybody thought that the Gaffer was going to leave more or less that day. Psychologically, the lads were thinking it was going to be his farewell game, so we put on a great show. We all thought he'd gone, and the club did really well to hang on to him. Then at the Tottenham game we saw what all the fans thought of him, and that was a bit of an emotional tidal wave which lifted us again. If the Gaffer had gone, I would have had a year left on my contract at the end of the season,

and after that I would have gone. If he'd gone and taken all his staff with him, then I think a lot of the players would have considered their position. A lot of the lads are here because of the Gaffer, and it would take a hell of a big man to fill his boots. Like everything else, you don't appreciate people until they're gone. He would have been a massive loss for Leicester."

Given some distance, how do you view the Worthington Cup final?

"We were well on top during that time between the break and the sending-off. Perhaps we should have changed things round a bit then, put an extra man up front, maybe. It's easy to say in hindsight. We didn't have any chance to recover with their goal coming so late. It was the biggest blow of the season."

The press really went to town on us afterwards...

"That was shocking, absolutely shocking. Frankly, I was disgusted by it, but it was a spur for us to go on to better things. These people don't seem to look outside of London, so how can they be unbiased in their reporting? We're always stereotyped as a good old, hard-working, tenacious team who'll give you a run for your money. We went down to Chelsea with them fighting for the title and we came back from two goals down, and all we heard afterwards was that Chelsea took their foot off the pedal. Steve Guppy scored one of the best goals of the season and it just seemed to be treated as an afterthought. It sort of rankles with you. The

League Cup final wasn't a great game to watch, but it wasn't just Leicester's fault. Spurs didn't exactly set the world on fire, either. But it all seemed to come down on us and, especially, Robbie – who, if anyone actually watched the game, didn't do a lot wrong. Edinburgh knew he'd have to go as soon as he lifted his hand. And then we had people like Steffen Freund and Allan Nielsen waving imaginary yellow cards... and Freund did it again two weeks later. He's got a lot to learn about the English game. It shows a lack of respect for other players."

It wasn't just Savage who was singled out for press attention...

"I wasn't trying to cane the board or anything. I was just hoping that the club realised how far the team had progressed, and that the Gaffer needed a bit of backing. He only spent about £5 million last season – not a lot when you consider that Wimbledon spent £7 million on one player. We're behind in the financial stakes."

The win over Spurs at White Hart Lane – sweet revenge?

"Yes, it was brilliant. On the front of the programme was a picture of Allan Nielsen with the Cup and someone had stuck it up on the noticeboard in our room. I don't think I've ever seen the lads as fired up for a game. Unbelievable. The reception we gave them on to the pitch was the Gaffer's idea and I didn't want to do it because I didn't want to give them any credit whatsoever. But he said, 'Go out there and show some sportsmanship. Then get things off your chest later!' We played brilliantly, it's just a pity we didn't play like that a couple of weeks before."

In April came the Chelsea game...

"It was on Sky, and we hardly got a mention in the build-up. When Chelsea

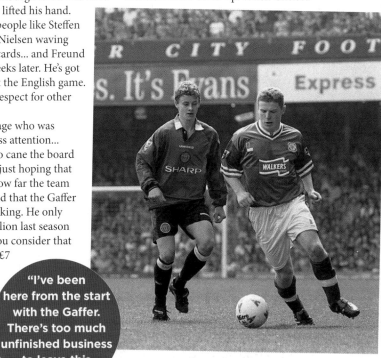

> "I've been here from the start with the Gaffer. There's too much unfinished business to leave this club."

went 2-0 up, it all seemed to be a foregone conclusion, but you know what the character is like in our squad – and there was the added spur that it was Chelsea, with one or two things that have gone on in the past. We came back at them, and that was the end of their title challenge. Then we went to Anfield and won there, and there was one stage where we were passing the ball round and played 25 consecutive passes. Marshy scored a great goal at the end. Perhaps we're not such a bad bunch of players."

What if? Neil had signed for Premier League Cov, rather than second-tier City.

Scotland Forever

Craig LEVEIN

When we met Craig Levein at Belvoir Drive, he'd only been City manager for four months. A year later, he was gone – back to Scotland, where he would soon take up the reins of the national side before returning to his beloved Hearts.

Why did you feel it was time to move on from Heart of Midlothian?

"Well, I'd been there 20 years, playing the same old teams in the same grounds. Four times a year in the League and then with the cup ties as well you can end up playing the same team seven or eight times in a season. I think I got a bit fed up with it. In Scotland, the only jobs bigger than mine were Rangers or Celtic. Even if I'd managed to get either job, then you'd still be playing the same teams week in, week out. I needed something fresh. I made no secret of the fact that I wanted to manage in the English Premiership. I couldn't see myself getting there from Scotland. So the other route would be to manage a Division One side and take them up there myself.

Leicester seemed to be the ideal club."

What was your first impression of City?

"It looked quite a strong squad with some very good players. There was obviously a reason why a side that looked good on paper weren't doing it out there on the field. I think it was that they lacked energy and drive. Then I added up the ages of all the players and I did wonder where the youth element was. Why weren't younger players pushing through? As a manager, I feel that the youth side of things should be constantly pushing up from below to give the squad that energy and that balance with the more experienced players. It just didn't seem to be happening.

How have you addressed the problem?

"Well, Rob Kelly and I had a chat very early on and said, 'Let's not do anything silly right away. Let's have a good look and see what we've got here.' It wasn't until around the Rotherham game that we decided that we had to get some fresh

faces in. Long term, we're trying to change the whole structure and thinking behind the club – it's the only way forward. If you're always continually trying to buy players to keep you in the Premiership or get you back up then you just have a constant turnaround of players. If you go down, you're paying Premier wages, and if you don't buy the right players to get you straight back up, then you've had it."

Early on, you decided you wouldn't be using the existing Director of Football set-up...

"I want to make my own mistakes. I always have done. If I

listen to somebody else or do something that somebody else tells me to do and it goes wrong, then I still end up blaming myself. I'd rather make my own mistakes and learn from them than take advice from someone else."

Many fans feel that players aren't here long enough to be part of the club. There's no one out there they can identify with...

"I understand why they feel like that and we want to get away from it. We want to try and put people out there on the park who have a rapport with the supporters. I think the supporters like the idea of seeing younger players coming in and watching them grow. We don't really have many players here doing that – there's Richard Stearman and perhaps Jordan Stewart, though he's a bit older. I see signs of improvement in Jordan since I came here, and I think he could turn out to be a decent player. He's one that I think could handle the step up if we went up. We'd want to be in a position where we'd be looking to add half a dozen players in the summer rather than 12 or 14. Guys like Maybury help, he's a wee tiger. Every time he goes out his attitude is spot-on. He has an attitude that rubs off on others, and we have a few players like that now. We're heading in the right direction."

How difficult is it to get players that you want, on long contracts, within budget?

"It's very difficult. The wage bill has been slashed this year and will come down next year and down again the year after.

"I want to make my own mistakes. If I listen to somebody else, I still end up blaming myself."

We want to get the right signings here in the summer but it won't be easy and we understand that. We want to bring in young, hungry players who would be able to take a move up to the Premier League in their stride, but we also need to get that supply of players from the youth set-up coming through. I have no doubt that Leicester people would love to see

12-game ban for punching a team-mate on the hooter.

Leicester kids moving up into the team. But in the shorter term, bringing players in is all about finding value for money. That's why I've gone to Scotland for signings up to now, because it's a lot harder to find a bargain in England."

Gary LINEKER

Running scared

In the midst of a busy day filming *They Think It's All Over* at BBC Television Centre, Leicester's superstar goalscorer reminisced about his formative years.

Can you remember any standout matches as a season-ticket holder?

"Oooh, one or two! I was at QPR for that quarter-final when Joe Waters got both goals. I went to the FA Cup final in 1969 when we lost to Manchester City – and cried all the way home. Peter Shilton was in goal for that game, and I was eight years old. I ended up rooming with him for England. Then I retired, and he was still playing! The semi-final against Liverpool which we lost. Some of them are bad memories, but you cling on to them. I was very much a fan, as much as anyone else… and then you play for them. You're still a fan, but it's a different feeling. It matters a bit more. Fans would think otherwise, but it's not the case. Then, after a period of time, you leave. It's hard to leave because it's your team, but then your allegiance instantly changes to your new club. What genuinely surprised me was that, as soon as I finished playing, that real fan thing returned – huge disappointment when they lost and elation when they won."

Tell us about the day of your debut…

"New Year's Day, 1979. Filbert Street, versus Oldham Athletic, frosty pitch. Three people made their debuts for Leicester – Bobby Smith, Dave Buchanan and me – and the other two scored. I played on the wing for pretty much the first time in my life, and I never had a clue. I fell over a lot and I was very nervous. The game after that, when Keith Weller came back in, was the famous day when he wore his white tights against Norwich."

How did you get on with Jock Wallace?

"He was certainly a great motivator and also a great man. Jock taught me how to live properly. I was actually quite scared of him, so there was no way I'd go out partying or anything. I remember the first time he came down to a reserve game. We sat down at half-time and Jock came in effing and blinding at us, but he was looking at me all the time he was doing it. I couldn't understand a word he was saying but I got the general drift. Then he came over to me, picked me up by the scruff of my neck and pinned me to the dressing-room wall. He said, 'You little English shit, you get yourself running.' When he put me back down again, I was trembling. I wouldn't have minded but we were 2-0 up

> **"Jock picked me up by the scruff of my neck and pinned me to the dressing-room wall."**

and I'd scored them both! I didn't score in the second half because I could hardly put one foot in front of the other. I just ran around like a headless chicken trying to look as if I was working hard. He called me in next morning and it was like sitting outside the headmaster's office. He'd calmed down then and he said, 'Don't worry about it, son, I was just making a point.'"

What are your most vivid memories of playing for City?

"Well, I think that Shrewsbury quarter-final was the most remarkable game I ever played in. I think the quiz question is: 'In which game were seven goals scored, and two goalkeepers kept clean sheets?' It was an incredible game. Larry May scored, and then Chic Bates put a stud in Wally's thigh and he conceded two. Then Youngy went in goal and got a bang on the head, so Steve Lynex went in. Then Youngy went back in. In the meantime, we were knocking them in at the other end. Jim Melrose got a couple and I got one. I mean, at home to Shrewsbury in the quarter-finals, you do think you've got a good chance. A bit like being drawn at home to Wycombe!"

And at the other end of the scale?

"The replay at Harlow. The day of the game, I started feeling ill and it turned out I had tonsillitis. I never dreamt I'd be playing, though, so I just toddled along with the squad down to Harlow. Then Jock reads the team out and I'm in it, starting, but I was too scared to tell him I had tonsillitis! And we lost. Not a great night."

You finally left us for Everton in 1985, but did you have other options at the time?

"To be fair, the club did come and make me quite a genuinely good offer, but at that stage it wasn't about money. I needed to move to a club that were going to win things and give me a better chance of playing for England. They're just the facts of life. It was still a very tough decision. Manchester United were in, but Big Ron was on holiday and wouldn't speak to me until he got back. At the eleventh hour, Liverpool came in. Bob Paisley wanted me but I didn't want to risk spending a year in the reserves. Everton were the best option – a very good side but I could see myself fitting in there more easily, so off I went to Goodison. Debut at Filbert Street!"

Photo: Neville Chadwick Photography.

Brian LITTLE

Little, by Little

In his Filbert Street office, Brian was still setting about the task of reviving the club – fresh from leading Darlington back into the League and to the Fourth Division title.

The favourite first quote of every new arrival at Filbert Street is always, 'It's a First Division set-up'...

"Well, yes. That's certainly the impression that the place gives, and in the long term that must be reflected on the field. One of my priorities is to make sure this isn't just a 'stop-off' club where people come in, earn a few bob and then move off somewhere else. At the moment most of the players don't live anywhere near the football club. In the First Division things are different – they're near their work. I don't mean they all have to live on Filbert Street, on the doorstep, but it would be nice to have them all in Leicestershire. At Darlington I encouraged the lads to live in the North-East. When they got home at night they read about themselves and the club they played for instead of driving home to a different area and not getting any feedback. Every time the players go out on the pitch they should be playing for: a) the club and community; b) themselves and their families, and c) for me. This instils pride and passion. It's good to have players living within the local community – to go out for a Saturday night pint and say, 'Oh, there's so-and-so who plays for City,' and there's a bit of banter. It's mutually beneficial for players and fans."

How far up the managerial ladder do you see yourself going? Could Leicester be another rung, like Darlington?

"Before I went to Darlington, I had one other managerial job, at Wolves. I got the sack after nine matches in charge. I had to sit down and think: if I took this job and Darlington were relegated from the Football League – which was the actual outcome – it might be the last job I ever get in football. Similarly, I looked at the job at Leicester. I can't kid myself, it's not going to be easy. Not when you look at where they finished last season – third from bottom isn't something to go home and shout about. My arrival isn't going to make these players better overnight. But I've brought a couple of people in, without spending a lot of money, which I feel will create a different atmosphere. Going on to the question, 'If I succeed here, will it be a stepping stone to somewhere else?' – I can't answer that. All I want to do is create as much success as possible, and what comes, comes. I am an ambitious person, but in the sense that I'm striving for success, not looking for the next big job."

Have you looked back at last season?

"I've been working my way through the videos. Something's definitely missing somewhere along the line when a team wins 15 away games in five years. That's frightening. I've got to find that missing ingredient. That's where myself and my coaching staff come in."

The training picture in the *Leicester Mercury* was a bit worrying – you were leading the sprint!

"Oh, I'm still quick! For the first 20 yards, anyway; but when I start twisting and turning my knee hurts. I asked Ricky Hill to run with me the other day, and he said, 'No chance!'"

How do you feel about your injury, and never winning a second England cap?

"I was 21 when I played for England, but I got injured and had an operation. In my next full season I scored 26 goals in the First Division but I still wasn't selected. A couple of years on, at 25, I played my last game in the First Division. It is a regret, but it's also one of my driving forces now. I look at my playing career and it just seems so long ago. It all passed so quickly. I still love getting out there in training with a ball and I love being a manager despite the hassle – but nothing beats playing. That's the ultimate. One thing about being the boss, though, is that no one tells you what to do. I've never enjoyed being ordered about. Ron Saunders always said I was the most awkward so-and-so he'd ever worked with, and I'm still the same now – but it's one of my biggest strengths. I'm not a nasty person but I know what I want and I'll work towards getting it."

What's your game plan from here?

"The modern game is all about skill, speed and stamina. Even when I was playing, Ron Saunders would say, 'When the ball's around you, chase it a little bit, but save your energy for when we have the ball.' These days, no one is exempt from hard work. The whole team has to be prepared to chase up and down. If you don't work as hard as the opposition, then they will beat you – more often than not. The old saying was that 'skill will win out in the end.' I'm not sure if that's still true. Arsenal are the team that

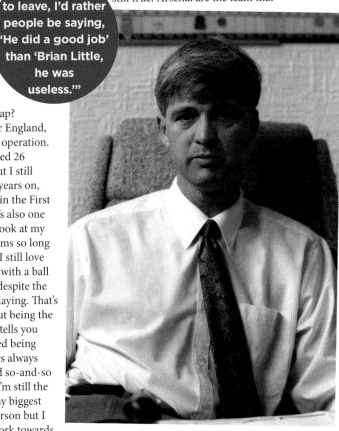

"If I'm ever to leave, I'd rather people be saying, 'He did a good job' than 'Brian Little, he was useless.'"

everyone's looking at now, and their team are all tremendous athletes – but they can play. They get the ball up quick but it isn't just whack, whack up the field. It's exciting stuff. Their players have real physical presence."

101

The life of Brian

We met Brian at the Hilton Hotel, off junction 24 of the M1, where he reflected on his time as City boss. He felt in limbo in just his second summer in 34 years without pre-season preparations looming large.

What were your priorities when you first arrived at Leicester?

"I think to try and let people know that I was in charge. I went to the training ground and I thought it looked more like a leisure area. There was a pool table, and I moved that out straight away. There were silly signs up about passing the ball around and I took them all down. I got the walls painted and changed as much as I could before anybody turned up. On the playing side, I still wanted to play with ambition and enthusiasm when we had the ball but there was a definite priority to try and

concede fewer goals. Hence you don't have to score so many to win."

Who would you rate as your best signings?

"Who came in my first year? I took

Fitzy – Paul Fitzpatrick – Kevin Poole, Colin Gordon, Steve Thompson... I could never afford any big names. It was always more of a collective effort. When I bought a lot of these players I knew what their strengths were but I used to look at their weaknesses and decide whether I could put up with them. They all did something, but they all frightened me at times. I can't single one out! Thommo was great. Iwan, I liked him a lot. I start to think of David Speedie now. And Ian Ormondroyd and Phil Gee coming in for Paul Kitson."

That deal kick-started the 1991/92 season and took us back up to the Play-off places, all culminating in that fantastic 5-0 result against Cambridge...

"I still think that's one of my favourite games. Especially in view of the 5-1 defeat at their place, earlier in the season. Night games at Filbert Street were very special. The atmosphere was great, when they still had the old wooden stand with everyone stamping their feet, and the players seemed to respond to it. It was a great occasion, and to get to Wembley that first year gave us all a chance to be part of the Leicester thing."

In your three consecutive Play-off finals, which side do you think was the best?

"That's a difficult one. I still think the first time we weren't ready to go up. The Swindon game, I still can't believe they beat us, to be honest. We played our best football that year. I must have sat for an hour and a half on the edge of a bath, totally and absolutely gutted. To have gone back the third year and achieved it says a lot about that group of players. Man for man, Derby were better than us so I

had to pick a side that could win in that one-off situation. I got labelled after that game, especially at Premiership level, as a long-ball manager. But I don't think I was. I was a result-orientated manager."

Early in the next season, Ron Atkinson was sacked as Aston Villa boss...

"I suppose everybody has a period in their life when they look back and think, 'Oh God, why wasn't that done right?' The whole thing really was an absolute shambles. From a personal point of view, it wasn't done right. All I would say is that everybody should look at it and be disappointed with themselves. It really was uselessly handled. I still think that I couldn't say 'no.'"

Nothing could have stopped you leaving?

"I felt I had to do it. I wish I'd come out and said, 'Look, I've really got to go and talk to them and see if it's right for me.' But I didn't. In the end, if they'd stopped me, I think I probably would have left Leicester anyway, in disappointment."

And then your second match in charge of Villa brought you back to Filbert Street...

"Yes. It's funny, I spoke to Steve Cotterill at the recent Play-off final. He obviously left Stoke and made the decision to go to Sunderland. He said to me, 'I got a letter off somebody and they were really giving me stick.' I said, 'Listen, son. I went back to Leicester with 20-odd thousand 'Judases' written in front of me. You've had one letter off a Stoke fan! You haven't lived.' I remember getting in my car that morning in Barrow. The phone went and somebody said, 'Have you seen the back page of *The Sun*?' It was horrible. To this day, it's had an effect on me as a person. I don't know if I can be bothered any more. I'd love to be a football manager but if you can't put up with that side of things then maybe I shouldn't be. There's an edge missing from me now, based on those experiences. Returning to Leicester that day was definitely the worst day of my footballing career. I say this now with total honesty, not just because people from Leicester will read this, but I love Leicester City. I still do, but that day hammered me, I tell you. It was horrible!"

And the pain continued when Leicester visited Villa Park...

"Oh, that was crazy! My Villa team had a really dicey end to the season, thanks to that game. Four-one up with 15 minutes to go and we let them in for the draw. It was a lesson for me. I suppose, underneath, I smiled about it."

"Leicester fans tended to look backwards to that '70s period. I think I probably overcame that in the end, in terms of where we got to."

Andy LOCHHEAD

Heads, Andy wins

We visited the Burnley home of former City striker Andy Lochhead accompanied by Alan Young, who was keen to catch up with an earlier wearer of the Leicester number 9 shirt and an old team-mate at Oldham.

Burnley was your first professional club, though you were from Glasgow. How did you make that journey?

AL: "I started out at the same club as Alex Ferguson did, Drumchapel Amateurs. I was offered a trial by a Burnley scout when I was 17. Then they offered me a 12-month contract – that's all I ever got, even when I came down to Leicester. You didn't get these four-year contracts like you do now."

AY: *"Me, neither. Each year I just signed a one-year contract. I hated it, each year I thought I was going to get binned."*

AL: "I didn't get a raise until I went to Leicester. I asked Matt Gillies for £100 basic and he said, 'No problem, Andy, we can give you that.' I managed to stay on £100 at Villa and even at Oldham!"

AY: *"Really? I was doing all your f***ing running for you and you were getting £100 and I was getting £30?"*

AL: "Sorry, did you not know?"

You soon earned a reputation as an uncompromising centre-forward. Everton defender Brian Labone described you as his toughest opponent: 'Kick Lochhead early in the game and he comes back and kicks you twice as f***ing hard and twice as f***ing often.' Is that how it was?

AL: "Oh yes, 100 per cent. It was a man's game and you had to be able to look after yourself. There was more going on off the ball than on the ball. A winger would be under orders to hang his first cross just under the crossbar so we could whack the goalie. Next time a cross comes over, the keeper has one eye on the ball and one eye on me. A good goalkeeper would always keep both eyes on the ball – you knew which ones you could get at."

AY: *"I remember Portsmouth away, I scored and was charging around going 'Yesss!' Andy got hold of me and said, 'This game's not finished yet, son.' Moments later I got pole-axed by their big Irish centre-half, Eoin Hand. The next thing I knew, Hand was lying flat on the pitch and Andy was walking away from him."*

AL: "It was only a friendly tap."

For the 1968/69 season you were teamed up with Allan Clarke. How did you get on with him?

AL: "Oh dear. Not very well at all. He was a very self-centred man, not a team player at all, and his attitude could

be shocking. After we'd lost the Cup final we had quite a few games left. We were in trouble and needed something from the last game at Manchester United. Frank O'Farrell held a big team meeting in

"It was a man's game and you had to be able to look after yourself."

preparation. He said, 'Right, I want Andy on his own up front and Allan to play ten or 15 yards behind him.' Clarke said, 'No, no. My job is in the box, that's where I'm going to play. Not him.' And he pointed at me. What a stinking attitude towards a team that was in trouble. Frank's idea was that they could launch balls up to me, I would win them and knock them back to Allan. He'd been tapped up by Leeds by then so he didn't care because he knew he was on his way."

Obviously, we were relegated that season, having done so well to get to the Cup final. What was happening in the Cup that wasn't happening in the League?

AL: "Ah, you tell me and you'd be a manager. When the whistle blows and that ball starts rolling, anything can happen. Going back to the '60s we used to play a team twice over Christmas. We played Man United at Turf and the next day we were at Old Trafford. We beat them 6-2 at

Turf and the next day with more or less the same 22 players, they beat us 5-1! That sort of answers your question."

You're still remembered by Leicester fans for the goal you scored at Anfield in a fifth round replay during the 1969 Cup run. Do you remember much about it?

AL: "A bit, it was a header. I was up against Ron Yeats that night. I recall it going past Tommy Lawrence, 'The Flying Pig' they called him. Don't bother going for it Tommy, it's past you."

The FA Cup seemed to mean more to the players back then than it does now...

AL: "It was a magnificent experience, walking out of that tunnel behind the goal and knowing you're playing in the FA Cup final. It was the only game in my career when I sat there and cried in the changing rooms afterwards – and not just because of my miss. It was such an occasion, right from the moment we stepped off the coach, and I really felt for all our supporters."

Photo: Neville Chadwick Photography.

Ian MARSHALL

Corridor of uncertainty

Scruffy socks and shinpads, custom-made extra-long shirt and mullet flapping in his considerable slipstream – that's how we remember Marshy at the end of the '90s. Despite some business setbacks in Canada, he was in high spirits when we met at the Holiday Inn.

Born into the red half of Liverpool, how did it feel to score a last-minute winner at Anfield in your last season at Leicester?

"That was my favourite ever goal that I've scored. As a boy, I dreamed of scoring at the Kop end at Anfield, albeit in the red shirt. But the next best thing was doing it as an opposition player."

What were your first impressions at City?

"It's only since I retired from the game and matured slightly and had time to analyse Martin that I get to understand him a bit more. He's the only person in football who's succeeded in making me

feel uncomfortable. I remember when I'd not long signed for Leicester we stayed in a hotel down in London. As I turned the corner to go to my room, he was walking down the corridor towards me about 50 yards away. I was looking at him and he was looking at me, and then he just walked past without a word! I was waiting to go, 'Hello, Gaffer,' and he just looked straight through me as though I was invisible. Bizarre little things that he used to do. He'd go round the dressing room saying, 'You were shit... You were shit.' Then he'd put his arm round Gupps and say, 'You were great.' He'd sit and talk to his favourites like Muzzy and Lenny, and I'd just be ignored completely. In his psychobabble sort of way he was trying to get me to prove him wrong. Possibly, it worked. As a football manager he has a bit of a side to him, but as a man he's very thoughtful and caring."

Many City fans' highlight of all time is going 1-0 up in Madrid. Do you realise how significant your goal was there?

"I do, because people come up to me and say, 'Best time of my life, that goal.' I'm thinking, 'But we lost that night.' I only played 35 minutes of the game before I was stretchered off. From what we heard, the fans were treated like cattle and had a horrendous time, so this was the moment that made up for it. My wife was there, and she was seven months pregnant. I looked up into the stand and she was standing on her seat! I thought, 'Christ Almighty, love.'"

You picked up a bad injury in that game.

"Yes, it was totally intentional. In a 20-year career I've felt completely in the zone only about five games. That game when you're invincible and everything you try comes off. I was beating players, every pass was to the man. I've got a photo somewhere of me being stretchered off by the Madrid people and one of the guys carrying the stretcher is giving a big thumbs up to the Madrid fans!"

Were you similarly 'in the zone' when we beat Derby 4-2 at home, and you got a hat-trick?

"No, not at all! I woke up that Saturday morning with a burning throat and I remember saying to my wife, 'The last thing I want to do today is play a game of football.' The 4-0 away at Derby was one of those, but for the whole team. For the first 20 minutes we murdered them."

could see cameramen up in the trees. It was like we were Hollywood film stars who had done something outrageous –

"I had mine first, and I wish I still had it. It was a real mullet and I loved it!"

What really happened at the infamous La Manga incident?

"Well, Stan took a fire extinguisher off the wall in the hotel bar and gave it a couple of blasts. I think at the time he was trying hard to fit in with the lads and thought a little joke would go down well. It was literally only a couple of seconds each but it was one of those CO_2 ones. As the white powder settled down we could see that the physio, Mick Yeoman, had got completely covered. He thumbed it out of his eyes and, because he was a bald-headed guy, he looked like Casper the Friendly Ghost. Everyone started roaring with laughter but, as you looked around, this white stuff was behind the bar, all over the place. The next morning we

unbelievable, and totally blown out of proportion."

How did Martin O'Neill react?

"Well I phoned him, which was my biggest mistake! There was a curfew of 12 o'clock but in my drunken state John Robertson let me use his phone. It went straight to answer-phone and I said, 'Gaffer, it's Marshy. We're having a great time here, really brilliant. Any chance of the lads having a later curfew? *Love yer!*'

When we got back, Martin marched straight up to me and growled, 'You, yer ****. Don't you ever, ever call me again.' I'm there thinking, 'Hold on, I only made a phone call. Stan here has caused absolute uproar in the international media and I'm getting slaughtered!' Typical Martin!"

Did you know? Following his Canadian adventures, Ian has now emigrated to South Africa.

Ali MAUCHLEN

In and out of love

When we met our '80s midfield hero at his house in Fleckney, Ali was still playing part-time for Ballymena.

It was August 1985 when you and Gary McAllister were signed from Motherwell...

"Yes, I really enjoyed playing under Gordon Milne, even though we were struggling in the First Division most of the time. He was a fair manager and a tremendous coach, and I don't think he got what he deserved at Leicester. The fans were split on him, weren't they? He had some good players – Ian Wilson, Tommy Williams, Alan Smith, Ian Banks, Bobby Smith, Bob Hazell, Ian Andrews, John O'Neill – but financially he couldn't tempt two or three extra players to the club, and had to make do with younger players."

Why was he moved upstairs to make way for Bryan Hamilton?

"That was a bit of a strange one. It was a bad blend because Gordon and Bryan never saw eye to eye. They were chalk and cheese. Bryan handled things rashly; Gordon would sit down and take stock and then deal with it quietly. As I saw it, Bryan put a buffer up. He didn't want Gordon's experience. And he made a pig's ear of it. There was a Simod Cup match, away at Charlton, and I decided to make a stand and not turn up for the bus. I was living in rented

accommodation on London Road, and I wouldn't tell him my address or phone number or anything. I phoned the office and told them I wasn't going to turn up. Bryan said I had a contract and I had to play. I told him that he'd pissed me off so much, I didn't care. I turned up for training the next day and he never even looked at me. He fined me two weeks' wages and said he'd put me back in on Saturday against Middlesbrough; but that was his last game. He was sacked. There was an actual deal for me to go to Chelsea on his desk, but when David Pleat arrived, he said he wanted me to stay, so I did."

Pleat turned the season around...

"He just got people believing in themselves. He brought his thoughts on the game, and had been in charge of some entertaining teams. We suddenly had a good spirit, everyone was getting a touch of the ball, and some lads, including me, discovered that they could play a bit. He encouraged me to use the ball more."

Why didn't the form go on next season?

"Well, David changed the side around. He made a big deal about signing Martin Hodge to replace Paul Cooper in goal. Russell Osman left as well, and Simon Morgan. Sometimes it's horses for courses, and David would never change his game plan. You go to some places and you know it's going to be tough, but we'd still be trying to play football. I think perhaps he still wanted to be at Tottenham, where he had Hoddle and Waddle, his five-man midfield full of stars, and Clive Allen scoring 40-odd goals in a season. We didn't have the sort of quality here that could open up a side and win a game just like that. We had to work hard to win games; we had to work hard to stop losing games,

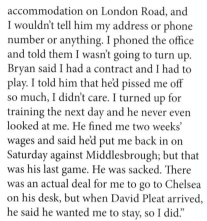

> "It was an unbelievable moment. I know it was for all the wrong reasons, but it was massive for the club."

at times. David was in a bit of a dream world and wouldn't change his beliefs."

Pleat left us in deep trouble, and Gordon Lee did a hell of a job in retrospect...

"Gordon was probably the best players' man I've ever worked with. When that final whistle went in that last match against Oxford, Gordon was even more elated than I was, and I was elated. The video shows me running all over the pitch. It was an unbelievable moment. I know it was for all the wrong reasons, staying up rather than winning something, but it was massive for the club. It was so vital for Leicester City to stay in that division. I think every player at the club wanted him to get the job, and it was a sad day when he left. Especially for me, because he'd given me a player-coach title and confided that if he got the job then he was bringing me in as his number two. We went to Portugal on an end-of-season trip. We were sitting in the hotel when it came on the news, the job had been offered to John Beck. Gordon and I just said, 'Well, that's the end of the road, mate.'"

You scored a goal in a similar situation on the last day of 1985/86...

"The end of my first season. Yes, we won 2-0 and we were waiting on a result from another game. I hit a 20-yarder in the bottom right-hand corner and Ian Banks scored with a penalty. It got us another year at the top."

How did you get on with Brian Little?

"I knew my player-coach position would go, but Brian never really gave me a chance. He stuck me in the reserves and gave Steve Walsh the captaincy. The hardest part was that, under Gordon, Rangers had come in with an offer for me. But Martin George, the chairman, was adamant that he wanted me to stay; offered me a two-year extension and a testimonial. I thought we had an agreement, and that was enough. I felt as if I'd been kicked in the bollocks, to be frank."

Game of consequences

Larry MAY

In an era when most centre-halves were built like Bob Hazell, Larry May offered a glimpse into football's future. Looking back, we shared some bittersweet City memories with Larry and his sports-scientist son, David, in a Hove café.

This is just a flying visit to England for you, Larry – all the way from the Algarve...

"Yes, I was working at Brighton & Hove Albion in their Community Scheme. Then it was decided that a qualified teacher needed to be doing my job, even though I'd been doing it for a decade! My wife works in finance and was offered a job in Portugal, so we decided to give it a go!"

Your first-team debut was in March 1977 against Bristol City at Filbert Street...

"Steve Sims was injured. I'd only started training with the first team the week before. I played alongside Alan Woollett because Jeff Blockley was injured, too, and we kept a clean sheet in a 0-0 draw. After a taste of first-team action, I thought, 'This is what I want to do.' I loved it."

But that was your one and only game under Jimmy Bloomfield, who soon left...

"Yes, my chances were limited in Frank McLintock's season because he brought in Dave Webb. But then along came Jock Wallace. He was straight-talking, and rough and ready, and he had this enthusiasm. Before a game he'd say, 'You be you, and go and win those balls in the air for me.'"

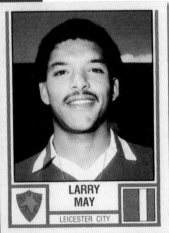

**LARRY
MAY**

LEICESTER CITY

You scored some important goals when City went up as champions...

"Yes, Jock always encouraged me to go forward and attack the ball at set pieces. You'd get a signal saying it was going to the near post or the far post, and I was quick enough to reach it. The Orient one came to me at the far post and I slid it in over the line. I can still remember doing it today. We were already up, weren't we? But that win clinched the title. I remember thousands of Leicester fans there, outnumbering the home fans. Some of the players got their kit ripped off in the pitch invasion at the end, but I got away with it. We went up into the directors' box to go and see the crowd on the pitch. I'll never forget it. We had some party that night!"

How did you find the top flight?

"There was obviously a jump up in quality. Suddenly you were facing players like Kenny Dalglish and Trevor Francis. You looked forward to pitting yourself against the best, but you could also get a bit panicky just because of their reputation. I should have just gone out and played my normal game. Jock wasn't the best tactician and while the blood and thunder could get you by in Division Two, it wasn't really enough when you went to places like Arsenal. Sometimes we were finding that we had to work it out for ourselves on the pitch. We were a very young side, as well. But we had some great days. We beat Liverpool home and away, and they were probably the best side in the country. We beat Manchester United. I think we beat Tottenham home and away. But sadly we couldn't produce it often enough, and we went down."

You played a big part in the Cup run next season. But Jock's final act as City manager was to sign Alan Smith, a great welcome present for Gordon Milne...

"Yes, Alan was different class and he went on to prove it. Gary Lineker was coming into his own then, too. It took him

made a young, rash decision on my own."

Alan Young was surprised you didn't go on to play for England and a bigger club...

"Yes, it's probably my biggest ever regret that I left Leicester when I did. It was a huge mistake. I think I was one of those players who needs to be loved a bit, and I'd got that from Jock. But I never felt that Gordon rated me. I'd played most of his first season, and we got promoted again. But then David, my first son, was born. He was ill, with stomach problems. I'd missed training and didn't feel mentally right for it, but I allowed Gordon to talk me into playing up at Grimsby. I really wasn't at the races and ended up getting sent off. He dug me out a bit for that, and things were never quite the same again. In the close season, Gordon told me, 'We've had an offer for you from Barnsley. You can go if you want.' I didn't want to, but their manager, Norman Hunter, said a couple of things that chimed with me and I ended up signing. Having got promoted with Leicester I was now back in the Second Division. I was Player of the Season for three years, but Barnsley wasn't a good move, career-wise. I did get back to the First Division with Sheffield Wednesday – eventually."

"I was slim, tall, quick and good in the air. Perhaps I would've been more suited to the modern game."

a while, he started out on the wing until they started to use his speed in the middle. And of course he went on to have a brilliant career, too. Perhaps I should have as well, but I made a bad decision. I remember I was captain one week and we beat Wolves 5-0. The next week the teamsheet goes up and I'm not on it. That's when you say to yourself, 'He doesn't like me.' I look back now and I can see that I would have got back into the team. I believed in my own ability and worked hard in training. But I didn't have an agent at the time, and my dad knew nothing about football, so I

Gary McALLISTER

A long time gone

There was so much to look back on with Gary McAllister. Aside from his priceless City memories, he went on to play for Leeds, Coventry and Liverpool. We met at a hotel in Harrogate, when he'd recently lost his job as Leeds manager. As an 'interview fee', Gary asked us to make a donation to LOROS.

How did your move to Leicester City come about?

"I was about 19 when Gordon Milne came up to watch Ali Mauchlen, who was also a target for Manchester City. But Gordon ended up signing both of us. To be honest, all young players in Scotland had a huge desire to play in England back then, especially in the First Division."

How did you find Gordon Milne?

"Brilliant, a typical Liverpool man. The best part of his career had been spent at Anfield and he had that ethos. It was music to my ears as a youngster and all his ideas fitted in with how I liked to play. He's a proper football man."

Early on in your time at Leicester you scored when City beat Manchester United 3-0 at Filbert Street. Do you think the days when that could happen are now over?

"I don't know. I mean back then a 3-0 win against Man United was obviously a great result – my dad still has a tape of the game – but it wasn't that unusual. Leicester had a decent record against the big clubs. They could beat Arsenal or Liverpool. The first week we arrived at Leicester, Ali and I sat in the stand and watched the lads beat the champions, Everton, 3-1 in the first game of the season. Ali and me turned to each other and said, 'Hey, this is some team we've joined here!' I think these days if you had to play the champions there would be a level of fear there that would prevent you beating them."

Who did you like to play alongside in City's midfield?

"Ian Wilson was a fellow Scotsman who was a talented guy. He pushed his way into the Scotland squad and got a move to Everton. The two guys who were perhaps labelled as a bit of protection for myself, for my style of playing, were Paul Ramsey and Ali Mauchlen. Paul was very unlucky with injuries and a very underrated player, but I think the people of Leicester appreciated him."

Relegation under Bryan Hamilton in 1986/87 was hard to take. We thought we were going to turn the corner, signing Mike Newell and Jari Rantanen...

"Relegation was horrible. I think we thought it would just be a case of coming straight back up, but that's easier said than done, isn't it? Jari was a big brute! He scored a couple of good goals and had a decent touch for such a huge lad. I used to really look forward to the confrontation between him and Walshy on the training ground. You'd pay money to watch them challenging for a 50-50 ball – like two steamrollers whacking into each other!"

David Pleat arrived in the New Year of 1988, and we enjoyed a superb second half to the season under his leadership...

"He'd come from working alongside fantastic players like Glen Hoddle, Chris Waddle, Ossie Ardiles. In terms of influencing my career, he's right up there. He was a manager who wanted to play

Photo: Neville Chadwick Photography.

football and win games by passing the ball. His emphasis was very much on attack and playing with a bit of flair. David might tell you this himself, that he neglected the other side of the game a bit. Keeping clean sheets, being ugly away from home."

You moved to Leeds in the summer of 1990. Would anything have kept you at Leicester at that time?

"I've got to say that, looking back, I should have left earlier. I was too loyal to Leicester City. I went along to a hotel to meet Brian Clough with my agent Jon Holmes and it was one of the most bizarre nights of my life. He was quite abusive towards us. I think we all know now what was affecting Brian. I moved to Leeds to get back into the top flight because I had a couple of wasted seasons in Division Two. As a player you have to try and play in the highest possible league for as long as you can, and look after yourself. As soon as you become surplus to requirements at a club you'll be out, that's for sure."

Your international career started that summer when you moved to Leeds. Those 57 caps must hold many great memories?

"I loved every minute of it, every game. And about halfway through that lot I was made captain which took it to another level. We qualified for Italia '90, Euro '92 in Sweden, Euro '96 in England, and France '98 so it was a good time. Playing for your country is the pinnacle for any footballer, I think."

You stepped out of football to be with your wife. Did losing her change your philosophy on football?

"Football pales into insignificance alongside that. It changed the way I looked at life. You live for today, enjoy yourself and try to smile because you're a long time gone and quickly forgotten."

> "Cruyff presented my Man of the Match trophy at the UEFA Cup final. That was a great night."

Leader of the pack

Paddy McCARTHY

At Belvoir Drive, we asked our young Irish skipper to take us through his relegation-threatened side's characters, 'Meet the Team' style. Paul Henderson, Richard Stearman, Patrick Kisnorbo, Nils-Eric Johansson, Darren Kenton, Alan Maybury, Danny Tiatto, Gareth Williams, Andy Johnson, James Wesolowski, Iain Hume, Elvis Hammond, Matty Fryatt, Chris O'Grady, Josh Low, Levi Porter, Stephen Hughes. In retrospect, it's telling how few made a mark at City, or in their later careers.

Although you did well personally, 2005/06 was a very disappointing season...

"You can't come into such a tough league as the Championship with almost a whole new squad and expect to take the league by storm. A lot of us were still learning the game and were untested at Championship level. We came from different levels of the game, from different countries and from reserve-team football. I think it was unrealistic to think that we'd be challenging for promotion last year.

Obviously, that's what we all wanted and what we tried to achieve but, looking back, with 15 new players walking through the door, it wasn't going to happen."

What was the difference in styles between Craig Levein and Rob Kelly?

"I really liked Craig as a man and as a manager, and obviously he gave me my big chance in football. I learned an awful lot from him in six months. But then Rob Kelly took over and I think he's taken us on to a new level now. He's a really good man manager and a knowledgeable coach. The lads really responded to Rob taking over, though I can't really put a finger on what it was that he did."

Rob Kelly has made you captain of the side. What do you say during the huddle?

"I think we did it for the Luton game, that's the only one I can remember. It's basically a continuation of the geeing-up in the dressing room, a lot of effing and blinding and telling people what's needed to be done. Everybody has their little say in getting us motivated. But it certainly didn't work against Luton so we put it to bed after that! There are a lot of big voices in the dressing room and a lot of strong characters. When you have these people saying their piece it really does get people fired up."

Do you realise that you're one of City's longest-serving players, after 18 months?

"That's maybe an answer to one of your previous questions. We've had a big turnover of players here, and there are a lot of youngsters. That's why, if we can hold on to the young, talented players I think we'll be a force to be reckoned with in a couple of years. We do have that inconsistency at the moment, but there are signs that we're progressing as a team."

The Fergie connection

Mark McGhee had only been manager for two months when we chatted over tea and cake in his Filbert Street office.

Alex Ferguson has spoken very highly of your recent work at Reading...

"I had five very good years under him at Aberdeen. I worked hard for him and he did a lot for me but it was a very turbulent relationship. I had a lot of run-ins with Alex, but he isn't a man to bear grudges. Every manager I've worked under has influenced me, but the game is all about good players, not fancy styles of management. I worked with Bill McGarry, an experienced and enthusiastic manager, who was very abrasive, and I would never be like that. Ernst Happel, a world-class coach at Hamburg, was also very abrasive. Managers like Alex and Jim Smith you can actually talk to, and those are the type of guys I would take my style from. Towards the end of my playing career, I had a chat with Alex and he said it was time I started thinking about managing or coaching, because ultimately that was what I wanted to do. He said, 'What about the Reading job?' Alex made a call and said to the chairman, 'Interview this boy.' I went along for an interview and was given the job the same day."

Idealistically, what style of play do you want to see out on the pitch?

"Passing and moving. Passing forward whenever possible. Quick movement of the ball, not slowly rolling the ball around. The best team ever, for me, were the Liverpool team of the early '80s. Because of the Fergie connection, people used to say that Reading were the Manchester United of the Second Division, but I always liked to think we were the Liverpool of the Second Division."

What are your priorities at Leicester, with the side threatened by relegation?

"Obviously, winning games. In many ways, things were worse than I imagined. Even among the players who are good enough to be part of my Leicester side, there was a lack of confidence. There's no magic wand that you can wave at players and they suddenly turn it round. It's more scientific than that. The best way is to bring in new faces with new ideas to inspire the players around them. There's no doubt about it, regardless of what anyone thinks, you can buy success. Dalglish, Ferguson, Keegan are all proving that. It's the easiest way to get a good side. If you can't spend, then you have to go out and get as good as you can, and make them as good as you can. You're never going to be as good as the guys who can go out and get the best players."

Mark McGHEE

The ten per cent solution

Mark McGHEE

We went to Belvoir Drive to meet Garry Parker, who sadly proved unavailable. But the Endsleigh League First Division Manager of the Month kindly stood in for a grilling – not long before he shocked us all by quitting for Wolves.

Are you surprised to have been top of the League for so long?

"No. I didn't particularly anticipate before the season that we were going to be top. But as things have unfolded and I've seen what we're like and what other teams are like, I'm not surprised, no. You have to take into account the fact that a large part of what we tried to do in the summer to improve things – Kalac, Kaamark – haven't played yet. Scotty Taylor and Steve Corica have been injured. What encourages me is that we've got all that to come, and I think that will make the difference between us and the rest."

To your mind, what have been the

outstanding displays of the season so far?

"I don't think we've yet put together a total performance, one where you could say that we've exhibited exactly what we're trying to do. That has only happened in spells, and we can do better."

What's the root of our inconsistency?

"We will lose ten or 12 games this season and still win the league. Newcastle or Manchester United, or whoever wins the Premiership, will probably lose eight or nine games. After those games Kevin Keegan, Alex Ferguson and myself, and every manager of a good team who loses a game, scratches their head and wonders why. Because you do everything right and you prepare right and everything looks the same... but it just doesn't happen out there. When the other team comes out a bit and there's more space and we're passing it about well, we can make it very difficult for the other side. When you play at home and space is more restricted and teams get behind the ball, then we sometimes find it difficult to make the space necessary. You're then looking for certain people to give you variety and options. One of the players we expect to step in and produce a moment like that is Steve Corica, and we haven't always had him there to unlock things."

Did you realise he was *that* good when you signed him?

"I knew that he was very good, and I have to say we still don't know how good he is. We're excited by how good he can become."

Another special player, Julian Joachim, has seemed a bit subdued this season...

"Well, it's funny, I've got this letter today: *'Under Brian, Julian was more effective*

116

with a more direct style, when the ball was put in behind people and he was asked to chase it...' There's no doubt that has been Julian's strength in the past. Possibly we could make him more effective by playing to that strength. But in the long

> "Look at Juventus v Rangers the other night. That's what we're looking to be like, and that's a fact."

run that isn't going to make Julian a better player. The way we want to build play, we need ten outfield players who are willing to contribute. He has to play as a midfield player, he has to link up and keep possession. Every time he gets the ball, he doesn't have to beat a man, score a goal or do something wonderful."

We've seen glimpses of your new Leicester City style. How close are we to seeing the finished article?

"We've only scratched the surface. You say we've seen glimpses of it, but it's only glimpses of a style. It isn't anything like what eventually we hope for. You have to look at Juventus against Rangers the other night. That's what we're looking to be like, and that's a fact. If you're looking for anything less, then you're looking for second best. Compare what you've seen

with some of our better moments and that display by Juventus in the first half, and that's how far away we are."

What percentage of the way there are we, would you say?

"Ten per cent."

There have been spells in matches when we've looked like pasting teams...

"Divide anything you see out there by two, because we're playing in the First Division. If you put a rating on a performance in this division and said that it was 8 out of 10, then divide it by two. If we were playing in the Premiership, it would have been worth 4 out of 10."

Are we ready for the Premier League?

"You need to be going into the Premier League with a realistic chance of winning matches and, until then, we'd be stupid to think that we were good enough just because we're sitting on top of the First Division. The best we are at the moment is the best First Division team, and we have to improve on that."

Eager Belvoirs: Mark attempts to turn City into Juventus (step 1 of 273).

Frank McLINTOCK

Fanatical, philosophical Frank

In his conservatory in leafy Enfield, our shining star of the '60s reflected honestly on his ill-fated return as manager.

You signed for City on your 17th birthday, moving down from Glasgow...

"It was all so exciting to me, becoming a footballer. I remember that badge of the fox on that blue shirt, and it was so outstanding to me. I loved it. I was also serving my apprenticeship as a painter and decorator, and going to night school. I was up at 6.30 every morning, cycling to work. Two nights a week training at Filbert Street. Then I'd be playing for Leicester on a Saturday and sometimes midweek as well. I played at Wembley in front of 100,000 people and then was back at work on the Monday morning. Unbelievable!"

You kept working even in the first team?

"Oh, yes! I finished work on the Friday and cycled home. I got washed, showered and shaved. Cycled down to the ground and got on the first-team bus down to London. Stayed at the Dorchester Hotel and met Elizabeth Taylor and Richard Burton. Played at Wembley the next day against Spurs, but got beaten because Lenny Chalmers got injured. Then, back at the hotel, I was dancing with Barbara on the dancefloor when I felt a tap on the shoulder. 'Hello son, how would you like to play for a *good* team?' Bill Shankly and  Ian St John, tapping me up! And then back at work on the Monday again!"

There was some controversy about Ken Leek being dropped for the final...

"We heard later on that Kenny had put a bet on himself to cover his bonus. He liked a bit of a gamble, although he wasn't a massive gambler. He was always a thorn in the Tottenham side and we were a bit of a bogey team for them. Suddenly Matt Gillies had us all in and said that Kenny was out and Hugh was in, and we were all gobsmacked. Nobody told us why."

And another Cup final was lost in 1963...

"As a team we didn't operate in the usual way, we weren't as free. I was choked that day, absolutely gutted. Getting beat is bad enough, but playing really badly is even worse. And when you play for a team like Leicester, all the shop fronts are decorated in blue and white with balloons and photos of the players, it's a massive thing for the whole community."

After some fantastic years at Arsenal at QPR, you hung up your boots in 1977...

"I hadn't really made any plans for a future in the game because I'd been so involved with playing. I still loved Leicester and, when I heard they wanted me, I let my heart rule my mind. I looked at that team and saw they'd finished eleventh, so it looked healthy enough. But Keith Weller was missing a lot of games through injury, and Frank soon left because he needed a signing-on fee and better wages. I look back on that time now and I can see where I went wrong. You need a bit of fear and distance with the manager, but I'd just come as a player from the changing rooms. I was given £100,000 to go and buy four players. I had to go and buy older players that I knew, just to

Frank
McLintock

try and get it a little bit better, like Davie Webb, Eddie Kelly and George Armstrong. And I was so used to winning all through my playing career that those defeats hurt me really badly. I think they ended up affecting me as a person, and my anxiety showed to the players. I now realise you have to serve an apprenticeship under somebody's wing as an assistant; it's just too hard to be a manager straight away. I made mistakes: I bought Alan Waddle from Liverpool for £20,000 and I hadn't even seen him play. But we had a midget forward line and the board thought we couldn't really lose for £20,000. But, looking back, you get a bit of pressure and tension on and you can't think as clearly. I think the players started to freeze as well. Because we had such a small team I made them keep the ball below the waist in practice games, and they did it brilliantly. As soon as the match came, they'd hit the f***ing thing 20 yards into the air up to Brian Alderson and Stevie Earle, who were both about 5'7". So in training they looked terrific, playing it on the ground, but in matches I couldn't believe how bad they were. They'd probably say the same about me, as well."

How did it all come to end?

"Mr Sharp told me he wanted me to come up and live in Leicester. Looking

> **"I still loved Leicester and, when I heard they wanted me, I let my heart rule my mind."**

back on it, it was probably just a clever way to make me resign. I was already up three or four nights a week, and going to games, and watching the reserves. I had a pub in Islington that was making me more money than my manager's salary. I was on 14 grand a year at Leicester, because I hadn't been interested in the money. I know it was only nine months that I was manager of Leicester, but it's stayed with me so much. I was so desperately trying to be a good manager of Leicester. I loved the club and the fans loved me as a player. They were very good, the supporters, even though they must have been bitterly disappointed."

Were there any positives to take away?

"I did give debuts to the lads in the Youth team that would make the grade. Larry May was one. Trevor Christie, Tommy Williams, Mark Goodwin."

Jock Wallace definitely benefited there...

"Yes, Jock said about me, I was 'in the wrong place at the wrong time.' He told Ian MacFarlane that. I had the knowledge but not the experience – two different things."

"I turned to Ian MacFarlane and said, 'I can't f***ing believe this! Where do we go from here?'"

Tom MEIGHAN

Firestarter

We met Kasabian frontman Tom in the Rutland & Derby with his dad, before a 2-1 victory over Blackpool.

Leicester City: is it a family thing?

"Yes, I started going down with my old man when I was about nine years old. My first game was Port Vale at home, I think we won 4-0. It was the ZDS or something, so there were only about 5,000 there. Shocking! We used to go in the old Members' Stand – in the middle bit, because we knew Richard Smith and some of the other players. We used to go in the players' lounge afterwards. The old man used to give the doorman a bottle of whisky once a year and that was enough for us to get the nod through every game! It was a little old place – there'd be Steve Walsh and all the players' wives crammed in. We'd have some good nights in there."

Did you go to any away games?

"My first away game was Millwall. Straight into the Lions' Den! It was really cool going down to London for the day. We lost, and I remember Teddy Sheringham scoring for them. We had tickets in the Millwall end, actually. They were a scary lot, but we were okay, just a dad and a lad."

Did you used to go to games with Serge when you were younger?

"No, not really. I used to see him down there, especially after the Carling Stand was built and then we were in the Premier League. We had season tickets in the bottom bit, and Sergio was a couple of rows in front of us. I've been to some big games with him, more often away games. We went up to Everton once, I think it was my 18th birthday. Instead of a party, the old man gave us the money to go up to Liverpool, go to the Beatles Museum, get wrecked and then watch City at Everton. It was 0-0. A good day out."

Isn't it great that 'Fire' is the new goal music at the Walkers Stadium?

"I've not heard it yet. I hope it's amazing. I got a call from the club – I thought that using 'Chelsea Dagger' was a weird thing to play. Not only because of the Chelsea link, but because every other club uses it. It's a real pleasure for me to know that 'Fire' is being used. It's unique to us, and it has a Leicester connection."

You're now a star yourself; but are you still a fan when you meet the old City players?

"I still get a buzz out of seeing Walshy. It's a bit bizarre because he's like my mate now. Walshy's a big hero for me, even though he can't pronounce my name correctly and calls me 'Megan.' Martin O'Neill called me up to say, 'Well done with 'Fire''. So I thought it would be good to ring him and say 'well done' on Villa winning 3-1 at Anfield. I asked if he wanted to come and see us at the

Bassett and Wigston. I had trials for Oadby Town and was accepted, but I never went back. I was a defender, a number five. Like Cannavaro – or maybe Walsh! I was all right; Serge was really good, like..."

We all saw Serge do his thing on *Soccer AM* when he volleyed the ball through the little target...

"I think he's sick of it now, people mention it to him every day. It was pretty good, though! He could never do that again, never. It was incredible to do it live on TV. His head's massive!"

How do you feel about the current City set-up?

"I think Milan means well, and eventually he'll get us into the Premier League and then bow out. It was all a bit crazy, that season with all the different managers coming in. It felt like no one had a grip on it. It's all there at the club, the set-up is ready – we just need to get back up there."

What's the daftest, most 'Fanatical Frank' thing you've ever done, watching Leicester City?

"Is he still in it, the little comic-strip guy? Oh, wicked. I love him. We got a busload up from Blaby for one of the Play-off finals, but there were no buses left in the whole of Leicester, so we had to hire a bus from Nottingham. We stopped at the motorway service station and there were about 400 buses from Leicester parked up – and then we rolled in, in a green bus with 'City of Nottingham' written on the side. Really embarrassing..."

> **"We'd have to be the size of U2 to put money into Leicester City. So give it about five years!"**

Wolverhampton Civic Hall. He said, 'I'd love to, I'd love to, but I've got to sign some players!'"

Do your gigs at the De Mont always feel special to you, too?

"Yes, well, it's a bit of a homecoming, isn't it? There are some seasoned Kasabian fans out there. They're proud that we're from Leicester, and we're proud, too."

You've wore City's green Ind Coope away shirt a couple of times on stage...

"Yes, I've got a red one from the '80s as well. The John Bull one from the Alan Smith era. It's incredible!"

What kind of footballer were you, as a kid?

"I used to play Sunday league for Dunton

Jim MELROSE

In the shop window

'One Jimmy Melrose!' they used to sing on the Kop. And that much was certainly true. For two seasons in the early '80s, he wore the blue shirt with pride. Then, 18 years later, came Jim's surprise return – when we joined him at Belvoir Drive to mull over past glories and upsets.

How did you become City's chief scout?

"As you probably know, I was Neil Lennon's agent, and I brought Neil here. On the strength of Neil doing ever so well, I got to know Martin O'Neill, and in the end I was doing more work for Martin than for my own agency. I don't think I've been happier since I was here as a player. I cover a lot of games. I do match reports, player assessments – and, to the directors' credit, they've now put the finance in place for a comprehensive scouting system."

Let's take you back to 1980, when you first joined Leicester...

"That was three stones ago! I could have gone to Celtic or Rangers from Partick. But Jock Wallace was a legend in Glasgow and, being a Rangers fan, before I went to meet him I was sold on it already. He was different class. The only man I've ever known who could get me to do bunny-hops up and down a double-decker bus. I wasn't the most skilful player, but I could look after myself and after my team-mates. Jock liked that – the up-and-at-'em. During the midweek between being beaten by Exeter in the FA Cup and beating Liverpool at Anfield, Jock had us in the dressing room. He put the team up on the board and went through, commenting on everybody's strengths, obviously to give us a bit of a boost. When he came to me, he said, 'The only man capable of breaking legs and not batting an eyelid.' I think it was a back-handed compliment! Jock was no monster. He ruled by respect. Nobody would dare upset him, but it wasn't through fear – it was through fear of letting him down."

It took some time to get your first goal...

"Well, I was only 21, and stepping up from part-time football was physically demanding. For a player who got 26 goals in 65 games for the club, it was amazing – I didn't get one until December!"

You almost put your life on the line for the cause, after a clash of heads at Spurs...

"All I remember is waking up in hospital, trying to work out why I had my full kit on. Apparently, I did take a fit on the park. In the changing rooms, there was a neurological boy who happened to be in the stands and he was sticking things in me to try and get a reaction. The incident happened at 4.20 and I regained consciousness at 6.35. Jock was so convinced I was dead, he was too frightened to come and visit me!"

The next season you were scoring goals, but still weren't a regular in the side...

"Gary Lineker and I started the season together, but I got an injury against Orient and was out for six weeks. Then Youngy got a partnership going with Gary. Not scoring many goals, but Jock was a creature of habit. He told me to be patient, and that I was coming on as sub and benefiting from their hard work. What really put a tin hat on it for me was when we played Derby and I was sub. Youngy got a knock on the head and was stretchered off. Jock said to me, 'Get stripped, wee man. You're on.' And then Youngy came running back down the tunnel saying, 'I'm all right! I'm all right!' In the latter stages, he was more interested in getting people to feel sorry for him than he was in playing. It's well known that Youngy and I don't get on, but I will say he had ability. And somehow he threw it away."

How did you feel when Jock left?

"Absolutely gutted. He never even came and said goodbye, y'know? I don't know why he did it. He was on about £50,000 here – a lot of money. He was out at the World Cup in Spain when Motherwell approached him. He was always preaching loyalty, and I told him later that the thing that upset me most was his loyalty to his wallet. Jock told me he would always regret what he did, and how he did it."

Gordon Milne was your new manager...

"It's fair to say I will never hold that man in high regard. It might have something to do with the fact that he swapped me for a bloke called Tom English. If he was a footballer, then I'll show my arse in Burton's window. I came to see City down here not long after, and when they read his name out over the

"I could look after myself and after my team-mates. Jock liked that – the up-and-at-'em."

Tannoy, supporters *laughed*. I see Gordon Milne as the man that caused me to have seven or eight league clubs. Whenever anybody put a pay cheque under my nose, I took it. I always thought, what's the point in being loyal to a club, if they won't be loyal to me? I was late coming back to pre-season training because my mother-in-law had

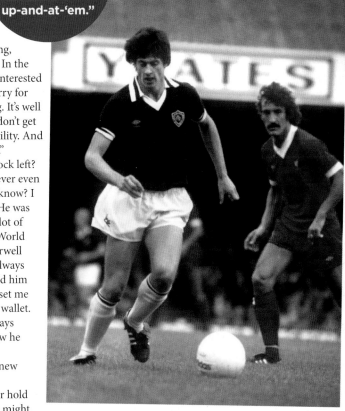

Photo: Neville Chadwick Photography.

died. I honestly believe that that's where the problems started. I came back fit and started batting in goals all over the shop, but he never really looked at me again. It broke my heart, to be honest, and I was never the same player again."

Gary MILLS

Discipline, respect, attitude

We met our ever-dependable captain at Filbert Street, at the time when his City side were closing in on their second successive Play-off final.

Your career began, shall we say, not a million miles from Leicester?

"I was in the Forest first team at 16, and was there for nine years altogether, including a couple of loan spells to Seattle which helped me grow up a bit – although I was out for a year when I broke my leg. Both my tib and fib were broken so my leg was sort of hanging off. But I got good treatment out there, which is more than I got when I came back. I had a bit of trouble with Cloughie regarding getting paid. They say he always gets the best out of a player, but I've seen some who just

couldn't cope with the way he was. He rules by fear to an extent. He has this great presence. You wouldn't see him all week, and then he'd arrive Friday afternoon and watch the five-a-side and everyone would

almost stand to attention. Not just the kids but the old pros. They knew if they didn't perform, they could be out."

After spells at Derby and Notts County, David Pleat brought you to City...

"After about a week here I realised there was a lack of professionalism, and I thought, 'Christ, have I done the right thing?' If the manager or coaches had a go at a player in training, they'd answer back. I wasn't used to that. We weren't going to get anywhere with that attitude. When we played Oxford in that last game to stay up... well, I never want to go through that sort of season again – it was a nightmare. But, with the lack of organisation and discipline at the club, it was inevitable.

There was a lack of respect from half a dozen or more players. Brian Little brought discipline into the club and the players respected him for it."

How big was Gordon Lee's contribution to avoiding relegation?

"He was very popular among the players and had their respect. He was the right man to take over from David Pleat at the time, and he proved it, even though it went down to the wire. Leicester should always be thankful to Gordon for that."

Last season, you said the Play-off final at Wembley meant more to you than your European Cup final...

"I was only 18 when I got a European Cup winners' medal, and it was a bit too early in my career to fully appreciate what was happening. I've been through more ups and downs since then. Now I'm 31, I desperately want success, and I was a big part of that campaign. I played in every game and really earned it. It was a shame we couldn't

Did you know? Over the past 20 years, Gary has managed eight clubs including Notts County, York City, Wrexham and Gateshead.

> **"After about a week here, I realised there was a lack of professionalism. It was a nightmare."**

quite do it in the end."

Could we ask you to put on your captain's armband and introduce us to your team?

Kevin Poole: "The Cat is so quiet that when he goes for a cross, he gives you sign language to tell you what he's going to do. He's a lovely lad."

Mike Whitlow: "He's got the strongest handshake I've ever known. When we wish each other all the best before the game, you have to get treated before you go out. People tend to just wave at him now."

Richard Smith: "Smudger's only a young lad but he's one of the hardest tacklers. He's recently bought a house, so we're a bit worried about his Pot Noodle diet."

Steve Walsh: "Walshy's a gentle giant, but when you've got a striker elbowing you in the face and treading on your toes, it's difficult to hold on to your temper."

Steve Thompson: "Thommo is the one that gets people laughing in the dressing room and gets everyone relaxed."

David Oldfield: "Imagine an Australian fella, an image of roughness, creased shirt, sitting there with a beer in the sun. Well, that's David. We wait for his famous 'foot-over' trick in training. One day he'll find another defender who hasn't seen it yet."

Julian Joachim: "Jules is only a young lad but his pace and strength are unbelievable. I tried to overlap him down the wing in one game but couldn't keep up. The bench were all laughing at me."

David Lowe: "We're all having lunch and we can see him through the windows walking round the field on his own – 'The Man on the Moon.'"

Phil Gee: "'Sonic Phil' is a computer freak. He'll come in and say, 'I got 108,000 on Sonic' or 'four under par on PGA golf.'"

Ian Ormondroyd: "Sticks gives his all in every game and, for that reason alone, doesn't deserve the barracking he gets from sections of the crowd. It gets to him. With the right service, he can do the job."

Lee Philpott: "On the Christmas night out he came in his trendy young gear. He looked like Betty Boo!"

Gordon MILNE

Square pegs in square holes

Leicester City's manager for four years in the '80s, Gordon Milne shared memories of his long career in football over a cup of tea at his home in Barwell.

Back in the '60s, you played right-half for Liverpool and England...

"Yes, Bill Shankly played for Preston with my father: he was right-half, my dad was left-half, and when I was a kid he lived across the road. When I came out of the military I signed for Liverpool. Shanks never really grew up, so he always kept that enthusiasm and that love of the game you have when you're younger. He seemed to be able to pass that on to the players. I was playing for England right up until the time of the World Cup. Coming up to '65/66, Alan Ball came into the squad and, looking back, you could see that he was a rival to me in that position, being a similar type of player. I got injured at Chelsea a couple of weeks before the FA Cup final.

GORDON MILNE
LEICESTER CITY Manager

Missing the final and then not being in the World Cup squad was a big disappointment, but you can't feel too sorry for yourself. I had lots of good times."

Including many at City...

"Well, obviously, I knew plenty about Leicester, living in Barwell, and it being Coventry's local derby. Instead of driving to the end of the road and going 13 miles that way, I was going 13 miles the other way! Jock Wallace had been very popular, and when I arrived at Leicester there were a lot of his own men in there who were in the 'Jock' mould. Which is all credit to him, but I needed to do things differently. There was a bit to go at there."

Which players did you need to 'go at'?

"Eddie Kelly, he was a good midfielder but definitely his own man. I thought his legs were going, but as a player that's very hard to admit. There was Alan Young, the big centre-forward. Bobby Smith, who actually turned out good for me. There was a group there and something had to change. Sometimes it's necessary when a new manager arrives. But you can't do it all straight away and you have to be careful."

You quickly made moves in the transfer market – some quite controversial...

"Yes, I knew Jim Melrose was popular but I swapped him for Tom English. My thinking was that Tom was young, while Jim was getting on. Dave Sexton later sold him to Celtic for good money, so there must have been more to Jim than I saw in him. Whereas Tom turned out to be a disaster and we got nothing for him. I remember Tom scoring a hat-trick against Leicester at Highfield Road, and we were very excited about this 18-19 year old who could produce goals out of nothing. But he let me down at Leicester. It didn't mean enough to him, that was Tom's problem. He was still very boyish and after a poor start he wasn't strong enough to handle the criticism. I think my best signing was probably Gary McAllister and Ali Mauchlen on the same day, especially considering what we paid for them."

We had an awful delay in promotion

after our 0-0 draw with Burnley...

"We just couldn't score that day. I remember everyone celebrating in the dressing room and then suddenly somebody coming in and saying the game at Derby is still going on. Then it came through that the Fulham manager, Malcolm MacDonald, was going to protest to the League because of the pitch invasion. I remember thinking, 'Oh, Christ Almighty!' We took the team off to Majorca, and were out there when the news broke that they'd given up their appeal. My real worry had been the League deciding to replay the game, then it was out of our hands."

We had a terrible start in 1983/84, before a sudden upturn in fortunes...

"Yes, Bob Hazell was a good signing at that time – a good example of putting a square peg in a square hole. Bob was Bob. He did a steady job as a centre-half but he also gave us good mileage as a personality. Not bad, considering we couldn't even get a pair of shorts to fit him! And Gerry Daly did very well for us at that time."

Did you see any signs of what Gary Lineker would go on to achieve?

"Every time he turned, his legs would get tangled up and over he'd go. It was a case of working on his control. There was no

point trying to turn Gary into a Shearer type who could hold the ball up, instead we had to work on players getting the ball into areas where he wanted it. Gary was always very focused. Even as a young lad he'd say, 'No, I don't want to do that.' You had to come up with a system that suited him, to provide the

"With Gary, it was touch and go. We might've been able to keep him for another year or two..."

ammunition and the decoys for him."

And Gary was followed by Mark Bright...

"There's a comparison to be made with Mark and Tom English. When Tom arrived he was a technically far better player than Brighty, but he had no appetite for it. Brighty came with lots of limitations but a big appetite. He came though the backbiting and the stick because he had determination and aggression and you could see that in his game. He was a satisfying signing because we recognised something at a very early stage."

Photo: Neville Chadwick Photography.

"After Shankly and Ramsey I worked with Joe Mercer, so I had a good education."

Keeper of the faith

Carl MUGGLETON

We met Carl in the Fox & Hounds in his home town of Syston, after he'd finished his day's work as a driving instructor.

It makes us feel old to see your son is now playing professional football...

"Yes, Sam's at Barnet now. Martin Allen took him there from Gillingham. He's a left-sided defender with an enormous long throw, which Martin loves."

Martin had a short, strange spell at City...

"I think he probably learnt something from his time at Leicester. He's calmed down now. I was with him at Notts County and Gillingham, and he was great. He was dealing with Mr Mandaric at the time, and lot of those deals were done before the pre-season started. Martin didn't fancy many, if any, of them. I think the main issue was that he really didn't fancy the goalkeeper, Jimmy 'Casino' Nielsen at all. I think if he got another chance at a higher level, he'd do all right now."

How did you first get involved at City?

"Well, this was long before the days of academies, but Youth-team manager Dave Richardson, Gordon Milne and Gerry

Summers set up a centre of excellence. Then I did one day a week at Belvoir Drive and got to join in with the goalkeepers. Mark Wallington, Ian Andrews, Jerry Roberts. It was absolutely fantastic. Sometimes I'd get to join in with the five-a-sides with the first-team players – Alan Smith, Gary Lineker."

You made your first-team debut away at West Brom in January 1989...

"David Pleat was the manager, and Martin Hodge was his new goalkeeper. But he got a hernia in his first game, and then Paul Cooper had a car accident on his way home from a match. I remember when we ran out, I could see my mates standing behind the goal, so I was trying not to look at them. They were shouting at me, so I was just hoping it all went well! That was probably the most pressure, when all your mates are Leicester fans and you're going to get some serious grief if you screw up!"

You became the first City keeper ever to be sent off, at home to Charlton...

"Yes, the new rule had recently come in. I came out and dived at someone's feet and brought them down – professional foul. For some reason back then, it meant a three-game ban and fined a week's wage. Which wasn't a lot in those days. Probably somewhere between £200 and £250."

Leicester never were big payers...

"No, all we got for that Play-off final in 1992 was our usual appearance money. No bonus. We were all spewing!"

During your time at Leicester there was always competition for the green shirt...

"Yes, there were a few. Martin Hodge left in the summer before Brian Little arrived, and I was suspended because I'd been sent off in a County Cup game. So Brian had to sign a keeper and he brought Kevin

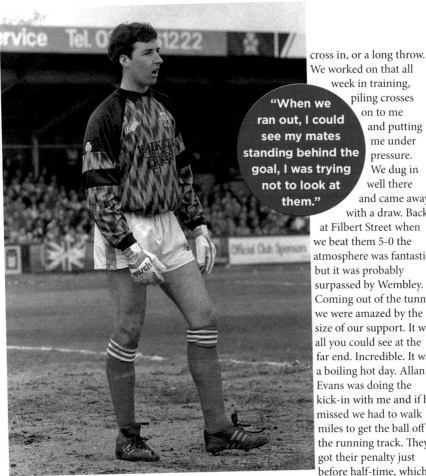

cross in, or a long throw. We worked on that all week in training, piling crosses on to me and putting me under pressure. We dug in well there and came away with a draw. Back at Filbert Street when we beat them 5-0 the atmosphere was fantastic, but it was probably surpassed by Wembley. Coming out of the tunnel we were amazed by the size of our support. It was all you could see at the far end. Incredible. It was a boiling hot day. Allan Evans was doing the kick-in with me and if he missed we had to walk miles to get the ball off the running track. They got their penalty just before half-time, which

"When we ran out, I could see my mates standing behind the goal, I was trying not to look at them."

Poole in. He was outstanding all season, very steady. But he got injured towards the end of the season so I back in for the Play-offs."

That night of the Play-off semi against Cambridge was very special for City fans...

"It was an absolutely incredible night. I remember walking round the pitch after the game with everyone celebrating the fact that we'd finally got to Wembley after all those years. And Cambridge had mullered us 5-1 at their place earlier in the season. What a good, strong side they were: Dion Dublin, Stevie Claridge, Lee Philpott. Bang it up into the corners, get a

was made worse by Mike Newell taking it, who I knew from his time at Leicester. It looked like we were going to score in the second half, but then I gave a penalty away. Thankfully, I made amends by saving it. It was bittersweet. A great experience, but we missed out on promotion. It seemed like as many City fans stayed behind as Blackburn fans, applauding us and soaking up the atmosphere. Funnily, the team had stayed in a hotel before the game, and the coach went off to Wembley without me! The days before mobile phones, eh? He didn't even miss me, Brian Little – the writing was on the wall!"

Richie NORMAN

Norman's conquest

When we met City's Geordie left-back of the '60s, Richie was still Nuneaton Town's physio at the age of 78. Spread on the table at the Field Head Hotel was City memorabilia covering 1958-68, one of the club's most successful periods. Richie picked out an article by Lawrie Simpkin of the *Leicester Mercury*.

"When I first read it, I thought, 'He's giving me a bit of stick here!' '*In goal for City was Gordon Banks, who remains the best keeper I have seen in a Leicester jersey. The midfield was superb: Colin Appleton, Ian King and Frank McLintock; and Ken Keyworth was the best passer of a ball over 30 yards after Johnny Haynes. Among the defensive talent was the highly skilful Richie Norman – the world's worst conventional tackler, who could never explain how he won the ball so often and so well.'"

What did he mean by that compliment?

"I just think I had my own way of dealing with it. In those days you were always facing a natural-born, out-and-out winger.

They were all internationals – Welsh, Irish, Scottish – so I had my hands full. These days a full-back will often not be facing a winger and they can bomb forward, but it was a different set-up entirely

back then. During the ten years I played for Leicester I only scored five goals, but that wasn't considered too bad. I always had a winger like Mike Stringfellow in front of me, and they stayed wide. My job was to defend and to get the ball to Mike. Full-backs were strapping lads and would whack a winger the first chance they got. I wasn't really like that, I dealt with the wingers in a different way, and it worked out fine. I think that's what Laurie meant."

Your full debut, in January 1960, was back in your hometown of Newcastle...

"Yes, I couldn't believe it. It was a great day. Leicester hadn't won up there for 33 years, and the previous Saturday, Newcastle had put seven past Manchester United. Anyway, we won 2-0. I started 1960/61 in the first team and I kept my place – 194 consecutive games, which was a record. I was pleased with that."

Who were the most troublesome wingers that you played against back then?

"There was Stanley Matthews, obviously, who was nearly twice my age but a fantastic player. The problem with Stan was that he was a bit of a national icon, and you didn't like to hit him too hard. I remember once there was a throw-in and I tackled him from behind, not too hard. And he turned round to me and said, 'Steady on Richie, I'm an old man.' Spurs' Cliff Jones would give any full-back a lot of trouble. John Connelly, the Manchester United winger, and the great George Best. I marked him a couple of times, but fortunately for me he then switched to the left wing when they signed Willie Morgan from Burnley. Mind you, Willie was still pretty tricky!"

What are your memories of the 1961 FA Cup final?

"The unfortunate thing for us was Len Chalmers getting injured, in the days before substitutes. With ten men against the team doing the Double, it was just too much. It's still a mystery why Ken Leek was dropped. If you asked anyone from the team, you'd probably get a different answer. My answer is, I don't really know. I wouldn't have anything said against Matt Gillies, because he picked me 365 times, but it was a mistake. Whatever the situation was that caused him to drop him, I'd have left it until after the Cup final. Ken scored every time he played against Tottenham, and he'd also scored in every round of the Cup."

"The world's worst conventional tackler, who could never explain how he won the ball so often."

We did at least qualify for the European Cup Winners' Cup...

"We got Glenavon, the Irish team first, and I think it was reasonably easy. Then we got Atletico Madrid. All we knew about at the time was Real Madrid. The home leg was first and we didn't really know what to expect. They had Spanish and Argentinian internationals. We were winning 1-0 and there wasn't long to go when Ken Keyworth got fouled. As he got fouled he chipped the keeper and the ball went in the net, but the ref gave the free-kick."

Just like the last time we played them!

"Just before the end, this Argentinian guy fired this shot right past Gordon and into the top corner. One-one to take over there didn't look as good as 2-0. We had a couple of injuries – I think it was Graham Cross's first game? They got a dodgy penalty – French referee, sounds familiar? When they scored again, that was it, we were out. We had a great time. We did the bullfighting and all that. After the game they took us up to the hills for a big banquet and we were presented with a Don Quixote statuette, which the club still have. I'm not sure what they'd have done if we'd won!"

What was your single career highlight?

"I think the semi-final second replay against Sheffield United at Birmingham when we finally knew we'd made it to the FA Cup final. That feeling was repeated two years later against Liverpool when we beat them in the semi. It's a fantastic feeling. My biggest regret is that we didn't win the Cup. Four final defeats is a record we could do without. But a lot of great players never played in an FA Cup final, and I played in two."

"Frank McLintock was so full of energy, it was almost annoying at times. He'd stray into my area and I'd say, 'Frank, clear off!'"

131

David NUGENT

Tangled up in blue

We have Sven to thank for signing striker David Nugent for four unforgettable years at the King Power. We met David in the Marriott Hotel at Junction 21, by which time he was playing for Derby.

What was life like under Nigel Pearson?

"Straight away, players started to come into training on time, and there was a strict timetable. It was the best team spirit that I've ever been involved in. Especially the year we got promoted, and then the year when we survived in the Premier League. We'd do stuff together on and off the pitch. Out for meals, nights out, team bonding trips. It was almost weird, how well we all got on. He drilled into players what was expected of them and they did as they were told, and it led to success."

The 2012/13 season ended at Watford. If only you or Harry Kane had taken pens...

"Well, Anthony had won the penalty and he was desperate to take it and be the hero.

He'd grabbed the ball and was intent on taking it, so no one wanted to distract him by taking it off him. His missed the pen, and the rebound – and then I watched it all unfold as I was running back. I was thinking, 'No, no, no, no, *nooooooo!*' as they they scored. I sat on the ground with fans running past me, screaming in my face, thinking, 'What the hell is going on here?' It was tough to take, and Anthony was inconsolable afterwards. I think it spurred us on for the following season."

You enjoyed a great partnership with Jamie Vardy in that promotion year...

"I think Nigel gave him a bit of a rocket once and he came back for the new season a completely different person. He took it all more seriously, and his speed, awareness and finishing all clicked into place. I dropped off into the number 10 role and always knew where he was going to be. We knew each other's game, almost like telepathy, and we really enjoyed ourselves, scoring a lot of goals. I was a bit shocked when he asked me to be his best man. I'd only known him a few years, so I must have had a big influence on him!"

City got promoted when we weren't playing. How did you celebrate?

"We all went round to Andy King's house. We got there about 11.00 watching *Soccer Saturday* and were there for about 14 hours! Kingy's house was a bit of a mess by the end. There was a good video on Instagram with us all celebrating, and beer and champagne flying around. Poor Kingy's mum and dad had to clear up afterwards. We had a bit of a weekend of it and then we had to play Brighton on the Tuesday. I felt terrible, and I think most of us were still a bit hung over. We lost 4-1. After that, we realised we had to knuckle down and get the title."

Craig Shakespeare is now caretaker manager. What did he do to become so well regarded as a coach?

"He's very easy to talk to. Obviously, players didn't want to be going to the manager too often, so he was a good middle man. He'd go and ask Nigel what he wanted to see from you and would report back. He was a fantastic coach and took all the training sessions. I think he deserves a large amount of credit for what they achieved last season in winning the Premier League. Obviously, Claudio gets a lot of the praise, but Shakey deserves a lot, too."

That season ended with the Great Escape, which apparently began with a meeting?

"It was a players-only meeting in the changing rooms. A few of the senior players spoke. Basically, it was, 'We've got nine games left. We've worked so hard to get into the Premier League, are we going to throw that away or are we going to do something about it?' We weren't not trying, we weren't playing badly, but we weren't winning. We scored three goals at Tottenham, but still got beat. We still had that team spirit, and we thought if we could push on then the luck would turn. The revival was crazy. It started against West Ham. I missed a penalty, but King's late winner saved my bacon. Then we won a mad game at West Brom. We had the quality and the belief, and there was also a change in formation to a 3-4-1-2. We had a bit more up top, so we were creating more chances. After Vards's last-minute winner at West Brom we believed we could pull ourselves clear.

> "I absolutely loved it at Leicester, but it looked like my time was up and I was gutted."

We looked unbeatable after that. If the season had been longer, we'd have been pushing for a place in Europe. And that momentum carried on into the next season."

Was it a shock when Nigel then left?

"I found it hard. I'd been under Nigel for years and I didn't really get on with Claudio's way of doing things in training. I was playing left wing in pre-season, then I wasn't even in the squad for the first game. It was mixed emotions for me, last season. I was delighted for all the lads but it was horrible for me, missing out on it all. I was watching all the results, going to games when I had time off. I'm a Leicester fan. I still go to games now, and still see the lads. I'm still part of that group."

100 per cent record: One cap, one goal.

Scoring four and losing five

Frank O'FARRELL

A classy wing-half for West Ham, Preston and Ireland, Frank O'Farrell had an eventful reign as City boss around the dawn of the '70s. At home in sunny Torquay, on a street lined with palm trees, he reminisced about times past.

As Torquay manager, you refused Bolton and Ipswich before deciding Leicester was the right move for you. Why was that?

"Well, although they were struggling, I thought they had good players. I liked Leicester's central location in the Midlands. You were within driving distance of a lot of clubs and you could keep your eye on things. It was December 1968, and Leicester were struggling down at the bottom of Division One. It was obvious there was work to be done; but with players like Shilton, Clarke, Cross and Sjoberg I was sure I could get better results. It was just before Christmas and the pitch at Filbert Street was very bad. It was difficult to play on. I think the sun and wind didn't get at it because of the big Double Decker at the Spion Kop end. It never dried out. We got involved in the FA Cup run and I think our fifth round

match against Liverpool got postponed five times. Bill Shankly came down every time for a pitch inspection. There wasn't a blade of grass on it. We got behind with our fixtures, and had five games to play after the Cup final."

What were City doing right in the Cup that they weren't doing in the League?

"I think the draw was fairly favourable to us, and we also had a bit of luck that perhaps we weren't getting in the League. I seem to remember Barnsley in round three hitting the bar, and if that had gone in it could all have been very different. Peter Shilton saved a penalty at Anfield. There are so many imponderables that you can't really explain how something happens. We were working hard, we had some decent players and the confidence was growing within them. The only problem I had was Allan Clarke was unhappy. He didn't want to play in the Second Division, and I found him quite troublesome. I think he knew that Leeds were coming in for him, although I can't prove it. I didn't expect him to be bubbling over, but he was always moaning. He had a long face with me because he thought I was asking him to play too defensively. All I wanted him to do was, when the opposition had the ball, do his best to get it back; but he didn't seem to want to do that."

How do you remember the Cup final?

"At that time it was the big event of the year and the climax of the season. To be part of that was really something in those days. We were well prepared and played quite well but lost to a great goal. The lads gave a good account of themselves, but it was a big disappointment to lose. And then we had to come back and play five more games to try and save ourselves. It was a double whammy, losing the Cup final and then losing that last game at United and getting relegated. That was the situation and we had to

> **"I got Carlin and Kellard, the little streetfighters. A lot of skill, a lot of ability and a little bit of nastiness."**

recover from it. The next season, we finished third...

"And then, for 1970/71, I got Carlin and Kellard, the little streetfighters, who gave us the competitive streak we'd been lacking. A lot of skill, a lot of ability and a little bit of nastiness. They had a voice, whereas the rest of the lads wouldn't shout the odds. They got stuck in and had a bit of yap and chat about them. The team developed, and younger players came in like Steve Whitworth, Rodney Fern and Paul Matthews. I had a few problems with Shilton because he didn't want to be spending his time in the Second Division. He was frightened he wouldn't get selected for England. I had to pacify him through a few little discussions."

That season, you were very strong defensively with a counter-attacking style...

"That was my philosophy, that you had to have a good defence before you could get anywhere. It's no good scoring four and losing five. We had enough quality in the team, with the likes of Lenny Glover and Andy Lochhead, that when we had possession we could make openings and score goals. Like all teams, they had their strengths and weaknesses, but you try and play in a way that your weaknesses don't get exposed. The basic thing is giving 100 per cent effort. I'd forgive a lot if I could see a player doing his best. I expected them to earn their keep."

We won the title, but you moved to Manchester United that summer...

"My contract was actually up at Leicester. I spoke to Matt Busby and he admitted he'd let things go; that there was a lot of work to be done. He offered me a five-year contract at £12,000 a year. But I later met United chairman Louis Edwards and found out the offer was £15,000. I think I should have turned the job down then: I didn't really trust Matt any more. I didn't really want to leave Leicester but it was too big a job to turn down. Right from my first day, some builders were building a small office down the corridor from the traditional manager's office – which Matt had been planning to keep! He was interfering and undermining my position, having given it up because he couldn't do it any more."

"George Best was a smashing person. He'd stay after training to do some more shooting. But you never knew if he'd turn up the next day."

135

Martin O'NEILL

Ever the magician

We met Leicester City's new manager in his office in the Carling Stand.

We noticed in Brian Clough's autobiography, he said, 'I looked upon O'Neill as a bit of a smartarse.'

"I did read that, yes, and I think that's how he genuinely did see me. I always seemed to have an answer, and sometimes managers don't like that. I'm not saying that I had a right answer; I just always had an answer. I think that he always felt that I was arrogant, with nothing to be arrogant about. Perhaps he was spot on."

Are you enjoying yourself at Leicester?

"Perversely, yes. We haven't won a game in seven matches, so to say that I'm absolutely enjoying everything would be a lie, but I am actually enjoying it here. Coming to Leicester mid-season is difficult. I don't want to chop and change too much because we're still in with a chance of promotion, though you might wonder after a couple of performances

recently. It's a difficult time because I'm trying to get to know the players, but in doing so, I need to try and win some matches."

Can you put your finger on why things haven't gone so well since you arrived?

"Having spoken to a few of the senior professionals, I think teams started to suss Leicester out. If I'd been in charge of Norwich, I'd have put Robert Ullathorne man-for-man on Garry Parker. I would have said to Leicester, 'Right, who are you going to pass to now?' That's what other managers were thinking as well. The results were beginning to show this – so, ever the magician that I think I am, I thought I could change this overnight."

Although it's early days, we've already seen a difference in footballing style...

"What differences have you seen?"

Like, three passes instead of seven?

"Okay, that's interesting that you say that. Alan Ball and Peter Reid both said, 'Nice footballing side, Leicester. But they don't hurt you.' Play it, play it, play it... If you're going to score a goal, then sooner or later you've got to play that ball into the penalty box. I genuinely believe that you can play with passion and have a side with lots of get-up-and-go about them, but you can still, when you have possession, play decent football. I feel that we only want to play here when we have the ball. We don't do enough to win the ball back quickly enough when we don't have it."

What's your managerial style, in terms of how you get the best out of the players?

"Come back and see me in four months and see what you think. Actually, the way results are going at the moment, I might not last four months, you'd better ask me in four weeks!"

Congratulations all round

In the midst of his preparation for a second Premier League campaign, we found Martin back from his holidays, catching up with his mail and newspapers at Belvoir Drive. We told him about a hot new TV series.

You made a brief appearance in *Match of the Eighties*, congratulating Archie Gemmill after a goal against Arsenal...

"That's me, one of the game's great congratulators. I didn't score that many but I was always first on the scene after somebody else had."

What have other managers been saying to you lately?

"I must say, Alex Ferguson has written me one of the nicest letters I've ever received. *'I just thought I'd let the dust settle before I write to you to say well done on a fantastic season... punters' favourites to go down,'* and that sort of stuff. George Graham also wrote to me, which he always does when we've done well. And Brian Clough dropped me a line congratulating us on winning the Coca-Cola Cup. He put 'Love to John' on it, to John Robertson, who was always his favourite, and obviously still is."

How valuable was it to play 'Boro in the League, just before the final?

"I deliberated the night before: shall we stick someone on Juninho, mark him man-to-man? They destroyed us, and any notion of letting him run free was put well and truly in its place. In hindsight, I'm very pleased that he murdered us in that game – it didn't cost us relegation, and it made me re-plan for the Cup final."

You have a great record of signings so far. Do you have a formula when you move for a new player?

"I wouldn't say I have a formula, more of an attitude. At £1.6 million, I thought Matty Elliott was something of a gamble for us, but it was necessary at that time. Around January, we were in need of a lift, and his presence was a big factor in us staying up. £1.6 million for a 28-year-old that a lot of people had looked at and not been too sure; takes a chance now and again; can head it all right, but a bit slow; has never kicked a ball in the Premiership. It was a gamble, like it is with every player. I've just paid £400,000 for Robbie Savage. Because he comes from Crewe, people are expecting Savage to be another Neil Lennon. I told them up in the boardroom, 'Wait a wee minute. This boy isn't in the same league as Neil Lennon. You aren't going to get someone who makes the difference between staying up or not for £400,000. I've said that my daughter, who is 13, is worth £400,000 at today's prices."

Martin O'NEILL

Martin O'NEILL

Extraordinary!

With just six months left on his contract, we found Martin O'Neill in a mood of millennial reflection in the manager's office at Belvoir Drive.

What's pleased you most about this season so far?

"Just about everything, really. I'm pleased with individual performances, pleased that players never know when to pack it in. An example of that was highlighted on *Match of the Day*, with Muzzy Izzet going from one penalty area to the other to make a tackle. He could have decided, 'Oh well, these boys are too far in front', when they broke away five against two. 'The manager won't be watching me now. I made my challenge on the edge of their box so I've done my bit, someone else will have to get back.' Instead of thinking that, he bust a gut to get back and make what might have been the most important challenge

of the day. He wouldn't have thought for a minute that anyone would even notice it. The fact that my players are prepared to do that sort of work for the good of the team is really something that you can't buy."

The media's treatment of City isn't always so positive. It probably bottomed out after the Worthington Cup final...

"I thought it was desperately poor. I picked the papers up the following morning... obviously, Robbie took a hammering individually, but the team also took a hammering over tactics. Someone called Graham Hunter, who writes for the *Daily Mail*, drew some sort of comparison with myself and Brian Clough being able to kill games off. He quoted Clough winning the European Cup final, having *killed the game*! Extraordinary! Savage took a dog's abuse. When they'd seen what the German player had done, going down after being missed in the challenge completely, I think they were almost too embarrassed to report it two days later, having had the chance to watch it again. In the second half, I think we deserved to win the game. For them to come up and score with a minute to go was particularly galling. Tottenham should be able to beat us, to be perfectly honest with you. And Emile Heskey was less than 30 per cent fit. If he'd been as fit as he is now, then we would have won it. I've seen Brian Woolnough since, and I told him his comments have inspired us to greater things – and he wasn't particularly happy about it when I picked him out at a post-match press conference."

Maybe the tide has turned, with awards for Izzet and Lennon, and international recognition for Heskey and Guppy?

"I can understand the players' annoyance

here because they can definitely play. I read that we are 'hard-working Leicester.' As if we're the only team that work hard in the League. Manchester United work as hard as anybody, so do Arsenal. For me, hard work is a prerequisite of doing well."

Have you been frustrated in your efforts to add to a squad that always seems to be shorter than that of the opponents on the back of the programme?

"Absolutely, every single week. I'm linked with everybody and anybody simply because I go to matches, especially in the divisions below us. But I know what I can afford. Somebody over on the commercial side there told me that I wasn't a great budget keeper. I'm the best budget keeper Leicester City has ever had, I tell you that honestly. I've never asked for money that didn't exist. But with the players making a big, big effort here, and us in a great position, *now* is the time to strengthen."

You said that Leicester City had become 'your club'. Could you expand on that?

"Well, I've been here for four years now – although you'd have got long odds for that in January 1996. I don't think you can be at a place for that length of time without getting an attachment to the place. It's born out of getting to know people at the training ground, getting to know the players and the people who have a passion for the football club. I know supporters can see managers as people who can come in and do a job without really getting a feeling for the club. I can understand the cynicism that leads to supporters feeling that way. A manager has to get his feet firmly ensconced under the table before he can start to think of the club as being part of him – and even if you do, it can be taken away from you in a second or two if you go six or seven matches without winning a game. But I have a good feeling for the football club and after four years I'm entitled to think of myself as part of it, and hopefully they feel the same way about myself. Next thing you know, I'll be gone in three weeks, and you'll be saying, 'He didn't know what he was talking about.'"

"Somebody on the commercial side said I'm not a great budget keeper. But *now* is the time to strengthen."

"You can't afford to rely on history, you have to make it."

Nigel PEARSON

The Fear Factor

It wasn't long into Nigel Pearson's second period in charge that we tiptoed into his office at Belvoir Drive. We found Nigel in an introspective mood – perhaps helped by our Shrewsbury-City programme from 1982, featuring a 17-year-old Pearson on the cover.

"Oh, my word!"

Inside, there's news about your dismissal for one of the first 'professional fouls'...

"I can remember that, it was against Wrexham. Roger Milford sent me off, the ref with the long hair. It was outside the box, and it was a tackle, not a cynical trip on the last man or anything like that. [Studies back of programme.] Look at that: no sub named. One on the day. I think we had about 14 players! Phil Bates, that was 'Chic' Bates; Colin Griffin – 'Chopper', the centre-half who taught me all the tricks of the trade; Graham Turner, the boss; and Steve Ogrizovic in goal, the ugliest man in football!"

You later played for Middlesbrough in the 1997 League Cup final against City...

"We felt we should have won the first time out, and I think Leicester deserved to win the replay. We had a very good team, but Leicester just managed to sneak a result right at the end. I think probably Middlesbrough beating Leicester 3-1 at Filbert Street about three weeks before the final meant that Martin O'Neill changed his approach."

When Leicester first appointed you, we'd just been relegated to the third tier...

"I had to get the right staff in, freshen the playing staff up. In all honesty, I think it's difficult to bounce back with the same group of players, you can have a real hangover from relegation. It was a very good balance we ended up with, and the players that remained were very positive. It was a case of getting a good team spirit, not just within the players, trying to get a bit of positivity around the place."

Was there a danger of the Leicester game being every other side's Cup final?

"Well, it was. It was a tough year because a lot of sides used to come and just shut the back door. Perhaps we drew a few too many games, we certainly didn't lose too many. We ended up with 96 points, I think? So not a bad job."

The following season we made it to the Championship Play-offs. Did you have any warning about Yann Kermogant's disastrous chipped penalty?

"Nobody saw that coming. We'd done a penalty shoot-out the day before in training and he smashed every one in the top corner. There's no accounting for how pressure affects some people. Unfortunately, we'll always be ruing the missed opportunity of that day. We fancied ourselves to go all the way if we'd got through, because we'd hit our stride. We'd ended the season with five straight wins. The players felt great about themselves."

You probably aren't going to say why you then departed for Hull City?

"No, I'm not going to say anything! There's no mileage in doing that. I'm back here now and I'm really pleased to be back."

When Sven left Leicester, did you immediately fancy a return?

"No, honestly, it really did come out of the blue. It wasn't something I'd considered and it was such a surprise. But if I'm totally honest it didn't take me too long to make the decision. I'm here because I want to be successful."

Richie Wellens talked about the return of the 'fear factor'. Are you a strict disciplinarian?

"I think there are a lot of misconceptions about me, but if people want to think that, then I'm happy to go along with it! I'm fair. And I think the players know where they stand. I do want them to have fun, but they've got to know when they're working, as well. The ground rules are there."

So you're not an ogre?

"I don't think so!"

What is a realistic ambition for Leicester City, from here?

"Well, we've got to get promotion. That's what my remit is. People will have their own opinions on the timescale and whether it's achievable this season. If everything had gone really well this season so far then I wouldn't be sitting here, would I?"

What's your hardest task as manager?

"Well, you tell me... everyone thinks it's media, but it's not at all!"

Brian Little said it was having to tell youngsters they're not going to make it.

"Well, that's not easy, but it's a damn sight better than leading them on.

> **"As a coach, it's important to be yourself. Everybody thinks I'm one thing, but I'm not really!"**

Big Nige makes his point to Little Jay Spearing.

You've got to be honest with them. I'm a parent myself so I know what it's like when they have their dreams shattered. For me, the worst part of management is losing games, without a doubt."

Kevin PHILLIPS

The turn of the screw

Legendary goalscorer Kevin Phillips' route to the King Power was a circuitous one, via Baldock Town and nine different League clubs. As a City player and coach, he contributed to the Championship win of 2013/14, to the Great Escape and the groundwork for our famous title season.

You scored twice in 12 City appearances, and broke the record as oldest goalscorer...

"I'd done a fair bit of warming up on the touchline that season and you could hear people in the crowd shouting, 'Time to retire, Phillips, you're too old.' And 'Where's your walking stick?' I hadn't planned the stick celebration, it just popped up in my mind after I'd scored at Bournemouth. It wasn't the greatest of finishes but it won an important game. I was 41 by the end of the season, and it was getting harder. My ankles were sore and it was getting more difficult to motivate myself in training, although I had no problem getting up for games. It just seemed the perfect way to retire, Leicester winning the Championship, last game at home so all my family could be there. It was a hugely emotional day."

Was Jamie Vardy your first project when you started your striker coaching at City?

"I suppose he was. He's certainly a handful. He always had something to say! I worked with Jamie, David Nugent, Leo Ulloa, Chris Woods, then Kramaric and Okazaki. We tried to recreate situations that they'd be faced with in a game. For me, it's criminal how Jamie is played out of position for England, and I'm not using that word lightly. For me, Jamie is an out-and-out striker. He's such a threat in behind. I know from talking to him that he hated playing out on the left. He'll do it for his country and give it everything, but he really needs to be playing down the middle. I wasn't sure if he could ever be a prolific scorer, but he's proved me wrong. He's getting better and better. He's still quite raw but he takes on board what he's told, like working on his hold-up play and composure in front of goal."

What was it that suddenly changed last season, when we suddenly started our run of form for the Great Escape?

"There was no change, we continued to do the same stuff week in and week out. Nigel was very good at keeping everyone motivated. If you come in and see that the coaching staff are still bubbling and lively and still have that belief, then it keeps you motivated and keeps your spirit high. What did happen was that we eventually found the 3-5-2 system that worked and suited the players we had. We'd disregarded Marc Albrighton for a long time, and he turned out to be one of the best players. It turned out that Jeff Schlupp could do a really good job at left wing-back. You can only do so much with a system, you

need the players to turn up. Once that run started and they had a sense that we could still get out of this, they were unstoppable. It was an unbelievable

thing to be involved in."

Esteban Cambiasso really stepped up...

"He struggled at first with fitness and the tempo we played at, but he could command things when there were players around him to do his hard graft. He's a very clever footballer. His experience, organisation and range of passing were some of the catalysts for us to survive."

It's said that there was a players' meeting just before things began to turn around...

"Yes, there was. Me, Shakey, Nige and Steve Walsh were standing out on the pitch at Belvoir Drive saying to each other, 'Where are they?' They'd locked the door to the changing rooms and ironed out a few home truths. Those sort of in-house players meetings aren't unusual. Maybe you'll think someone isn't pulling their weight and they get told. They can either take it on board or kick off, whichever. From what I gathered, they got things off their chest and it was a very good meeting. We'd got to the point where we had nothing to lose, so we really went at teams

with a very positive attitude."

What a shock when Pearson then left the club – and what a shock replacement...

"He flew out to Austria to join our pre-season camp. The coaches knew who was coming, but the players weren't sure. Top flew over and introduced himself and told us we had a new manager: "And it is... Claudio Ranieri." And he just walked through the door. The lads were all, 'Ahh... right!' He's certainly a well-respected manager and he's getting the best out of them. He made it quite clear that he wanted to keep everyone on board. He was keen to keep everything the same, which was pretty sensible when you looked at what happened last season. It's paying dividends now, because they're flying."

And you're now Derby's assistant coach...

"Well, I have aspirations to be a manager. I liked what I was doing at Leicester but couldn't see much room for me to progress. I've been promoted out of the Championship five times, so I know it well. Big things are happening here."

143

The battle of wounded knee

Matt PIPER

At the Marriott Hotel, we heard a frank account of flying winger Matt Piper's career, sadly ruined by injury. Matt now runs the Football and Sports Diploma Academy, helping kids get into the game.

You were with Leicester City from the age of eight…

"I played through every age group with City and then signed up to the Youth team. Everything had gone well for me until it was professional contract time, and I had a meeting with Peter Taylor. He told me, 'We think you're a good player and we'd like to keep you because we think we'd be able to sell you, but I don't see you in our first team.' Garry Parker was the reserve-team manager, and he told me to sign the contract. He said, 'If Peter Taylor ever loses his job and they put me in charge, then I'd put you in the first team.'

In October 2001, Garry duly gave you your debut: 0-6 to Leeds in the League Cup! And after a loan spell at Mansfield you got your place in a struggling team…

"It sounds a bit selfish, but it was a

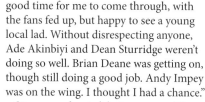

good time for me to come through, with the fans fed up, but happy to see a young local lad. Without disrespecting anyone, Ade Akinbiyi and Dean Sturridge weren't doing so well. Brian Deane was getting on, though still doing a good job. Andy Impey was on the wing. I thought I had a chance."

City were relegated, but you scored the last goal at Filbert Street, after 110 years…

"Over the years since, I've realised what an honour it was. At the time, I was thinking about something that had happened that week. I'd been in to see Dave Bassett with an agent about a new contract – and Dave had thrown him out. I rang my dad, who's an old Londoner, and he got straight into his car and drove over. My dad said, 'Listen, Mr Bassett, I respect you as the manager of this club, but you know this boy here, he's not asked for so much as a *chocolate biscuit* since he's been at this club from eight years old!' Dave started laughing and said, 'A *chocolate biscuit*? I'll tell you what, he does deserve a new contract. But I want a goal out of him.' My dad said, 'Okay, if he scores this weekend, make sure you have a new contract set up for him, for next season.' And they shook on it."

You got your contract – but by then Micky Adams was manager…

"I went to Portugal on holiday and it was the best summer ever. I was a Leicester lad, born in the Royal. I'd made the first team and scored the last ever goal at Filbert Street. The pre-season games had gone well. Micky named the team for the first game at the new stadium against Watford, and I was in the starting eleven, right wing. Brilliant. But the night before the game I caught a bug and was sick all night. He said, 'I'm going to rest you,

because there are bigger and better things coming for you on Monday morning.' I was thinking about that all weekend, wondering if I'd been picked for the England Under-21s. Monday morning, I was called into his office and he told me, 'The club has accepted a £3.5 million offer for you from Sunderland.' I was stunned. I was only 19. I said, 'I don't want to go!' I held out for a week at Leicester, but wasn't allowed to train. They told me the club was close to going into administration and they needed to sell me, because no one had come in for Muzzy or the bigger players. In the end they wore me down, and I said I'd go to Sunderland. It was awful. I'd been there eleven years and was gone within a day. Before I finalised the deal, Ade Akinbiyi rang me and said, 'You can't have your dad doing a multi-million pound deal, you need an agent. Use mine.' I thought, well, he'd got Ade some great moves! So this agent flew up on the day and he was very good. He got me more money and a five-year deal. He personally made £165,000. He'd been my agent for 18 hours. I hadn't even signed up to him. I said, 'I'll sign for you if you give my dad half what you got today. He's been my agent since I was eight, and he's driven me all over the country and been there for me all that time.' He said, 'I can't give your dad 80 grand!' He went and phoned his business partner, and came back and said, 'Okay, deal.' And he gave my dad half."

You started promisingly at Sunderland...

"But in my 15th match, I got my first knee injury. I got hit from the side and there was cartilage damage, cruciate ligament damage. I knew it was a 12-monther. A year later, I was back and training, and then my other knee went, and it snowballed from there. I ended up having 15 knee operations. I'd been at Sunderland for four years and

> "Emile Heskey is up and coming. And we're really excited about this 15 year old, Matt Piper" – Brian Little

made about 40 appearances. My contract was terminated by mutual consent. I was still only 24. I had kids by then, but I split up with my wife. Within a year of quitting the game I was in Tony Adams' rehabilitation clinic. When I was a pro, I hardly drank, never gambled and was really fit. My playing weight was 11 stone. I'm now 14 stone. When I went in there I was 18 stone! Luckily, they sorted me out. Then Jon Rudkin offered me a job coaching kids at City. As soon as I started that, I realised it was my calling, what I was meant to do."

Matt went to England Under-14 trials with Gareth Barry, Joe Cole and Jermain Defoe.

David PLEAT

Board games

Not a lot of people remember David Pleat as an England Schoolboys wing prodigy, before injury at Forest set him on a lower-league path and into management at Nuneaton Borough – and so to Luton Town. We spoke to the great football analyst on the telephone, at his house in Nottinghamshire.

Is it true that you were a Leicester City fan in your youth?

"Well, yes, I have very early recollections of going to Leicester and sitting in the high stand behind the goal. I saw the likes of Arthur Rowley and Derek Hines, Derek Hogg, Ken Keyworth... I lived on a big housing estate called Clifton on the main bus route down to Loughborough, so I certainly knew a bit about Leicester City."

And finally you arrived here as manager, from Spurs, in 1987...

"We did very well for about the first 18 games. We were bottom of the league when I took over, which I think people

Official Players Collection 92 PANINI CARDS

DAVID PLEAT

tend to forget, and we did wonderfully well shooting up the league, culminating in the last game of the season when we beat a Middlesbrough side going for promotion in front of their own fans. At the end of

that game I told the players that if they all stuck together then we'd have something very special going forward into the next season. But Russell Osman decided that Southampton was a better bet for him. I was left with some decent players – Nicky Cross playing off Mike Newell; Peter Weir at outside-left; I had McAllister, Mauchlen, Ramsey and Walshy – but I'd lost my main centre-half, and it was crucial. I failed to replace him adequately and as a consequence we had a very average season – so then Gary McAllister wanted to leave when his contract was up. The following season Mike Newell wanted to go, my workaholic centre-forward."

Having to sell our best players every season was weakening the side...

"Well, yes, as time moved on results got worse, I'm afraid. After my last game I got a most wonderful phone call from Mr Shipman. He said, 'David, I've got bad news for you. You've done wonderfully well in the transfer market in terms of keeping the club afloat, you've made us many pounds but unfortunately you haven't got enough points. The board have taken the decision we've got to replace you.' I said, 'I'm very sorry, Mr Chairman, but I understand. That's the way life is.' And then he said, 'But it's even worse, David – the board want me to leave, too.' That still makes me laugh, to this day. One of the funniest lines I ever heard. The board were very good, but they had no money. Now, there was a man called Trevor Bennett who wanted to put money into the club, but the board resisted him. He was a great entrepreneurial figure who gave very generously to the cricket club to build a new stand at Grace Road, but very sadly for Leicester City he took his

money up to St James' Park and gave it to Newcastle. The club lost out on a great opportunity there because they didn't want to disrupt the balance of power and wanted to hang on to their democracy."

We were selling players but few prospects were coming through the ranks...

"Well, I have to admit that our recruitment wasn't too good. We actually had a massive opportunity to sign David Platt from Crewe Alexandra. Martin George went up with Sammy Chapman, the chief scout, to go and watch him and, as it happened, he didn't have a very good game. We delayed on our decision and Aston Villa nipped in ahead of us. That's an absolute fact, we could have had him and we let him go."

Who would you rate as your best signing for City?

"Well, we never spent much on them! Nicky Cross, I think we paid about £15,000 to Walsall for him, and he was a bargain."

You did well in the loan transfer market in the 1989/90 season...

"Oh, Kevin Campbell did very well for us, he was fantastic. George Graham let us borrow him at the time because he'd been knocked out of the Arsenal side by Niall Quinn. He scored something like six goals in 12 games for us, and I still remember his last game when he had to do a lap of honour at Filbert Street. He carried us during his time at Leicester. But I can assure you that signing him was absolutely out of the question!"

What would you say is your favourite memory of your time at Leicester?

"Probably beating Leeds 4-3 was one of the best games. They were going for promotion under Howard and they really resented that defeat. There are always good memories as well as bad!"

In retrospect, is there anything you might have done differently?

"I still hear some of my ex-players saying, 'He never worked with defenders, he was only concerned with attack.' Maybe they were right. I didn't think it was the case at the time, but a few of them have said it."

> "Quite frankly, the signings I made didn't match up to the players I started with, and it drifted."

147

Kevin POOLE

Goalkeeper drops award

We interviewed Kevin in a corporate box at Burton Albion where he was goalkeeping coach, and still making the bench at the age of 50.

The first question is from Brian Little, who wants to know 'if you're still the quietest man in the world?'

"Ha! I suppose I didn't really used to say a lot when I was a player. But now I've moved over to the other side and I'm a coach, I have to be a bit more vocal. I was vocal enough out on the pitch but in the dressing room I kept myself to myself. Me and Brian go back a long way. He was Youth-team coach when I was first at Villa, then we were both up at Middlesbrough."

Was there ever a moment in a match where you wished you were taller?

"Never really a thought that crossed my mind. I thought I was good enough, and agility was more important than height. Y'know, Fabien Barthez – 5'10" and a World Cup winner. Some of the taller keepers aren't so good at getting down to shots. If you're agile enough and

good enough then you'll get by, without a doubt. At Villa, I talked to Graham Taylor and asked him if height was an issue, and he admitted that it was, and he wanted someone of more stature. He actually said to me, 'You won't make it in the game.' So it was nice to prove him wrong."

You missed the Play-offs in your first season at City, but were in for our Wembley date with Swindon...

"It was unbelievable, I've never played in a game like it. At 3-0 down, you're really thinking, 'It's over.' Then we gradually came back. Got one, got two. Then 3-3. And you think, 'We're going to win this now, because they must be really hurting.' To get done by a penalty again for the second year running was so frustrating."

What's your version of the incident?

"Well, I've hardly touched him. The ball came over the top, I came to the edge of the area. Steve White was chasing it down and I just brushed him on the shoulder. Absolutely nothing to make him fall down like that. David Elleray gave it, and there was no way we could come back again at that stage. You see a lot of it now, diving. It's cheating, that's all it is. It's not right, but it got them promotion to the Premier League, didn't it?"

You were Player of the Season in 1994/95 when we did make it to the Prem. Is it true you dropped the award?

"Yes, it is! Me and my wife stayed in the Holiday Inn after the awards do. I had it in a box which I got out of the car. While we were still in the car park the bottom fell out of the box and it went straight through and smashed on the floor! It was cut glass. I didn't actually drop it, I blame the box, but 'Goalkeeper Drops Award' is obviously the headline there. I took a little bit of stick

for that, as you can imagine."

Did you have to pay for a replacement?

"No, the club got me another one, so it was okay."

In the middle of that campaign, Brian Little departed...

"I had the jersey, and when Mark McGhee came in he didn't change much at first. After a while he told me he was getting someone else in – and it turned out to be Zeljko Kalac. He played two games, didn't he? At West Brom in the League we won 3-2, played some really beautiful football, and Kalac dropped a couple of clangers! And Bolton in the League Cup when he cost us the game. Then Mark had to come crawling back to me and say, 'Sorry, I've done the wrong thing.' He was good enough to apologise to me!"

Did you know Martin O'Neill was going to sub you for the penalty shoot-out in the Play-off final against Palace?

"No, it was a total shock. I hadn't seen Spider warming up as I was concentrating on the game, so the first thing I knew about it was when I saw my number being held up. There it was, number 1. What's going on here? I was so utterly dejected when I came off that I didn't even see Claridge's goal go in. But as soon as it did I was jumping around with everyone else.

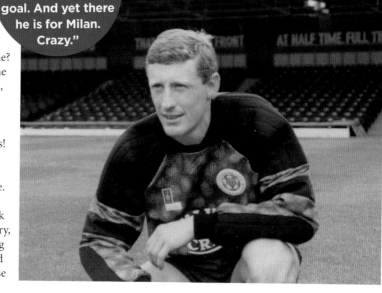

"His height was the main thing. He just looked big in the goal. And yet there he is for Milan. Crazy."

Deflation to elation in 30 seconds. He never discussed it with me afterwards but we had a do on the night and my missus went up and had a right go at him! It would have hurt more if he'd got a great save in the shoot-out and got all the credit, but of course Claggy's goal ended all that."

Back in the Prem, you were vying with Kasey Keller. Do you remember a farcical goal against Everton, which was dissected on *Match of the Day*?

"Oh, yes. We got awarded a free-kick and Garry Parker knocked it back to me so I could take it. The ref said, 'No, you've taken it,' and awarded handball against me outside the area. I thought I'd better get back in goal quick, so I dropped the ball and ran back. But they took it quick and played it from inside the box, when it should have been outside the box. I should have kept hold of the ball but I didn't see any danger because it wasn't where the free-kick should have been taken from. Not a great one to concede!"

Three into one will go

Chris POWELL

Chris Powell may go down in history as City's oldest ever signing, but that's far from the whole story. He earned a winner's medal for our League One campaign. And, when we met at Belvoir Drive – the day before his 667th, and last, game – his onerous job on the pitch was just one of three he'd undertaken.

"I came on and scored in my last game for Charlton and I actually thought I was going to retire. I'd more or less decided in my head that was it; but then suddenly I ended up here. I was supposed to be on a week-long trial but after two days Nigel said, 'I want to sign you.' I think they wanted to make sure I was up to it at the age of 38. It wasn't a hard decision. I liked the club; I loved the way Nigel worked with Craig; I loved the attitude of the players, they seemed hungry; and I could just smell that we had the right ingredients to get out of League One."

Not all of the bigger, better-supported clubs have managed it at the first attempt...

"I think the initial problem is that you're a target immediately. Teams go to Elland Road, the Valley or the Walkers and they love it because the majority of grounds aren't like that. They want to prove that they can match you. We had the right manager who knew how to organise things. We had the skill, the fitness, the stamina, a good support behind us – everything was in place. We stamped our authority on a lot of those games. And when things did go wrong Nigel deflected any negativity away from us."

How did winning the title compare to success in the Premier League and your international games?

"It was as big as them. It was an achievement and an honour. Pulling on a white England shirt is the pinnacle of anyone's career, but this was very special coming so late in my career because I thought those times had gone."

Do you still get a buzz from playing?

"I cherish it more now, because every time I pull on the shirt I'm thinking this could be the last time. This season really is my last, so I've sort of programmed myself to realise that it will be over in May. If I don't play again, I can't complain. I've had 750 games. Last year, having won the title, I was again thinking that it was time to retire. Nigel said, 'I'd like you to be registered as a player, just in case, and I see some qualities in you to become a coach or a manager.' I couldn't have asked for any better way to start a new career."

In 2001 Sven-Göran Eriksson picked you to play for England. The *Evening Standard* weren't very kind with their 'Chris Who?' headline. Did it come as a surprise to you,

at the age of 31?

"When Sven first came in, he said he was going to watch every club, and I believe that he did. I know he'd been to a few Charlton games and I was playing very well at the time. But Charlton players didn't get chosen to play for England... I remember Gareth Southgate, who was a year younger than me as an apprentice at Villa Park, coming up to the hotel before my debut against Spain at Villa Park. He was injured at the time and it was great to see someone I knew. He shook my hand and said, 'I bet when they delivered the training kit to your room, the first thing you did was put it on and look in the mirror.' I said, 'Yes, how did you know that?' He said, 'Because everyone does it! I did it.' Well, he was right, it was the first thing I did. I remembered my England kit that I had when I was small. But this wasn't a replica, it was the real kit. I can't express what joy it gives you."

You moved over to the coaching side in the summer, what does that currently involve for you?

"I'm a player, I'm the player development coach and also Chairman of the PFA."

"My title is player development coach, and it involves filling a few different roles. I'm still a player, so I'm a link between players and coaches. I try and judge how a player is thinking, even though he might not be expressing it. I'm developing as a coach myself, in the midst of getting my 'A' licence. It's a new environment for me because I'm now in on all the team meetings and discussions, which is invaluable to me as an aspiring coach. I'm learning on the job and Nigel is giving me that insight that not a lot of people get. I'm a player, a coach – and also Chairman of the PFA."

That alone must be a big job?

"Yes, we're the governing body for the players, and we have to look out for ex-players. We always try and impress upon players that they need to think about their future. We don't want them falling by the wayside and struggling with gambling or drinking addictions when they fall out of the game. Sporting Chance is there to try and deal with that aspect. Not everyone can stay in football."

Back to My Roots (Hall): Chris has returned to Southend United as manager.

151

Paul RAMSEY

Rambo: first blood

Paul Ramsey was a tiger in the Leicester midfield for 10 years and over 300 appearances, during which time he also played for Northern Ireland in the 1982 and '86 World Cups. We met Paul in his squash club's bar on Frog Island.

Jock Wallace was in charge when you first arrived in Leicester...

"Yes, he was scary. A big guy with a real aura around him. I left the security of home and my mum and dad at just 16, and was quite homesick. The first thing I remember about Jock was him watching me train a couple of times and then he put me straight in the big gym at Belvoir Drive with the first team along with Eddie Kelly and those guys, and told me to get on with it, which I did. I think he liked my aggression... ever since then, until the day he died, we were friends. I was still a young lad then, but I think that much of the person I still am today owes something to Jock."

PAUL RAMSEY
LEICESTER CITY

Gordon Milne arrived and we went straight up; he left and we went back down.

"Gordon was a great wee guy. He used to tell us stories about playing for England and Liverpool, and he always liked to join in the five-a-sides.

He was quite a character. Then Bryan Hamilton came along, and I had a terrible time under him. I couldn't stand the bloke. He came in and said, 'Right, there are going to be changes. You're too old...' I thought, 'Hang on a minute, you can't be rude.' It's not the way to be. Bryan couldn't command any respect and, once you lose that, you have no authority. I know he was only a young manager but he was too arrogant. Finally, he came into the little players' hut that used to be at Belvoir Drive one Friday and said to me, 'Right, you pick the team and get yourselves ready for tomorrow.' He knew he'd lost it."

Then David Pleat arrived on the scene...

"For a while he was the Magic Man. He came in, took training a few times, and a little spark happened. We'd just see him briefly and then not again for two or three days. Gordon Lee would take the training and we didn't feel like the manager was watching over us all the time. Whatever it was, it worked. David made me captain and I was really enjoying my football again, but after that successful back end of the season, he changed things. He started to come in to training every day, and you could feel uncomfortable. You could look across the canteen and see him staring at you and you'd think, 'What are you looking at?' There was something about David that really wasn't quite right. Then he got into all these silly mental exercises, trying to make you think really deeply about things. You'd have the names of cars up on the wall, 'Ford' here and 'Citroen' there... silly stuff. It all went pear-shaped."

One game stands out from 1989/90, the 4-3 against Leeds. What fans still think of as 'the Paul Ramsey match'...

"Oh yes, I still get bought drinks now on

the strength of that game! It was a belter, the week after my testimonial game. Yeah, I came on as sub when we were 2-0 down. As I was going on Pleaty came over and kissed me and said, 'Go on and change the game.' Gary Mac sent me through for my first one, which I lifted over the keeper; then I volleyed one in from a rebound. There was a fantastic atmosphere, I think it was a big crowd that day. I'll never forget that game."

Were you primarily a full-back or a midfielder?

"First and foremost, I regarded myself as a player that would give 110 per cent. I'd go out and give everything I had to the people that were paying my wages. They knew what they were going to get from me: put the shirt on and I'd go for it. I would hope to put my influence on every game I played in, and there are plenty of different ways of doing that. Talking to your team-mates; putting in that first hard tackle; placing the ball down and taking a quick free-kick. I suppose my strengths were tackling, having a lot of energy and being vocal. I really don't think I was a dirty player – Walshy was, though! You could tell from this odd look on his face when the red mist had come down. And do you remember Mick Kennedy? He was evil. He was bought to replace me. Plymouth away was his debut, and I turned up to get on the bus. Pleaty said to me, 'You're not going today. Mick

"I'd always give a new player a good kick first day to see what they were made of."

Kennedy's playing in your place.' I had to walk back off the bus in front of everyone and back to my girlfriend. I felt about two inches tall. My goal then was to see him off, and that kept me going. I knew then I'd bounce back. Mind you, I always felt a bit threatened every time a new player came in. I'd always give a them a good kick first day to see what they were made of. Walshy, Gary Mac, Ali – they'll all tell you! But in those days you trained how you played. You really went for those 50-50 balls. I don't think they do that so much now. We had some really good players over the years I was there: Lineker, Alan Smith, Kev MacDonald, Gary Mac – but we never quite had the team. There was never a four-year spell when the club said, 'Right, we're not going to sell anyone. Let's try and keep these players and build a good team.'"

Did you know? Rambo's real nickname is 'Penya'.

153

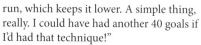

Shoot for the moon

Bobby ROBERTS

In his pristine front room in Anstey, we looked back half a century on the Scottish midfielder's time at Leicester, which spanned 1963-70 – and then back again as coach at the end of the '80s.

Having moved down from Motherwell, it took you a while to find your position at Leicester. Was that a bit unsettling?

"I always thought of myself as a midfield player, but managers liked players that could fill in elsewhere and I was moved up to centre-forward when Ken Keyworth got injured. I played at left-half and inside-right. But after Frank McLintock had gone, I was always in midfield. Davie Gibson was the playmaker, but I never thought of myself as the anchorman. I liked to get forward, too. The coach, Bert Johnson, always wanted us to be an attacking side."

Of Fossils & Foxes refers to your ritual long shot that usually sailed over the bar...

"Yes, it was only years later when I started coaching that I realised what I'd been doing wrong! Mike Stringfellow very rarely put one over the bar, and I should have been doing what he was doing. When

I was about 25 yards out and lining up a shot, I would plant one foot and hit it with the other, which makes your body lean back and the ball goes up. What Mike did was keep running and hit it on the run, which keeps it lower. A simple thing, really. I could have had another 40 goals if I'd had that technique!"

When you came to City we were actually in contention for the Double...

"I think we were a pretty good side from when I arrived up until about 1967. And then it went downhill the year we reached the Cup final but got relegated. We had four or five good seasons, but the only criticism would be that we never kept players when we signed players. I came in and Frank went. Gordon Banks was allowed to leave because we had Peter Shilton. Derek Dougan was a terrific player. They signed him for £25,000, got two very good years out him, and sold him for £50,000. If we could have kept all these players at the same time, then we might have been a real threat. But it never happened. They had to balance the books. It was the same with Jackie Sinclair, a goalscoring winger. He scored 20-odd goals two seasons on the trot, and was then sold. Just when you thought we might be on top of the job, somebody went."

1968/69 was a real watershed season...

"We hit the woodwork about 20 times, that season. If four or five of them had gone in, we'd have stayed up. It was a bit of a sickener when Matt Gillies left. Frank O'Farrell came in and got us to the Cup final, but between the semi and the final we played seven matches. And then we played five matches after the final, which is unheard of, before or since. It had been a bad winter and the fixtures had piled up. It was hard because Frank came with Malcolm Musgrove, and it was intensive coaching for every individual match."

You played every game in the Cup run...

"Yes, although we weren't a defensive

team, we only let in two goals on the way to Wembley, both against Barnsley. We beat Millwall 1-0, Liverpool 1-0, Mansfield 1-0 and then West Brom 1-0 in the semi-final. One-nil at Anfield with the crowd behind them, we had to defend for nearly all of the game, but we didn't have much option because it was backs to the wall. Mansfield, at their place, we knew would be a tough one. The pitch was terrible and they'd beaten West Ham 3-0 in the previous round. It was a real battle. The fans were right up to the touchline. Rodney Fern got our goal – he went up for a far-post header and put it in with his shoulder. It wasn't a beautiful goal, but it was the winner. Then I suppose the highlight of my career was at Hillsborough, when we'd beaten West Brom and knew we'd made it to Wembley. It was a horrible, rainy day on a bobbly pitch and not a good game to watch. Frank O'Farrell did a few tactical things differently that day, and it really nullified Albion. I couldn't really see a goal coming for either side, but then Clarkey popped up with the winner in the 87th minute. The whistle blew and that was it, we'd made it. Marvellous!"

Manchester City at Wembley. Is it true that Cup final day passes in a blur?

"Yes, Davie Gibson told me to make sure I enjoyed all the build-up to it. He could hardly remember anything from the final he played in. I think Manchester City were better than us on the day, but we had the better chances. Sadly, none of them fell for Allan Clarke, who was a natural goalscorer. This was also when the pitch was being used for the Horse of the Year Show, and it wasn't at its best. I did enjoy the day, it was a huge occasion in those days."

You later returned to work with David Pleat – then helped Gordon Lee stave off relegation

> "If we could have kept all these players at the same time, then we might have been a real threat."

to Division Three on the final day of 1990/91...

"Yes, we only just survived by the skin of our teeth, but we did it. Then we were called in to the chairman's office and were told that was that. It was going to be all change: new manager, new coaches. It was no surprise, really. They had to start fresh."

155

Iwan ROBERTS

Iwan is a Welshman...

We first interviewed City's Welsh international centre-forward in the dugout at Filbert Street, shortly after he'd opened his Premier League account.

Your first ever hat-trick, against Derby – that must be your City highlight to date?

"It was special, but the best day ever was against Derby at Wembley – well, after the final whistle, anyway. There was too much pressure for the players or the fans to enjoy that game. A third defeat on the trot would have been too much to take. The League game was special, too. Two-nil down after 13 minutes, but the crowd got right behind us and we got an early goal back. Every time we attacked, we looked like scoring."

Have you ever scored a better goal than the equaliser?

"No, I've never struck one better. As soon as I hit it, I knew it was in."

Did you even expect to come back from injury to play in the Rams Play-off final?

"I honestly thought I'd be on the bench, with Sticks, Waller and Julian up front.

The Gaffer said, 'Go out there and run 'til you drop,' but in the second half I could feel my legs going. It was the warmest day ever, and there was no air in the stadium."

Just between us, did you foul the keeper?

"Well, I did catch him a bit, and I was surprised that the ref didn't blow for a free-kick. It should have been cleared off the line. I look at the video and I still don't know what Paul Williams was trying to do. It was so important that we didn't go in at half-time a goal down. You could tell, when Harkes missed and their heads went down, that we were going to win. And what a difference between the two sets of supporters – there was so much colour and noise at the Leicester end. Their fans never really got behind them, did they? I first heard my song at Wembley, and it still makes me laugh now whenever I hear it."

How did it feel? A Wembley win, at last...

"We could start enjoying it after the final whistle. Knowing that you've won, and going up those stairs... you can't buy that feeling. Knowing that there are 40,000 Leicester fans there, a lot of them grown men in tears. I even thought the Gaffer was going to start crying when they interviewed him afterwards."

How does Brian Little compare to your previous managers?

"He doesn't rant and rave at you when you're losing, and he doesn't slag his players off. He has an enormous amount of respect. That's one thing that convinced me to come to Leicester when I met him. The missus was impressed with him, and even my little boy. He kept pointing at him, saying, 'Fireman Sam, Fireman Sam!'"

He wears a Welshman's hat

Iwan ROBERTS

We caught up with Iwan again on the phone from Norwich, before he had to jet off to Montenegro to cover a Euro qualifier for BBC Wales.

Can we check the validity of the lyrics to your song, which still gets the odd airing today. 'Iwan is a Welshman' is obviously right. 'He wears a Welshman's hat'?

"Yes, I've been capped 15 times!"

'He lives next door to Joachim'?

"We both bought a house in Countesthorpe, on the new estate there, but we weren't next-door neighbours. We lived about 200 yards from each other."

'And he lives in a council flat...'

"No, definitely not, not with three kids!"

After relegation, you had a great 1995/96 season but this time didn't make the Play-off side...

"No, I broke my ribs again, against West Brom. Not four seconds after the kick-off. I went up for a challenge with Stacey Coldicott and got two broken ribs and a punctured lung. The last time I'd done it, two years earlier, was against West Brom with six games to go, and I had a strange feeling that something might happen to me again. I knew then we'd do well in the last six games, get to the Play-offs and win at Wembley... which we did. Its spooky!"

On that day at Wembley there was an incident with the chairman that tipped you into wanting to leave the club...

"It was a stupid comment, really. Alan Birchenall was talking to my missus, asking if I'd be fit enough to make the bench. Martin George wasn't even in the conversation, he was just walking past and said, 'He doesn't deserve to make the squad, the people who deserve to be in the 16 are the people who got us here.' I thought for someone of his position to say something like that was ridiculous. I was still the club's top goalscorer with 20 goals. I think I'd played my part, and it left a nasty taste in my mouth."

At what point did you decide to leave?

"I was out of contract, but had a new offer from Martin O'Neill. David Speedie, my agent at the time, had been speaking to Wolves. They made me a good offer so I decided to give it a chance there. Hindsight is a wonderful thing, and I don't have too many regrets in my career, but leaving Leicester at that stage was probably the biggest mistake I ever made. When you look at the success they had after I left, becoming a force in the Premier League, some great Cup runs and trips to Wembley..."

> **"I'd been on Creatine a week. I swear it made me really aggressive that time I was sent off."**

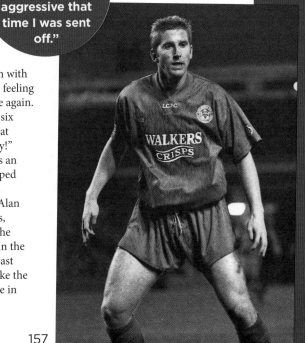

Keith Weller saved my stag do

Dennis ROFE

Our favourite Cockney full-back enjoyed eight seasons at Leicester, and went on to become a successful coach. When we met at his house outside Southampton, he was the Football League's Youth Development Officer for the South East.

Was Jimmy Bloomfield a big influence on your career at Orient and at Leicester?

"Oh yes, he was a massive influence and a tremendous man. Jimmy had a lovely philosophy on football. He wanted to play with style and entertain the paying public. Keep the ball on the floor and pass it. That was mirrored in the players he brought to Leicester. Discipline, meanwhile, probably wasn't Jim's strong point! He had a belief that we'd turn up for training in the morning and we'd be all right, having had half a shandy the night before. Well, with the likes of Frank Worthington running wild round Leicester, that wasn't always going to happen, was it? Jim kind of let you get on with it. He was always amazed if we lost a game. He'd say, 'Why did you lose that one? You're better than them.'"

Was it a culture shock, moving up from London in 1972?

"Well, I thought I was going to the industrial north! Obviously, Leicester was a bigger club but I wasn't sure where I stood. I went round all the senior pros at Leyton Orient and said, 'Look, I'm on 30 quid a week. What should I ask for?' In those days there were no players' agents, so it was just me driving up to Leicester in my Vauxhall Viva, murmuring, 'Go for 70 quid. Don't take the first offer. Go for 70 quid. Don't take the first offer...' I walked into Filbert Street and I was overawed by the lovely old oak-panelled boardroom. Jimmy told me, 'Look Den, I'm not going to beat around the bush. I want you here. I'm going to give you 100 pound a week.' I went, 'Get me a pen Jim, quick!' I signed for £112,000, which was a record for a full-back then. It lasted about 24 hours before Leicester sold David Nish to Derby for £250,000."

Do you remember your debut for City?

"Yes, it was 0-0 at home to Coventry. When I came off the field at the end of the game, I thought to myself, 'Yes, I can handle this level, I'm going to be all right.' Then came a magnificent game against Liverpool. It was also my stag night! When I came up to Leicester in August, me and Sue were planning to get married the next summer. We decided to bring the wedding forward to the 5th of November. I had a big night out planned after the Liverpool game: Granny's, Bailey's, the lot! But we found ourselves 2-0 down after about 19 minutes. Keith Weller then saved my stag do with a magnificent hat-trick! Imagine going out after we'd beaten Liverpool. It was a great night."

Was there a little bit of a divide between Jimmy's signings and the local lads?

"I think we had a reputation for enjoying a night out, which we did. I think the home-grown lads were a bit more quiet and reserved. But any dressing room with Birch in, spouting away, you really did

DENNIS ROFE

John Sjoberg, you won't find better defenders."

When Jock Wallace came in, a new era began...

"He very quickly made a big impression on everyone with his presence, his preparation, his work ethic. In Jock's words, if you did a shift for him then he'd take care of you. I had tremendous respect and admiration for him. The biggest problem we had was understanding him! Again, as Jimmy had brought in Londoners, Jock brought in the players he knew – from Scotland. It was a difficult time because a lot of my pals were drifting away. There was a new crowd coming in, and some of them were very young, like your Buchanans and Linekers. Me and Wallington were about all that was left. I got on very well with Bobby Smith, as well."

In February 1980 you made the big decision to leave Leicester for Chelsea...

"I was desperate to get back into the First Division because I'd reached 30. I was pretty certain that Leicester would go up under Jock, but I wasn't sure when. Basically, I made the wrong decision, because Leicester went up as champions and Chelsea missed going up on goal difference. Jock was tremendous about it. He even gave me his Championship winning medal. He was a terrific man in every sense of the word. I can still see him now: he'd put one fist up and then the other, saying, 'You can have sudden death, or six months in hospital. Which one do you want?'"

"I spent 5 months in the Holiday Inn with Frank. I was 22 when I went in and 35 when I left."

have to give him as good as you got. Some of the local lads like Alan Woollett, Graham Cross, John Sjoberg and Malcolm Munro were smashing lads but they weren't quite capable of doing that. Perhaps our quick wit and our banter gave some of them the wrong impression sometimes. And it so happened that a lot of Jim's side had come up from London clubs – Birch, Keith Weller, Steve Kember, Chris Garland, Jon Sammels, Steve Earle – it was only natural that we sort of clicked together. I think that distinction did become less later on. Certainly, I know there was a mutual respect for each other in that they knew what we brought to the team and we knew what they brought to the team. Y'know, the likes of Crossy and

Jon SAMMELS

Playing for the badge

Jon was working as a driving instructor when we visited him at home in Countesthorpe to look back on his football career with two League clubs.

Tell us about your time at Arsenal...

"I joined Arsenal at 15 and left with a League Championship medal. I had a lot of disappointment in the last six months. I broke my ankle in the season they won the Double, then I got back in halfway through the season and played every round of the Cup, but I was left out of the final. I left because I was a bit disillusioned – I'd got a bit of stick from the crowd. I'd been there nearly eleven years and it was time for me to go."

Why did you come to Leicester City?

"Really, I suppose it was because of Jimmy Bloomfield. I knew Jim from his Arsenal days. I remember the first Arsenal match I ever went to. Outside Highbury, at a stall, I bought a little shield badge with a photo of Jimmy Bloomfield in the middle, because he was my favourite player. I've still got it now. I knew the way he liked football to be played, and I knew it would suit me. I was 95 per cent certain I was

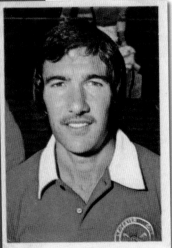

going to sign for Ipswich, where I was born. Then I got a call from Jimmy out of the blue and he said, 'Don't sign anything until you've spoken to me.' I was training with Arsenal in Bournemouth and Jim sent a car all the way down to bring me to Leicester. I was Jim's first signing."

And you won a trophy in your first game!

"Yes, the Charity Shield, with a rare goal from Steve Whitworth. A good start!"

Did Bloomfield command respect from everyone who played for him?

"The thing that saddens me is that a lot of people wanted Jimmy out. He was a successful manager for City, especially compared to what's gone on since he left. I really got cheesed off – we finished seventh the season before. One or two idiots started shouting, 'Bloomfield out!' and a lot more joined in like sheep. The majority of the players were behind him."

We now think of it as a golden era. How close were we to winning a major trophy?

"Close! If we could have had more competition for places. I played roughly the same number of games for Arsenal and Leicester. Without degrading Leicester, it was a greater achievement getting into that Arsenal side because of the competition. Jimmy had about 13 players to choose from. There was, at one time, a lack of team spirit."

How did you see your relationship with the fans at Filbert Street?

"I always thought I was a good player but there were people who didn't think I was. Part of the reason was that I could never just whack a ball. I always wanted to pass it to someone. When I started at Arsenal the two inside forwards were me and George Eastham – we couldn't tackle a fish supper between us. Jimmy Bloomfield used to pick players for what they could do rather than what they couldn't do. I wasn't the best tackler in the world, so there would be someone nearby who could. He blended things well."

Action replay: Villa Park '74

Twenty-three years later we returned to Jon's. By now, he was happily retired.

What was your role in that '70s City side?

"Jim's philosophy for the midfield was one to get it, the ball-winner; one to play it, which was my role, and one to go through, which was Keith Weller. I was more of a provider than I had been at Arsenal – I didn't score as many goals for Leicester as I would have liked."

Do you have a favourite one?

"Probably a half-volley against Burnley that I made really sweet contact with. It was a way out but I knew it was in as soon as I hit it. It was my 50th league goal!"

The Bloomfield team probably peaked in the FA Cup run of 1974...

"It was an attractive side, but we could be quite inconsistent. We could play brilliantly in a game and the next week we could be like a different team. We were lucky to have players of the calibre of Keith Weller and Frank Worthington and Len Glover. You always had a chance with players who could produce something special and win a game. The shame was that out of a semi-final line-up of us, Liverpool, Burnley and Newcastle, we didn't manage to avoid Liverpool. I'm sure we'd have given them a much better game at Wembley than Newcastle did. When we played Liverpool at Old Trafford, Peter Shilton was brilliant and kept us in the tie. They were overrunning us at times. But in the replay at Villa Park I thought we were unlucky. We played a lot better. At 1-1, Keith went clear on Ray Clemence, and he was the one you'd chose to score for you in that situation, but Clemence made a great save. Then Kevin Keegan got that one out of the blue, and they got a third at the end."

If only Jimmy had managed to complete the signing of John Toshack...

"I actually roomed with John while that was supposed to be happening. He was in the hotel room talking to Barry John, the rugby player, a lot. I was there when they told him they couldn't sign him after the medical showed something up. He knew about it, but didn't think it was enough the stop the deal. It certainly didn't do his career after that any harm."

The side was crying out for investment...

"Yes, it probably was. And I think Frank McLintock discovered that quite quickly. It wasn't a crisis; but Keith had his knee injury and there were a few others with problems, ready to move on. In the end, I think I left for Vancouver just before Christmas, and we were already in a bad way then. It was a terrible season. It was hard watching a friend like that struggle."

Robbie SAVAGE

Welcome to my world

After training, we were asked to follow Robbie's supersonic sports car home to Stoughton. But not until he'd squeezed in a parking altercation with Pegguy Arphexad, and then jokingly led us up the driveway of the local manor house.

Do you remember what Alex Ferguson said when he let you go from Manchester United, back in 1994?

"Yes, he said obviously there are a lot of centre-forwards at the club. Brian McClair, Dion Dublin was there, Paul Scholes, Mark Hughes. He said, 'It'll be tough for you to make it here, but I expect you to go somewhere else and prove me wrong.' I'm not a centre-forward now, but hopefully that's what I've done."

You then crashed your car, driving home – not the best of days, overall...

"No, definitely one of the worst. My mind wasn't fully on my driving. I was working out how I'd

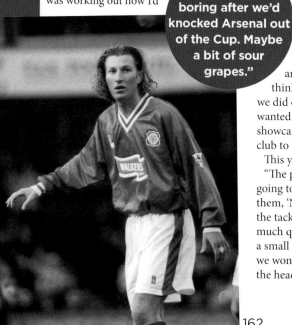

> **"Wenger said we were boring after we'd knocked Arsenal out of the Cup. Maybe a bit of sour grapes."**

break it to my family that United had let me go. Crewe came in for me when I was lying in my hospital bed."

You first rose to national infamy after the Worthington Cup final against Spurs...

"The press can ruin people's lives. I got a taste of it, but it's much worse for the likes of Stan or David Beckham. They just can't do anything. The coverage of that game changed my life. Some of the stuff written after the game, especially Jeff Powell's article, was ludicrous. It wasn't about football, it was a personal attack on things like my appearance – that's what hurt. Does it matter what I look like, even if I've got pink hair, if I go out on to the field and do my best? He even had the cheek to phone up a Radio Leicester phone-in and say he'd been right to write what he did. I wouldn't mind meeting him."

What did you take from the experience of being picked on?

"Well, I certainly couldn't change the way I play. The Gaffer gave me and Rob Ullathorne a job to do, and it was to stop Ginola from playing. You have your instructions and it doesn't matter what the crowd think or what journalists think. I think we did our job that day, but the press wanted Ginola to make the game into a showcase for his talents and the London club to win, so they had a go at us."

This year's final was much better...

"The press were all asking me, 'Are you going to change this year?' And I told them, 'No, I'll get stuck in again. I'll make the tackles, I'll die for the cause. I had a much quieter game at right-back. I played a small part but it was much better because we won. That's better than me making all the headlines for the wrong reasons."

Never say never, ever, ever

Ten years on, we met Robbie again – this time at his friend's house in Anstey, while Derby County's finest reclined on a chaise longue, watching athletics on TV.

Towards the end of the O'Neill era, didn't you feel something special was going on?

"Well, at the time Martin kept getting linked with other clubs and the feeling deep down was that if he left, that would be the end of it. He was that much of an influence on the team and the players, including myself. No matter what people say, Leicester will never have that same amount of success ever again."

We might...

"No, it's a fact. You won't. Never, ever, ever. It might not have been Leicester's best ever but it was a great side, finishing in the top ten four times, winning trophies, playing in Europe. It'll never happen again, unless they get the guy who bought Man City; but they won't."

How did you get on with Peter Taylor?

"I liked him. I thought he was a great guy and we had a very good start under him. We went to West Ham and won 1-0 – Darren Eadie. First time we'd won at Upton Park in years and years. We wore the white kit and I got the guy Stimac sent off. Well, I didn't get him sent off, he got himself sent off because he fouled me. Like I didn't get Justin Edinburgh sent off. He raised his arm and he had to go. I was sad to see Peter go. I still see him a bit now. I don't think he was given long enough. Managers never get long enough these days. I think he didn't help himself with his signings, though."

You moved to Birmingham when we were relegated due to Taylor. Was there anything Micky Adams could have done to keep you at Leicester?

"No. I didn't want to be dropping down to that level at that stage of my career. I'd had some great years at Leicester, and think I had a good season the year we got relegated. I needed to move. Leicester should have got more money for me than they did. I think I was a bit of a snip at £1.7 million, really. I'm a bit disappointed by the reactions of the fans now. I gave them five great years and won Player of the Year trophy twice and gave it everything I had. So for them to boo me when I played for Brighton was a complete and utter joke. It was shocking for me. I think they could have shown me a bit more respect when I was at my lowest ebb. Singing 'Savage is a w***er.' I thought that was wrong of them. For me, that was the love affair with the Leicester fans over."

Was there any truth in the rumours linking you with Leicester last season?

"Yes, I would have jumped at the chance to go back to Leicester at that stage. I was phoning Paul Dickov saying, 'Get me to Leicester!' But Pearson didn't fancy me. As it turned out, maybe that was for the best."

Blue Sky thinking

Alan SMITH

With 84 goals in 206 starts, Alan Smith was one of City's true stars of the '80s. We met today's roving TV reporter over a cuppa at St Albans' Noke Hotel.

Coming to City from non-League Alvechurch, you formed a very fruitful partnership with Gary Lineker...

"Our respective games just gelled together naturally, we didn't even have to work on it that much. He liked to face goal, and run at goal; I liked to have my back to goal and was good in the air, flicking it on and all that. We clicked pretty much straight away."

City were promoted under Gordon Milne, but it was seven games before you got a point – at home to Stoke...

"Ah yes, I'd controlled the ball on my chest and as it popped up to head height,

Steve Bould tried to kick the ball away from behind and he caught me in the face. I didn't realise straight away but he'd kicked my four front teeth out. As I sat there, I was watching Mark Chamberlain picking teeth up off the pitch and showing them to the ref. I didn't even realise they were mine because I couldn't feel anything and I was in a bit of shock. Gerry Summers, the coach, said, 'Oh you're all right Al, get back out there.'

I said, 'I've lost all my teeth!' Because they'd all come out by the roots, the Royal Infirmary could put them back in for me."

Bob Hazell's arrival shored up the defence and sparked a much better run...

"Yes, he was a big, solid youth. He had to have some shorts specially made for him. But even the biggest size Ind Coope shirt was tight on him. He used to get nipple-burn off it and had to put two plasters on before the game! He was a powerful presence. I was quite close to Bob because all the Birmingham lads used to meet up at Corley services and take it in turns to drive up the M69 to training. Stevie Lynex, Peter Eastoe, Mark Hutchinson from the reserves. There were five of us at one time. Bob had to have the front seat."

Gary Lineker left in the summer of '85...

"Well, there'd been so much speculation about him that it was inevitable at some stage. I was able to drift into areas where he would have been and get more opportunities, and I think my goal tally increased. Gary McAllister and Ali Mauchlen were brought in with some of his fee and Gary Mac added real quality to our midfield. Steve Moran came in. Mark Bright was pushing for a place, but he was too similar to me for us to play together."

One standout in 1985/86 was beating Man U 3-0, playing them off the park...

"I certainly remember my two goals! I got one on the follow-up, from a really tight angle, and I whacked one into the top corner from the edge of the box. It was one of those days when it all came together and it was great. Ron Atkinson locked them in the dressing room for about an hour afterwards, it was a bit of a crisis for them. They were a side full of household names, and they were tough opponents. I think it was the season before when Peter Eastoe got his jaw smashed in about 50 places in an off-the-ball incident with Gordon McQueen. I remember jogging back for a corner with Joe Jordan and he elbowed me in the Adam's apple!"

Having paid £800,000, it was odd when Arsenal agreed to loan you straight back...

"I was placed in a really weird situation that I didn't feel happy with at all. At Highbury, both sets of fans were singing my name and I was waving to both ends of the ground! Gary

> "At Highbury, both sets of fans were singing my name and I was waving to both ends of the ground!"

McAllister gave me a bollocking and told me to concentrate. It was a situation that I shouldn't have let happen. Then, at the end of the season, Alex Ferguson rang me and asked if I wanted to go to Manchester United. But I'd committed to Arsenal by that time."

There's a photo of you throwing your shirt into the away end at Oxford, after the last game of the season. How did that feel?

"Arsenal had an end-of-season dinner at Park Lane. I'd taken my dinner suit with me because I was driving straight down there. The lads were all distraught in the dressing room, all staring at the floor, and I was putting my dicky bow on. I had to say, 'Best of luck next season, lads, I've

got to go.' Paul Ramsey said, 'F***ing hell, Smudger!' Off I went, and I scraped my car getting out of the tight little car park at the Manor. It was a horrible way to end my time at Leicester, where I had loads of great memories."

Do you still have a soft spot for Leicester?

"Obviously, I got immersed in it all in that incredible season. Arsenal fans gave me some stick when I changed my Twitter photo to me in a Leicester kit. I said, 'Hey, I did play for them for five years!' It was lovely for the fans; to be greeted by supporters who'd been there when I was there, on the way up to the gantry. It was a complete one off – a fantastic story, and an example to other clubs that they can maybe achieve more than they think. Now Leicester need to use this momentum and increased profile to attract top players to the club and try and establish themselves maybe among the top seven or eight clubs. That would be a fantastic legacy of the title-winning year."

"Milne didn't purposefully clear out the Scots... but he wanted to bring in his own players."

The confidence of youth

Richard SMITH

We spoke to our 21-year-old centre-half at Filbert Street, soon after his goal saw City's first FA Cup win in six years.

Did you feel that the Youth team of your time were held up by David Pleat?

"We used to think there was no chance of getting in. I suppose it would have been a lot of pressure on young shoulders. He obviously didn't dare take the gamble and stick us in there. He could certainly talk a good game – he knew an awful lot about football – but he found it hard to get the right blend with the players he had here."

How is Brian Little's style different?

"As a young player, I didn't feel that I could approach David Pleat. Brian is obviously a lot younger than Pleat; he certainly gets more involved in the training side. I think Pleat was really lacking the respect of a few players. Brian has that respect and has certainly done the

but he doesn't get wound up and shout at us. He gets his message over, though."

Are you conscious of the support coming from the terraces while you're playing?

"Yes, you always are. Well, I am, anyway, because I've been a Leicester City fan all my life. I know what it's like standing there. I've done my time in Pen 3 for a few years, and in the Double Decker."

You were in with the City fans at Derby...

"There was no way I was going to miss that one. I could have gone with the team but Brian isn't keen on having injured players on the coach. I suppose it doesn't look too good if everybody's getting wheeled off the coach! Anyway, I like standing with the Blue Army. You can't beat the atmosphere."

Where do you think the future of Richard Smith lies?

"In the First Division with Leicester

City. And then hopefully in an England shirt. The club I've always supported have given me the chance to play for them – it's a big enough club to spend the rest of your career with, especially if it's in the First Division. I was down at City doing schoolboy training when I was nine years old during Jock Wallace's days. You could say I'm the longest-serving player, being here 12 years! I suppose I've got to start thinking about what to do after my playing career's over. I definitely want to stay in the game. I've got my

job up to now. He's always calm – he'll talk constantly, jogging your memory about what to do at free-kicks and corners, etc. –

preliminary coaching badge – if I get my full badge, I'd become a qualified coach. That's worth looking at."

The power of hindsight

Richard SMITH

Our second interview with Richard was conducted some 16 years after his final City appearance, in the shadow of the great wind turbines which overshadow his skip hire business near Gilmorton.

We recently watched the highlights of the Swindon Play-off final – it was brilliant for about three minutes in the second half...

"It was bizarre. What a crazy day. We went 3-0 down and I thought, 'It's gone. We've given ourselves too much to do.' But then somehow we turned the tide and managed to pick ourselves up. As soon as we got one, I thought there was only one team going to win it. And having got back to 3-3 it took a dodgy penalty again to beat us. I guess it just wasn't meant to be. There was a lot of emotion that day, for everyone. The City dressing room was completely distraught. Although there was also a bit of pride in the way we'd come back, even though it came to nothing."

Then you missed out on the Derby Play-off final...

"I spent a lot of time with David Speedie that day, as he was suspended. Ironic, given what happened in the Blackburn game two years earlier."

You played a dozen games in City's debut Premier League season before Brian Little left...

"To be honest, I never saw eye to eye with Mark McGhee at all. In fact, I found him to be the most arrogant person I'd ever met. He didn't last too long before Martin O'Neill came in. Martin was very honest with me. He said, 'I like you as a person and you always

work very hard in training; but you're not part of my first-team plans at present.' At 26, having had a taste of regular first-team football, I couldn't face life in the reserves. So I made the move to Grimsby."

How old were you when you retired?

"I was 30. It was my back that finished me. Scary. It was all I'd ever known, being involved at Leicester. It becomes a part of you and you don't think it's ever going to end, naively. You don't really plan for it. So when it happens you're left there thinking, 'Oh, shit. What am I going to do?'"

What did you miss most about the game?

"Going into training, keeping fit, working hard, being healthy. The camaraderie of the changing room. I fell completely out of love with the game for a good four years after I retired. Didn't even watch it. I finished on a sour note and that's probably what killed it for me. I was sort of angry at the game. Moneywise, I always say I was born five years too early! Don't think about it, because you can't change it! I tried a few things out along the way and here we are now. It's funny how things change, isn't it?"

> **"My back finished me. In the end, I thought, 'Let's get away, let's leave it while I can still walk.'"**

High Noon at Belvoir Drive

David SPEEDIE

Billed as 'an Appointment with the Devil,' our encounter with City's Play-off nemesis of 1991/92 confounded all expectations. Speedie was small, almost delicately framed. He signed kiddies' autographs obligingly. The 'Tartan Terror' beloved of Chelsea, Liverpool, Blackburn and Coventry proved unnervingly affable – with a soft-spoken Yorkshire accent. And he played a big part in the season's campaign, which finally ended with Play-off success.

What's your version of the penalty incident in the City-Blackburn Play-off final, 15 months back?

"I know a lot of Leicester supporters round where I live, it's a big Leicester area, and I say to them that if that had happened anywhere else on the field and a free-kick had been given, there wouldn't have been any complaints. I would have been happy with a free-kick in the area for obstruction, but I didn't give the decision,

the referee did that. At the end of the day, I was doing a job for my club, as I'm going to do a job for this club. What people are still sour about it is beyond me. People keep saying, 'If it wasn't for David Speedie, then Leicester would be in the Premier League.' But Leicester never scored a goal on that day. Rovers missed a penalty and had other chances saved. You've got to put the ball in the back of the net to win a game. I've had blatant penalties turned down because of the reputation I got from that game. It's a sad way to go out, but at the time I was a Blackburn player."

What made you come to Leicester?

"I only live 25 minutes away! They're a good footballing team and they want to do the right things on and off the field. After I'd spoken to Brian Little for a couple of minutes, I had no hesitation in signing. The Gaffer's a breath of fresh air. He knows what he's talking about, which some of them don't. The training is different class – it's like going back to school, the enthusiasm on the training ground. It's the best I've ever had, and they're a great set of lads."

Did your unpopularity with a lot of Leicester fans make you think twice about signing for City?

"No. I heard a few of them on Saturday, but they don't bother me. If they can't see that I'm wearing a City shirt and I'm going to do my very best for their club, then they can't really be called supporters. It's their problem."

Do you think your media image is unfair, or at least distorted?

"It's unfair in as far that they never let it drop, no matter what you do. I can get kicked from pillar to post for 89 minutes, but if I lose my rag for one minute then you can guarantee what will be written in the paper. I don't do anything to anybody unless they do something to me first, and that applies to any walk of life, not just football. Being aggressive and being involved is all part of the game. It's not done my career any harm. Really, it comes down to people wanting to have a pop at me because of my reputation, but I'm not the sort to walk away from things like that."

Have you thought about what you'll do when your playing career is over?

"Not beyond lots of golf and lots of holidays. I don't fancy being a coach – they don't seem to get much respect from players these days, although that isn't true of this club. I've heard things said to coaching staff on the training ground that wouldn't have been dreamed of when I was a young player. I wouldn't mind being a manager, though."

Did you enjoy your debut on Saturday?

I enjoyed the fact that we won, but we're capable of playing a lot better than that. I was just pleased that Iorfa couldn't finish for Peterborough! The grass was a bit long and the ball was getting caught under my feet. Gavin Ward had a splendid game. I've only played one full game with Steve Walsh; I played five halves in Norway, so it's something we'll build on,

striking up a good partnership."

Like with Kerry Dixon at Chelsea? What is it that sometimes clicks between players to create that goalscoring partnership?

"It's just knowing what each other is

"I've had blatant penalties turned down because of the reputation I got from that game."

about and being friends off the field, in that case. If you're at loggerheads with somebody then the partnership is never going to work."

A lot of sides have been spending big money in their team-building this summer. Can Leicester get promoted despite their lack of serious investment?

"Yes, of course we can! Just because clubs have spent money doesn't mean anything. When Kenny Dalglish came to Blackburn he brought in million-pound signings like Roy Wegerle and Duncan Shearer, and they couldn't get in the team. It doesn't guarantee success."

Did you know? David is now a taxi driver, based in Nottinghamshire.

Gerry TAGGART

Taggs's tactical talk

When we met up with Gerry Taggart at Belvoir Drive, his knee was in a brace and his season was already over.

You were in and out of the side last season. Were you surprised to get the nod for the League Cup final against Spurs?

"Well yes, in a way. There was a disciplinary problem with Frank Sinclair, if you remember. I asked the Gaffer later, 'Would I have played if Frank hadn't messed up?' and he said 'No.' I wasn't very pleased to hear that, but then nothing Martin did surprised me!"

Was that the turning point when you made the first-team spot your own, and the fans began to take to you?

"The first season, I was travelling down from Yorkshire on my own every day and that got on top of me. In the summer I moved down here and things got better. I wasn't cooped up in the car, stuck in traffic every day. I'm sure that led to me picking

up silly little injuries as well. Suddenly, I could understand why I hadn't been playing so well. The hunger was still there, but I wasn't firing on all cylinders out on the pitch."

"You've been sent off a couple of times for Leicester, though they were both for two bookable offences. The one at Spurs looked very harsh...

"It was very harsh because I never touched the guy at all. I obviously mistimed the tackle but he skipped over me and then decided to fall. For someone like myself who was brought up on tackling, it's not so easy now. Now the tackle from behind is outlawed even if you win the ball, there are times when you have to draw back. Stand up and jockey. A few years ago you'd have flown in and hoped that you'd come out with the ball. Defenders have had to change their game and adapt, or they'd spend all their time serving suspensions."

We perhaps got a glimpse of the good old days last week, with Roy Keane's challenge on Alfie Haaland?

"That looked like a case of revenge."

Have you ever gone after anyone like that? Or has anyone ever gone after you?

"Both! I remember Billy Whitehurst punching me in the face, so I ran straight after him and kicked him right up the arse! I've had a few run-ins. I'd never start something like that with a forward, but if he elbows me or something like that then the red mist descends and I'll try and get my own back. They have to know that they aren't going to get away with it. There's a lot less of that in the game now. You still get elbows flying around but they nearly always get caught on camera, these days. There don't seem to be as many 'hard' centre-forwards around. The most annoying thing that can happen now is they nutmeg you!"

Who are the strikers you least look forward to

"I played in a three at Barnsley, a back four at Bolton and a three at Leicester for two seasons."

playing against?

"Obviously, at Manchester United, Dwight Yorke and Andy Cole are very good at the minute. Thierry Henry at Arsenal. But you don't wake up and think, 'Oh no, I'm playing against him today.' You think, 'Right, I'd better be sharp today against him.'"

There's been a lot of talk about formations under Peter Taylor. Do you have a preference for 3-5-2 or 4-4-2?

"Not really. I used to play left-back at Manchester City. I played in a three at Barnsley, and in a back four at Bolton for three years. Obviously, I've played in a three at Leicester for a couple of seasons now. It doesn't make any odds. You can talk about systems all you want, but you have to have the right players to play in those positions. It doesn't really boil down to systems. If your team's good enough, then they'll win games. I don't think, at the minute, whether we play a three or a four, we're good enough to win games. It doesn't make a blind bit of difference at the minute."

How did you feel when Martin O'Neill left last summer?

"I was a bit sick, like everybody else. It was a big blow to the club and at the time it felt like the heart was being ripped out of the place."

A great deal of Leicester City's recent success has been based on team spirit...

"Well, the list of injuries at the minute has brought us down a bit. Certain players might be lacking in confidence as well. A couple of years ago, we had players like Walshy and Marshy about the place, and now Lenny has gone, so some good characters have left the club; but I wouldn't say the team spirit as a whole is gone."

We can't talk about this season without mentioning the disappointment against Wycombe in the Cup...

"That's probably the worst I've ever felt in my whole career. It was worse than getting relegated. It's difficult to put a finger on why it happened. We just weren't up for it – although why, I don't know, because it was the quarter-finals of the Cup. I don't even like to think about it."

The gloves come off

Gerry TAGGART

Seventeen years later, our rock-solid reader of the game looked back with the benefit of hindsight on his years with City, and on more recent triumphs.

The last time we spoke, Wycombe had just knocked us out of the Cup...

"I think we'd been riding our luck up until that stage. And me personally, I'd been carrying a serious knee injury all that season. I'd been managing it by not training. The week before that Wycombe game we'd beaten Liverpool at home and gone up to fourth place; but we'd been papering over the cracks and getting away with it. The Wycombe game was probably a crack that turned into a crevice. We weren't sitting round in the dressing room thinking, 'We're going to finish top six this year.' We were more like, 'We're shit, but we're getting away with it!'"

It's probably fair to say that history won't be kind to Peter Taylor...

"No, and neither will I."

He inherited a very good squad of

players. Where did it all go wrong?

"Well, he got rid of Steve Walsh for a

start, who really could have helped him. He got rid of Tony Cottee. He got rid of Stan Collymore. And he brought in young players that weren't good enough. He brought in Trevor Benjamin from Cambridge United and Kevin Ellison from Altrincham. Junior Lewis from Gillingham. When Martin O'Neill was here, he brought in quality and experience. Peter Taylor was building for the future, but there is no future in football. It's always about the here and now. He sold Neil Lennon, he nearly sold me. I nearly went to Celtic that summer, because Martin wanted to take Neil and me up there. We both decided not to go and both signed new contracts, but then Lenny couldn't get on with Peter Taylor, so he left. That was a big blow. And bringing in Matt Jones and Junior Lewis to replace Lenny – I'm sorry, you just can't do that. But also I think the job was too big for him. There was a lot of testosterone in the dressing room, some very big characters. That may have been one of the reasons he got rid of Steve Walsh. If you can't control your dressing room, then you've lost it. He tried to compensate by signing Dennis Wise, but his legs had gone. Peter spent a lot of money, but his signings weren't good enough."

You played a big part in the 2002/03 promotion...

"Fair play to Dave Bassett who'd brought Paul Dickov and Brian Deane in, they were brilliant for us. We still had Muzzy, Ian Walker in goal, and me and Matty Elliott at the back. You had to think that we had a chance.

#FEARLESS

And the club's financial problems meant we had wage deferrals, so our backs were against the wall and we came out fighting."

Still, you left for Stoke the next season...

"Yes, I really didn't want to leave Leicester, but my relationship with Micky Adams had come to a head. He wouldn't listen to me and I wouldn't listen to him because I thought I was right. I thought his training regime was archaic, and the fact we got relegated proved my point. We had a lot of older players – Ferdinand, Nalis, Hignett, me and Matt Elliott. I thought that should be managed in training. With the sports science in the modern game, if the computer says you aren't up to it, you don't train. The older players were struggling, and then they were expected to go out on a Saturday and perform for 90 minutes. Look at the stats and see how many late goals we let in. I let Micky know my thoughts, but he wasn't listening. I'm not one for sitting on the bench. I didn't want to go, and felt bad about it – but then a week later came La Manga!"

As a coach, how do you analyse our Premier League title win?

"It was Slaven Bilic who said, 'Everyone knows how Leicester play, but it's different coping with it when you're out there.' One

"I nearly went to Celtic that summer, because Martin wanted to take Neil and me up there."

important thing was that the majority of the players who started the season finished it, as well. Robert Huth was fit for the majority of the season, so was Danny Drinkwater, Jamie Vardy, N'Golo Kanté. They were a very good team. Fuchs was brilliant. Simpson was brilliant. The defensive unit was very strong. Because they knew they weren't going to get a lot of the ball, they concentrated on that. They had the quality of Mahrez, Drinkwater and Kanté, and the pace of Vardy. Too many teams came with a plan, thinking, 'This is how we're going to turn them over,' when they should have been thinking about how to stop Vardy scoring. Teams didn't adapt their tactics to play against Leicester. Whenever Leicester lost the ball there were immediately seven or eight players back in defence, and I think Robert Huth should take a lot of credit for marshalling that."

It was beautiful, wasn't it?

"*Yes!* Yes, it was."

"Me and Frank Burrows were put in charge for a few weeks. I wasn't ready for it and I didn't really want it."

Balls to the five-year plan

Andrew TAYLOR

We sat in the Gordon Banks Lounge with the City chairman, enjoying a chat over a cuppa and an LCFC-branded biscuit. Which one of us still has.

How would you describe the current financial health of Leicester City?

"Here are the facts: three years ago in the Premier League the club had a turnover of nearly £40 million. Last year in the Championship, with a parachute payment, it was £20 million. Now we're having to do without the £7 million parachute payment. When you drop two thirds of your revenues, it's a pretty unpalatable situation. Rob Kelly is the one man who can really transform this, so he's at the epicentre of everything we do. The majority of fans probably don't know who the chairman is and probably don't care. They know who the manager is, and they want a manager who can drive the team forward."

Are you involved in signing new players?

"Yes, every one that we've done latterly.

Tim Davies does the guts of it all and then I'm the one who's there to play nasty cop. As season-ticket holders, you wouldn't like to think that we were giving your money away loosely. I look back over the last few years at the approach we adopted where we had short contracts for players... My kids have got bloody drawers full of shirts with players' names on the back who played for City 20 times. Its crazy, isn't it?"

Chris Makin. We wouldn't know him if he was sitting there in the corner...

"On the top floor of the Banks Suite there's a Legends thing where the players have the programme from their first game and their last game. I'm really struggling to remember who some of those players are from around 2004, and I went to probably every home game at the time."

From a business sense, how soon do we need to be back in the Premier League?

"As of August 2007. You know, 'We have a five-year plan to go up' – that's all balls. I can't plan beyond the next transfer window at the moment. I think Rob has got an opportunity with this group of players to go for it this season. I think one of the things in his favour is some good young kids coming through. James Wesolowski emerged so strongly and so quickly. Richard Stearman. Look at Chris O'Grady, as well. People said he went to Rushden a boy and came back a man. I can't help it, I'm optimistic. I don't think we've had a City manager since Martin O'Neill that's going into a new season with as much support as Rob has got. Rob plays to win. Some coaches play not to lose – five across the middle of the park, one up front. Take a striker off and put a defender on to save a point. Rob's got a very counter-intuitive approach to football, I think."

The beginning of the end

"Have you seen *The Sun* this morning?" Peter Taylor greeted us. Yes, front pages were stuck all around the Belvoir Drive canteen. Page 3 girl Jilly Johnson was doing 'The Bump' with a young football star – who, 26 years on, was not only City's but also England's new manager.

Did your new England role surprise you?

"Very much so, yes. I made it very clear straight away that I wasn't ready for it, didn't want it yet, but always said I would help out if needed. I never thought that it would involve being manager for a game."

Have you enjoyed your time here so far?

"I'm enjoying it. I haven't enjoyed the last two games, but the players have responded very well and it's been as difficult for them as it has been for me. For me to follow Martin was very difficult, and it was difficult for the players to have someone else come along. But to have the start we had was terrific. I think that after eight games we deserved to be top of the table."

The players seemed to switch on to your new methods fairly quickly...

"You've got to have players that are willing to change. Leicester City for four years have played 5-3-2. At the moment, I've carried on the 5-3-2, apart from one game, but I'd like to change things round a bit more so that we can play different systems in different matches."

Some players, such as Savage and Impey, have flourished under your management...

"It's all different styles and opinions. I might have a problem with a particular player that another manager wouldn't."

What can you tell us about Stan?

"Oh, how long have you got? I told him I was looking forward to working with him and how much I rated him. But everything changed when Stan came to me wanting a new contract. I felt he should have got himself 100 per cent fit, got back into the side, score half a dozen goals, and then come looking for a new contract. But Stan was thinking that the club had promised him something before I got here. I think he signed with a view to looking at it again if he did well. Five and a half games and four goals later, Stan thought he'd done well."

Did you know Jim Bloomfield once saw you as the 'missing piece' in his jigsaw?

"No, I didn't. He was a gentleman, and always got the best out of people at Orient. Oh well, he got me in the end! Perhaps not quite the same player by then..."

> "My only reservation was looking at what Martin achieved, thinking how much further can it go?"

Peter TAYLOR

Mark WALLINGTON

Keeping up appearances

Three hundred and thirty-one consecutive starts, Wally made for City – before Chic Bates put a stud-hole in his thigh in that epic FA Cup quarter-final of 1982. When we visited our hero at home in Heckington, Lincolnshire, Mark took us to the pub and wouldn't let us pay a penny for our meals or drinks.

Do you remember your debut for City?

"Wooooh, do I?! West Ham at home, 11th March 1972? I remember getting my hand trodden on by the centre-forward and I jumped up, not really to have a go, but just to say something. I realised it was Clyde Best, so I just said, 'Sorry'. I was extremely nervous because it was a huge step up from Walsall to the First Division. I'd been thrown straight in so I didn't know any of the lads. But they wanted to help me settle in and they'd do anything for me. Fortunately, I kept a clean sheet, and Nishy got two."

You were an understudy to Peter Shilton for a few seasons...

"I was very appreciative of Peter's time, and the work that he put in on me was first class. I think he could afford to do that, for one because I wasn't a threat. He was so well established, and he's one of the most confident, self-believing chaps that you'd ever meet. It was what I needed because I'd missed out on all that professional training before

and I needed to catch up very quickly. To work under the England keeper was super for me. But I knew at one stage I'd be pushing him, because I also had great self-belief and great self-confidence. I wasn't there to be his understudy forever. After I'd been at the club about a year he made it clear that he wanted to move on and Leicester wasn't big enough. I'm not sure that Stoke was any bigger, was it? It wasn't the Liverpools or Manchesters that I thought he would have gone for."

You came into a fine Bloomfield side...

"They were some of the best players that I ever had the privilege of playing with. Playing against the top sides, they seemed to draw it out of us; but we couldn't always turn it on against the lower sides. If we met a more physical side, then they could ride us a bit. Possibly we didn't have the mixture quite right. I always thought, and Jimmy would say this too, we were always two players short."

A number that grew considerably under Frank McLintock's management...

"One memory that stands out was in training. Roger Davies came up with a cracking plan where he'd do a special whistle when we were to push up. That might have worked all right on the training ground but if you were somewhere like Old Trafford with 60,000 people in there and his mouth was dry, you could sort of just about hear a raspberry sound: *thruuuurpp!* Another classic – I shouldn't be telling you these, and I shouldn't be laughing – we had a free-kick worked out where one would run over the ball and down the side of the wall; the next man would run over the ball and go to the left; the third man would backheel it and the fourth man would have a shot. So we tried it. The first man's gone right, the second man's gone left, the third one's run over it, the fourth backheels it... and there's nobody left. I'm stood in the goal with my white handkerchief out because there are eight of them running at me!"

How did you get on with Jock Wallace?

"He's probably the man I've admired most in the game. He taught me so much about life. As skipper of the club, one of my jobs was to check the apprentices' bank books on a Monday. He had as great a concern for those boys as he did for his first team. We couldn't understand a word he was saying for the first two years and we got promoted, and then as soon as we worked out how to understand his accent, we were relegated! Manchester United were interested in me at one stage. Ajax were interested. Chelsea asked Jock about me and he said, 'I want £200,000 for Mark, it's as simple as that.' They offered £200,000, so he upped the price to £250,000. They offered £250,000, so he upped the price to £300,000. I said, 'Gaffer, what's going on here?' Jock said, 'I've not had any bids.' I said, 'I know for a fact you have because Chelsea are on the phone saying they've offered £325,000 and you've still turned it down.' Jock went all gruff then and said, 'Well, you just get them on the phone to me and I'll have a word with them.' I think he just didn't want me to leave."

Was there a time in your years at City when you felt you were playing your best?

"Yes... from about 1972 to about... 1985. Just those 13 years. You always used to

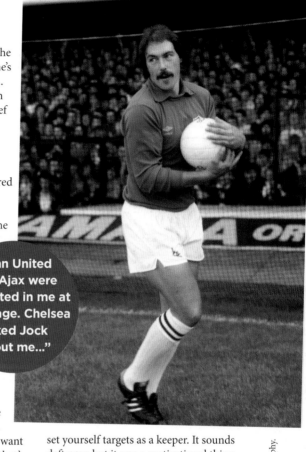

"Man United and Ajax were interested in me at one stage. Chelsea asked Jock about me..."

set yourself targets as a keeper. It sounds daft now, but it was a motivational thing where I set off to be the first keeper not to concede a goal all season. After the first couple of games, I'd say, 'Okay, we'll try and keep it to 20, then!'"

Have you got a favourite save of yours?

"You do need luck as a keeper. I remember playing at the old Victoria Ground, Stoke. It was a mudheap, like Filbert Street. This lad whacked the ball from 15 yards, bottom right-hand corner, and I'm thinking, 'Well, I've got to go after it even though it's beaten me.' But it stuck in the mud a split second before I got my hand to it. Everyone thought it was a fantastic save, but I could have walked over and picked it up. It was stuck fast!"

Photo: Neville Chadwick Photography.

Jimmy WALSH

The Mk.I Walshy Deluxe

With 91 goals in 199 appearances up to 1964, Jimmy Walsh was a nippy, quick-thinking inside-right. At one time, he used to shift 300 copies of _The FOX_ from his news shop near the Clock Tower, so finally we persuaded Jimmy to talk old times in his home near Western Park.

Did you have any hesitation in coming down to Leicester from Celtic, your boyhood favourites?

"No. The move to England was what all young players were looking for at that time, because the money was a lot better. In fact it was two pounds better! A week! In the end, we got a rise from £12 a week to £14. I think I finished on £20."

Was there a goal bonus or appearance money to boost that?

"No, you're joking. Sadly not. Maybe we didn't worry about money enough. We were quite happy to be getting paid to play

football. It was a good life. When I look back, I think, 'Where did we go wrong?'"

What was Matt Gillies like as a boss?

"He'd been the coach before David Halliday was sacked so he already knew all the players. He developed a style that had a deep-lying centre-forward. It was the kind of thing the Hungarians had. He was a very likeable chap, as well. He was the best manager Leicester ever had, until Martin O'Neill came along. I think Martin pips Matt to that title."

What did the training consist of then?

"It was mostly running. And then on a Tuesday we'd have an eleven-a-side game – Scots v English. It was easy to pick, and a good way to give a wee bit of edge to it! The Scots usually won, unlike the Home Internationals."

Early on, you played alongside Arthur Rowley...

"Yes, I did. How to describe Arthur Rowley? I've never seen anybody who could hit the ball harder. That was number one. If he got the ball anywhere near the box then it was a goal. If he got it in the middle of the field then he'd maybe fall over it! He was a powerful chap but he could turn on a sixpence and – _bang!_ – the ball was in the net. He was deadly accurate, I've never seen anyone who could hit the target like Arthur. The balls were like cannonballs then and they flashed into the net."

What were your strengths as a striker?

"I would say I was quite quick and I could nip on to chances. If there was a loose ball, I'd get there first. I should have scored more goals than I did, and I blame my eyesight for that. I did score quite a few goals. But it was only near the end of my career that they found out that my eyesight was bad."

You were one of the first players to experiment with contact lenses...

"They were nothing like the ones they have today. These were hard, and the size of your whole eye! After you'd been running around for a bit you'd get fluid on them and you wouldn't be able to see at all. It was a disaster."

You led City out at the FA Cup final in 1961. How did that feel?

"It was a strange day because we were a bit bemused by Matt's team selection. I still don't understand it to this day. He dropped Ken Leek, who had scored in every round. I don't know why he did it. That's something I could never quite forgive Matt for because I think it cost us the Cup. Every time we'd played against Spurs, Leek and I had always scored goals. So they were quite happy when they found out Leek wasn't playing."

Could it have been for disciplinary reasons?

"As far as I know, Ken didn't do anything wrong. Having thought hard about it, the only little thing I could come up with is that Ken could be a bit daft sometimes. When we got to the final, Ken said, 'Right, I'm only going to play in FA Cup finals and international matches for the rest of the season!'"

1962/63 was the season of the big freeze. At one point we were top of the league and in the Cup final...

"City came up with this chemical pitch treatment that meant we could keep playing while everyone else was frozen off. But it ruined the pitch for years to come. It was like clay, there was hardly any grass on it. Because we'd kept playing, we had an advantage. When they had to play us, they were a bit rusty."

Do you have one moment that was the high spot of your City career?

> "Johnny Morris was a very clever player. He could find you perfectly with a ball from anywhere."

"When I scored the opening goal in the FA Cup semi-final second replay against Sheffield United. Howard Riley was on the right wing and he fizzed the ball in. The goalkeeper spilled it and it span a wee bit away from him. I don't know how I got to it but I scooped it in. As that went in the net I thought, 'That's it, we're at Wembley.'"

We've got a DVD with that goal on it...

"I'd better not watch it, it might not be as good as I remember!"

Do you still enjoy watching City?

"I haven't been down that much this season. I'm still a bit shocked that we're in Division Three. It isn't right is it? We were always up there. If not in the First Division then at least challenging to get there. It's very sad. Now we're playing Yeovil... I used to play them when I was manager of Rugby Town!"

"David Halliday used to say, 'Ah well, go out and do the best you can.' If we were winning then nobody bothered us with formations."

179

Steve WALSH

Tough at the top

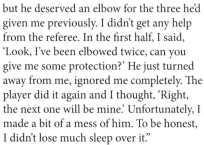

Walshy was out with a torn cruciate when we visited him at home near Loughborough, where his wife juggled children and a Lancashire hotpot.

The first thing Bryan Hamilton did as City manager was to sign you from Wigan. Did you get on well with him?

"I did at Wigan, but not so well at Leicester. I don't think he quite managed the step up to the First Division. At Wigan he tended to run the show but at City he didn't quite treat the players right."

Did any of the older pros help you out when you arrived as a young lad?

"Ian Wilson, Ali Mauchlen and Russell Osman were the main ones, but I was old enough to handle most things by then. I learnt quite a lot from Russell and we were beginning to really click together, but then he left. I think he was asking for too much money, so they let him go. Looking back through my career though, I think Colin Hill and Richard Smith compare with anyone that I've played alongside. Their strength and awareness are brilliant."

Back in Division Two, the season started badly for City, and for you personally...

"I wouldn't say David Geddis deserved what he got, but he deserved an elbow for the three he'd given me previously. I didn't get any help from the referee. In the first half, I said, 'Look, I've been elbowed twice, can you give me some protection?' He just turned away from me, ignored me completely. The player did it again and I thought, 'Right, the next one will be mine.' Unfortunately, I made a bit of a mess of him. To be honest, I didn't lose much sleep over it."

That eleven-match ban for breaking his jaw seemed to create an image for you...

"I suppose my mistake is thinking that if people can give it out, they can take it as well; but football isn't like that. The only time I've ever got into trouble is when someone has been out of order to me. Maybe I'm a bit cumbersome in the way I do it – the ref always seems to be looking at me. The refs treat me like crap, turning away or blanking me. Some will even wind me up, saying something sarcastic or laughing at me. They aren't really supposed to behave like that. If a player's trying to kick you or elbow you, then you have to do something to protect yourself."

What about Steve Bull? Would you shake hands and have a drink after the game, or is there real animosity there?

"I would do off the field, but when you get out on the pitch things are different. He provoked me first in both the sending-off incidents. He should have been off already for an elbow at Molineux. The ref turned away again. I wasn't quite discreet enough, but I hardly touched him. He made a meal of it and got me sent off, but that's his job. That's football. Whatever anyone says, if we get someone sent off, we're pleased. Bully didn't hurt me when he swung a punch at me at Filbert Street, but he deserved to be sent off for that, so I stayed down."

What did David Pleat do right when he first took over as City manager?

"He didn't upset anyone, and we did different things like playing golf or going to health places and things like that. We were well looked after. But after that, the way he treated and talked to players made him unpopular, and the way he wanted the game played was out of another world. He thinks he's a very clever person, and anyone who doesn't come up to that gets a bit of contempt. One of his training routines was having players warm up in the 'D' of the penalty area, and he'd be asking you questions like, 'What's the capital of Norway?' while you were doing your exercises. He absolutely destroyed Alan Paris, because he was a bit dozy. The only way to combat it was to come straight back at him and speak your mind."

Brian Little is working out well, so far...

"His organisation and discipline are his strong points. He knows how the game should be played, and he picks a team for a certain game. Sometimes you wonder why he's picked a certain player, but he knows how to get results better than anyone. How we've won some games, I'll never know, but it usually works. He's got everybody battling for him. You want to win for him."

When you came back from suspension last season, you were suddenly playing up front. How did that come about?

"I always play up front in training

matches, and I enjoy scoring goals. I always thought I could do a job up front, given the right service. I'd always enjoyed steaming in for headers, but now I don't have to run back down the field and get exhausted!"

We were back at Wembley last season against Swindon. Did you think we were dead and buried at 3-0 down?

"Yes I did, really. But you just keep thinking, 'Let's get

"I wasn't quite discreet enough, but I hardly touched him. He made a meal of it and got me sent off."

one back,' and then keep driving at them. When we got the third, well! It's hard to describe how we felt, with the supporters going mad. I was really pleased for them because at one point it had looked like it wasn't worth their while coming. I hope nobody went home at 3-0! I thought we were going to win it then, but the penalty was a real kick in the bollocks. We were gutted. I was thinking, 'Right, let's get another one,' but it was too late and we were out on our feet."

Steve WALSH

Blue blood spilled

Fifteen years in a blue shirt, and an amazing 53 goals – not to mention a League record 12 red cards. Steve Walsh was Leicester City royalty. We met in the Old Crown in Fleckney, and Steve told us about the end of days.

How did you feel when Martin O'Neill finally left the club?

"It was a really sad day for Leicester City. A terrible day. We had disagreements at certain times but I think overall we had faith in each other. Anyway, there isn't really any arguing with him because he has to be right! I wish Martin had stayed – because then I would probably have stayed as well. I signed a one-year contract and he did say to me that, whatever happened after that year, I would either be kitman, washerwoman or whatever, but I would have a job at the football club. In hindsight, I really wish he and I had

stayed because I should never have been allowed to leave Leicester. People say that I left Leicester – well, I did leave, but I was forced out, that's for sure."

Once O'Neill left, you applied for the manager's job. What led to that decision?

"I think because I'd been at the club such a long time, and I thought that I could keep together what Martin had built up. I wouldn't have unravelled the team like Peter Taylor did. There was a very special spirit about the side on and off the pitch, and I was part of that spirit. Once that spirit was gone, the team had gone as well. There was money there to buy the right, good quality players. Tony Cottee and I had sat down together and put a lot of thought into what players we would try to buy in if we were given the chance. We had to put our plan forward to the board of directors, and I think they were quite surprised by how thorough we'd been with our plans. But I think they'd made their minds up before we'd even got into that meeting."

Did you and Tony Cottee actually go through a formal interview?

"Yes, I think they were impressed with our presentation but used the excuse that we didn't have our coaching badges. Well, Martin O'Neill didn't have his coaching badge, either."

In came Peter Taylor...

"I knew from the very first day he arrived that we were going backwards. I knew for months and months that City were in big trouble. I don't know who okayed that much spending on players, or who decided they were the right ones to bring in. Martin had always been very, very shrewd in the market and wouldn't mind taking

a year to buy a player. But Peter Taylor rushed it and wasted it. To me, he killed the club and he knows it. I'll never speak to him again and he'll never speak to me. And the way he back-stabbed me as well was completely bang out of order. His right-hand man, Steve Butler from Gillingham – I don't think he liked me anyway, I played against him once and stood on his foot – every morning he'd tell me a different club were supposedly in for me. They were desperate for me to go, and in the end Taylor just asked me, 'We want you to leave.' Simple as that. He said, 'I'm going to make it hard work for you.' I didn't deserve to be treated like that."

What tipped you over the edge?

"I ended up training for a day with Wolves. *Wolves!* I thought, 'What the f*** am I doing here?' I couldn't do it to Leicester fans and I couldn't do it to myself. I had to cancel that one. Tony Cottee told me that Norwich would offer me a year's contract. I thought I could handle that; I wasn't wanted at my club. There was no response from the chairman. I think I had enough value to be kept on – run the Youth team, or whatever, but be involved around the club and in the dressing room. I wanted to contribute to that spirit even if I wasn't playing. But I was allowed to go by a manager who wanted me out and those upstairs not saying anything. Me, Tony and Stan Collymore were all forced out of there. I just think that I've been wasted, really. I think I had a lot to offer."

Who was your best defensive partner?

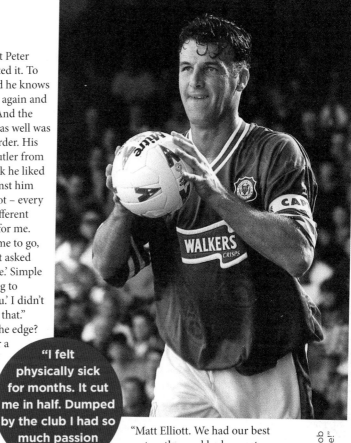

"I felt physically sick for months. It cut me in half. Dumped by the club I had so much passion for."

"Matt Elliott. We had our best years together and had a great understanding. I had a few good defensive partners but it has to be Matt, without a doubt."

And your best game in a blue shirt?

"It has to be the Play-off final against Derby when I got two goals. I think that game was the making of me. Also, lifting the League Cup at Hillsborough was very special for me. As far as the best feeling goes, Steve Thompson's equaliser at Wembley against Swindon to make it 3-3 takes some beating. That was fantastic. And also Fulham at home in the League Cup when I scored the equaliser after making such a balls-up earlier on. And the equaliser against Arsenal as well – put that one in for Ian Wright!"

"I've applied for the Leicester job every time it's been available!"

183

Arlo WHITE

The voice of soccer

In the Marquis of Wellington, we talked Leicester City with Arlo White – now the voice of NBC Sports' live coverage of the Premier League in the USA.

These have been great times to be a City fan, how have you enjoyed it?

"Well, it's been brilliant, hasn't it? I did a few of the European trips. I didn't make Madrid though, as my wife had emergency surgery just before we were due to go. As she was coming round from the operation she said, 'You must go. Go to Madrid.' I said, 'I appreciate that, but you are still heavily sedated!' Now City have asked me to do a magazine piece, but I'm not much of a writer. I think my writing peaked when I was doing articles for *The FOX* in the early '90s! I always preferred talking. When I was a kid I used to sit in the East Stand doing my own commentaries into a Goodmans recording Walkman. This was during the David Pleat

era. It wasn't as embarrassing as it could have been because there was so much room you could pick your seat and sit on your own. Usually it was appalling, but there was one brilliant game that stands out – the 4-3 against Leeds United. We were 2-0 down at half-time and then Paul Ramsey came on and inspired us to a 4-3 win. I bought the video of that game, the one the club brought out with the single camera."

Your career started at Radio Derby...

"My first game was Mickleover Sports against Bedlington Terriers in the FA Vase, which generated quite a lot of interest because there was a floodlight failure – and the same again at the replay! For the third game I was pitchside with a radio car and a microphone instead of a mobile phone. The real thing! When I went to my first Derby County press conference, I sat there thinking, 'I really want to do this'. When we got back from travelling, I answered an advert in *The Guardian*: 'Two broadcasters required for 5 Live'. I got a phone call on the train on the way back. I thought, 'Bloody hell, they let you down quick, the BBC'. It was Duncan Jones on the phone and he said, 'We'd like to offer you a six-month contract at BBC Radio Sport'. I was absolutely gobsmacked. I rang my mum and she was crying. I was 27 then, and I thought back to my time with a tape machine in the East Stand. It was what I'd always wanted to do."

After a spell on *Test Match Special*, how did you break into football commentating?

"I went to Seattle. That came about because I covered five Super Bowls for 5 Live. I met someone who covered Seattle Seahawks, and he told me they were launching an MLS team and we should keep in touch. They started talking to me about taking over the commentator's job in 2010, but I gave the BBC one more chance. They said, 'Can you do the World Cup?' Up to then, they'd given me Torquay v Yeovil on 5 Live Sports Extra and Bristol City v West Brom on Boxing Day. So I did five games for them in South Africa, and then moved to Seattle."

Does your fan status ever bias your broadcasting?

"When I moved to Seattle I was less bothered about being neutral. I was Tweeting things about Leicester as a way of keeping in touch with home. But when I got the job covering the Premier League with NBC, I tried to keep it a bit quieter. But then, as we were closing in on the Premier League title, suddenly the *New York Times* and *Washington Post* and ESPN all wanted to interview me as a Leicester fan."

Where were you on the big night?

"I was at Stamford Bridge. What an incredible night that was. I'd done the Man United game the day before and, although we got a point at Old Trafford, Danny Drinkwater was sent off and Robert Huth looked like he'd be getting some retrospective action against him. I was still convinced that we were going to lose out somehow. If Spurs had reduced the gap with a win at Chelsea, we'd have been going into that Everton game with a weakened side. Of course, Tottenham were 2-0 up with about 20 minutes to go and then Cahill got that header. And then Eden Hazard came on. As soon as that shot left his boot you knew it was

"Favourite City match? Everton at home, when we were presented with the Premier League trophy."

going in. I remember trying to keep a lid on it and do the job right, while inside I was thinking, 'Oh my God! We're going to do this!' I feel like I missed out a bit on the unprecedented scenes back home in Leicester, but on the other hand I was actually there calling the moment."

What did you do once you were off air?

"I went with Graeme Le Saux to his favourite Italian restaurant on the Kings Road and we shared a couple of bottles of red. On the night I couldn't quite compute what had happened, and I still can't, really. I wouldn't swap our story over the last ten years with anybody. It's been astonishing. Ten years ago we were in the process of getting relegated to the third tier. I spoke to Iain Hume about that, and he said missing that penalty against Sheffield Wednesday was the worst moment of his career. He moved to Barnsley, because at that point in time they were a more alluring prospect than Leicester City. After the Stoke game when we went down, I remember thinking, 'Where do we go from here?' We had no money. The best players in a poor side were leaving. Eight years later we won the Premier League."

Bukta Boys: Arlo and college-mate Martin Crowson, now Tigers correspondent at the *Mercury*.

Let's get physical

Mike WHITLOW

We caught up with Leicester City's fiercely committed left-back in the dugout at Burton Albion, where Mike was head of the club's Academy.

How did it begin, back at Witton Albion?

"I'd started out as a centre-forward, and wasn't known for tackling or heading, but after six months at left-back I was flying in and smashing anything above ground. We played against Bangor City, and I was up against this old pro as a cocky little 18 year old. I went round him once and he said, 'You won't do that again, son.' So I did, and he nailed me. Tackling was tackling, then. I tried it again and he hit me again, and then again, until I thought, 'Sod this.' When he got it, I nailed him and thought 'Yes!' I felt great, and it was a big turning point in my career. Going from a big girl's blouse to a left-back that loved tackling."

A natural fit for Leeds United?

"I'd only been playing at left-back for a few months but Howard Wilkinson saw something in me. After a couple of days' training he threw me into the Leeds side

for the Simod Cup. That team went on to win the last ever League Championship. But when they bought England left-back Tony Dorigo, I knew my chances would be limited. Fortunately, Leicester came in for me, and that worked out fantastically well."

Six months later we were at Wembley...

"Yes, Steve bloody Walsh gave a penalty away and David Speedie dived and Blackburn scored. I'll remember that for the rest of my life! With all those Play-off finals and the League Cup, there's always one vivid little bit that you'll remember out of the whole day. The Swindon game was the moment they got that penalty, and I hammer Pooley for this because he still says he never touched him. I tell him, 'You nearly knocked his ruddy head off, like Carl Froch!' 'I never touched him!' There was also the Claridge shin against Crystal Palace. He still swears it didn't go in off his shin! And Paul Williams missing that header on the line in the Derby game..."

Did you know you're the only player who appeared in all of City's 12 Play-off semis and finals?

"No, that's good! Simon Grayson must've been close?"

Having come back from 3-0 down against Swindon, and then still lost, you looked traumatised out on the pitch...

"I was absolutely gutted, because we were dead and buried at one point. Let's be fair, Glen Hoddle was incredible in the first half. He was pinging it everywhere, 40 yards, on a sixpence. But to go down to another penalty like that was gutting. Another opportunity to get into the

Premiership was missed. They grabbed it and we didn't."

One year on, we faced the Derby County 'Dream Team' at Wembley...

"I think we were just physically stronger than them. They had some very good players but they couldn't deal with our physicality, lads like Jimmy Willis and Gary Coatsworth. Coatsworth looked like a mass murderer: he'd kick himself, never mind anyone else! I think the ball went out to Simpson very early on and Coats just absolutely buried him. They knew what was coming."

Halfway through that first Premiership season, it was all change, managerially...

"Yes, Brian Little came back for Simon Grayson, and there was also talk that he wanted to take me to Villa. So I sat down with Mark McGhee and he said, 'No, you're not going, you stay here.' And then he'd gone! Football always surprises you. He thought Wolves was a better option, and off he went."

And we got stuck with Martin O'Neill!

"It took a little while for him to get things moving, but wasn't it great when he did? Martin kept all the letters he was sent, telling him how rubbish he was. Believe me, he kicked every ball with you. He headed every ball. He made every tackle. You'll never meet a manager like him for passion, as well as being a raving nutcase. He must have covered 20 miles per game. He loves it. And that passion and enthusiasm rubbed off on the players, who would have done anything for him. Ask anyone who's played for him. Half the players wanted to fight him when he

> "The keeper dropped it, a yard out – but I scored at the Stretford End, where I used to stand."

first came in, because he was such a different personality, and he'd rave with that Irish accent. But what he did for the club was absolutely magnificent."

After the Palace Play-off, we were much better prepared for the Premier League...

"Yes, we had players like Muzzy Izzet and Matt Elliott coming in. Emile Heskey was maturing. And Steve Guppy came in."

Was that another Tony Dorigo moment?

"It was interesting. A bid came in from Bolton and Martin said, 'If they don't offer you a stupid contract, then stay here.' He wanted to keep me as part of a three centre-back role, but I still wanted to run up and down that line. A few years later, Sam Allardyce said to me, 'Whoever told you that you could cross that halfway line wants f***ing shooting.' He said, 'Stay at the back and head it and kick it, because that's what you're good at.'"

"If there's anyone you want on the end of a scruffy chance, it's Claridge, socks rolled down and a piece of cardboard for a shinpad."

187

Right back where I started from

Steve WHITWORTH

Coalville lad Steve was a fixture at right-back throughout the '70s, winning seven England caps before moving on to Sunderland. When we spoke on the phone to Steve at home in Bucks, he was still a black cab driver, covering Wembley.

You broke into the City side in a Second Division title season. What made our home-grown defence such a tight unit?

"The easiest answer to that was having Peter Shilton in goal, because I think he was worth about 20 goals a season. He really was sensational. There were days when he was unbeatable in training. You couldn't get the ball past him no matter how close you got. And it was a good balance. David [Nish] was a top quality defender with a superb football brain. Crossy was maybe the best centre-half never to play for England, and you knew exactly what you were getting with big John [Sjoberg]. He was never a great footballer, but he was a very strong and competitive defender."

Was the First Division a big step up?

"When we were in the Second Division, Frank brought in Bobby Kellard and

Willie Carlin and they were tough, focused players who also knew about the dirty side of the game, and they taught me a thing or two. They were a part of our defensive unit, really. When we took a step up we were facing players who could win a game however you were set up, because they were top players. Players like Stevie Heighway of Liverpool, John Robertson at Forest and Leighton James of Burnley. I had lots of personal battles with these players, which I thoroughly enjoyed. I was quite fast, so they couldn't beat me down the outside, which was always their primary aim. The one time I got taken to the cleaners in that first season was Ian Storey-Moore against Forest. I had no idea what he was going to do next."

Frank O'Farrell got City promoted, but then quickly left for Manchester United...

"Yes, I don't blame Frank for that. But then in came Jim and he was a complete class act, for me. A great footballer in his own right. He could watch a first half and then come down at half-time and change a couple of things round and you'd have a completely different game."

The season started with the Charity Shield, beating Liverpool 1-0 at Filbert Street. Your only goal for Leicester...

"Yes, I don't know what I was doing up there, to be honest – and, even weirder, it was with my left foot, which was normally only for standing on. I'd bombed forward and put a low cross over; Rodney Fern had gone in but Ray Clemence came to meet him. As I'd kept running, the loose ball fell for me a yard out and I couldn't miss it."

You held that number 2 shirt for nine years. Did you never have any challengers?

"Not really. Only when Jock came along, with a new philosophy to Jimmy, did I feel that maybe I wasn't playing so well. It became apparent to me pretty quickly that I wasn't his cup of tea. He liked players that got stuck in, but that wasn't really my style. It was different to Jimmy's time, when it had been a real pleasure to play. Suddenly these wide boys arrived and the whole ethos of the place had changed. We became a team off the pitch doing everything together, and it was a wonderful time. You had all these strong, noisy characters like Alan Birchenall and Dennis Rofe – and then Frank Worthington arrived! They were great players, too. I couldn't really go wrong, either giving the ball to Keith on the right, or Frank in the middle."

What games stand out for you during that time?

"Well, that Cup game at QPR was a bit special, with Joe Waters scoring two pearlers on his debut. Every dog has his day, and Joe was superb in that match. It was a wonderful game. But maybe overall we lacked that bit of discipline to hold on to what we had in a game. We were gung-ho!"

Did Jim's exit come as a surprise?

"It was absolutely shocking, and I was desperately sad to see him go. Eleventh place, and he got sacked. Says it all. And what happened after that, eh?"

Frank McLintock arrived...

"Oh yes, I'm sure I saw his first game when he came down from Scotland. A brilliant player, both as a midfielder at Leicester and a defender at Arsenal. He was a great leader on the pitch, I'm not sure why it didn't work out."

Did you sense trouble at the time?

"I think that from quite early on Frank was panicking a bit. Admittedly, results

"We were overrun with Cockneys! They wanted to go out all the time, and the social side really took off."

were bad so perhaps he had to try something new, but he kept changing the team every week. He was a lovely chap, but was very, very honest. If a player was having a nightmare, then perhaps it wasn't always best for them to be told. Man management is knowing who to coax and who to bollock. But we'd gone from playing under a hugely experienced manager in Jim, to someone with no experience at all. Like throwing a kid into the first team before he's ready, you can do more damage than good."

I am the law

Tommy WILLIAMS

At the end of his football career, no-nonsense Tommy made a sideways move from bossing defences to policing the streets of Leicester. We spoke to him on the phone while he was in his car. And, yes, he did pull over into a lay-by.

People are sometimes surprised to find out that you were born in West Lothian...

"My dad moved us to Leicester when I was about nine years old. He was an officer at Leicester Prison. I definitely had my accent back then, but I suppose when you're a kid you tend to lose it more than an adult does."

How were you first spotted by Leicester?

"Strangely enough, my mum used to go to the same school as Davie Gibson. A few years after we'd moved to Leicester she, completely by chance, bumped into Davie while she was out in town shopping. They got chatting and he arranged for me to go to Belvoir Drive with the young kids. That's how it started with me at Leicester."

How many of your Youth team-mates went on to make a career out of the game?

"Just about everybody in that side went on to play first-team football, if not at Leicester then elsewhere. Winston White, Larry May, John O'Neill had quite long careers. It was a very successful time. These days you have the Academy director who

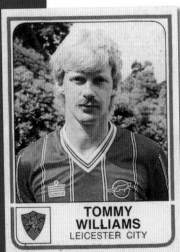

TOMMY WILLIAMS
LEICESTER CITY

has several coaches underneath him and more part-time coaches during the week. But George Dewis did all that by himself. It was quite an amazing job he used to do."

Frank McLintock gave you your debut, which was one of the era's few plus points...

"Frank signed a few players approaching the end of their careers and it didn't work out, but as a young lad it was a brilliant experience and I loved it! I scored three goals that season. One more and I'd have been joint top scorer with Roger Davies and Geoff Salmons. Pathetic, really!"

How much of an impact did Jock Wallace have on a young player like you?

"Big Jock was unique. In all walks of life you come across people with a good eye for man management, but I have yet to meet anybody who could deal with people like Jock did. He could build you up before you went out for a game and you'd feel ten feet tall when you came out of the tunnel. You expected to win."

Clinching the Second Division title on the last day of the season at Orient must be one of your career highlights?

"You perhaps don't quite realise it at the time. I remember the open-topped bus tour, and we went to Town Hall Square for a reception. I remember Eddie Kelly saying we had to enjoy this as much as we could, because you don't know when it's going to happen again. As a young lad, you just think that sort of thing will happen perhaps every other year... and it doesn't."

That side was relegated after a season in Division One. As a 23 year old, you were one of the older players...

"I can't remember how many points we went down with but I think we did okay. We had some good results. We took Liverpool's home record away. Was it 85 games they'd gone without losing at Anfield? We did the double over them that year. We had a really good group of young players, and if we could have just sustained it a little bit more through the season, it could have been different."

The following season's FA Cup run came to a terrible end at the semi-final against Tottenham...

"It was a freak accident. Tony Galvin was on about the halfway line. He had his back to me and had his foot on top of the ball. I went through him to take the ball and his heel hit my shin and broke it. Normally you'd just get a bruise but it just happened to break. To rub salt into the wounds, as I was being carried round the pitch Ian Wilson scored his own-goal."

Seven months later, you made it back for just four games...

"We were playing a game in the gym and I went to have a shot and one of the lads came in a little bit late and it went again. That set me back another eight months. It was quite difficult for me because there was a change of manager, with Big Jock leaving. Gordon Milne didn't really know me and hadn't seen me play. I don't think I was a big favourite of Milne's, and I wasn't a big fan of his, to tell you the truth. He didn't speak to me over a six-month period until I was fit. Virtually his last words to me were, 'It would probably be better for you and better for the club if you go.' He wasn't my favourite person."

Which strikers caused you most trouble?

"I like to think that nobody ever really turned me over. You used to raise your

> "To rub salt into the wounds, as I was being carried round the pitch Ian Wilson scored his own-goal."

game when you came up against the likes of Ian Rush and Kenny Dalglish. Frank Stapleton was a great striker, too. Knowing that you'd played against the best in Europe and not embarrassed yourself was a good feeling. The best wide man I played against was probably John Robertson. He was the type of player where you knew what he was going to do but you still couldn't stop him. He was that good."

Do you still get recognised by City fans, now you're in the police force?

"Yes, just a couple of days ago I was in uniform, I got out of the car on Uppingham Road and these four lads across the road started chanting my name! Everyone who recognises me wants to talk about my days playing for City. It's better than just being shouted at or abused!"

191

Frank WORTHINGTON

Hello, hello

**We spoke to one of Leicester City's truly
legendary performers on the phone to
his home near Halifax – at a time Frank
was still turning out for his village team.**

Was it always going to be professional
football for you?

"There was no alternative, really. I used
to eat, drink and sleep football. It was
steeped in our family because my dad
used to play for Manchester United. He
was also a trooper at the Battle of Arnhem
in World War II. He was one of the lucky
ones who came out of it with his life.
When I started out with Huddersfield we
used to play our pre-season tournaments
in Holland. One time we played Vitesse
Arnhem, and I went to visit the war
cemetery there, to see the graves of all
the British lads who had lost their lives. It
really put everything into perspective for
me – 18-, 19-, 20-year-old guys going over
there and dying for their country. And
there we were, another group of young
men from Britain only about 20 years
later, but we were there to play football
and have a great time. It really puts your
feet on the ground when you think about
it like that. How lucky were we?"

Before your Leicester move you almost
signed for Liverpool...

"I'll never forget what Bill Shankly said
to me, and I think it's a little illustration
of why he was one of the most successful
people in British football. He said, 'Do you
want to come and play for Liverpool?' I
nodded at him, because it wasn't a difficult
decision. And he added, 'Because we need
you.' They *needed* me? Can you imagine
the impact of that on a young player?
It was fantastic. I went up there, signed
everything, did TV and radio interviews,
and it was all subject to the medical.
Everything was perfect on the medical
exam except for the very last thing I'd
done, which was blood pressure – and it
was high. Now, I was a bit of a rascal at
that time and I was living fast. I was having
a good time on the pitch and a good time
off it, as well. I used to go to this very
select little club in Leeds, the In-Time
club in the Merrion Centre. I used to go in
there, see the dancing girl in a cage, have a
drink – though I was never a big drinker –
have a dance at the disco. Leeds has always
had a very high standard of good-looking
females and it was a brilliant place to go."

How did you feel when Liverpool pulled
out of the deal?

"Well, at the time I thought it was their
bad luck. Ultimately, when I think about
it now, it was my bad luck. Liverpool
were going to pay around £120,000, but
Jimmy got me for a knock-down £80,000.
Leicester was a brilliant move for me."

What were your first impressions of
Leicester?

"Mainly of the Holiday Inn, where they
housed me. All the stars that played at
Bailey's nightclub would stay there. Tom
Jones, Engelbert... We had some fantastic
nights – and as much as we enjoyed
meeting the showbiz stars, they were
interested in meeting the football stars."

How did you get on with Bloomfield?

"Jimmy was the Cool Hand Luke of English football, he oozed charisma and class. He'd drive up to the ground in this massive Jaguar. That came out in the way his team played: we were just about the most watchable team in English football at that time. We used to play a lot of five-a-side football in training. Our first touch was very good, apart from Birch! Weller, Lenny, Jonny Sammels. We loved going in to training at that time. It was a joy-to-be-alive sort of club."

> "I wasn't interested in defenders. If I got the ball into my feet I could do whatever I wanted with it."

Many City fans remember your warm-up routine. Did you used to practise?

"As a youngster, I used to go and kick a ball against a wall – we didn't have a garden – and play keepy-uppies all day long. I can still do five minutes without the ball touching the floor when I'm warming up before five-a-side. Flick it up, catch it on the back of my neck, roll it down my back and flick it back over – easy!"

The 1974 side was probably Jimmy's best. What could he have changed to win some silverware?

"We weren't defensively orientated enough. We were just a little bit short

of toughness in our back line. Frank McLintock played in the previous era for Leicester and I think if he'd played in our era then we would definitely have won something."

You left not long after McLintock took over as City's manager...

"Times were tight, then. I'd just gone through a divorce and things were changing at Leicester, so the right time had come to make a move. It was the gypsy in my soul. I'd always liked moving around and seeing new places here, there

and everywhere. After that it became a constant cycle. Bolton, Birmingham, Leeds, Sunderland, Southampton, Brighton, Tranmere, Preston. Then the doctor told me to get as far away from football as I could – so I signed for Stockport."

"One of my all-time heroes, and I used to baby-sit for him, was Willie Carlin."

Photo: Neville Chadwick Photography.

Doubting Tommy

Steve Walsh's young son charged around Tommy's Melton garden like a two-foot version of his dad, while Elliott Wright and his new sister, Brogan, slumbered. The 'For Sale' sign was all about the kids, see? Our Scottish winger wasn't looking for a move away. Here's why he left City for Middlesbrough later in the summer.

Do you get bored in the close season?

"I have been this summer because we've been waiting on Joanne having the baby, and we've not had a holiday."

You did go away with the club, though?

"Ibiza – that was a good laugh with all the lads but the weather was rubbish. It was all right at night because we went out drinking but during the day we had to keep drinking because there was no sun."

Didn't the management mind?

"No, not for that week. None of them were there. It was just 23 players on our own. The coaching staff went to Majorca."

What do you think of your cult status among Leicester fans?

"It's nice to be like that. The clubs I was at before, I was generally liked. But I tend to find that 95 per cent really love me and five per cent really hate me. There's a bloke stands behind the dugout, behind Brian Little, and when we beat Cambridge 5-0 in the Play-off he was still shouting for Brian Little to get me off! Playing left wing, he can be ten yards away from me, and you can hear it all right. I think Paul Reid hit him in the face with some mud once as he came off the field. I think he's a professional moaner."

Where did you get the idea for your shirt-over-head celebration?

"Actually, I saw it in the Copa America. I think it was a Uruguayan who did it, but he didn't fall down on his arse like I did at Southend. There was this little grass bank behind the goal and obviously I couldn't see where I was going, and I fell over. But then Rooster dived on me and it didn't look so bad."

What were the main factors that turned the club's fortunes around last season?

"Tactically, Brian didn't change that much apart from putting five at the back. The difference was that Brian can sit down and talk to the players. David Pleat couldn't. He was a very good coach, but he couldn't put across to the players what he wanted. I didn't always see eye to eye with him and I was nearly away because of it. You'd walk away from him and maybe hear a sly remark. I got fined a couple of times for having a go back. You don't like to see anyone get sacked, but I knew he'd get another job – I wasn't too sad! When I first got here, he mystified me a bit. He'd write something on the board like, 'One swallow doesn't make a summer,' after we'd won a game. I think that was our one win that season."

What are your recollections of Wembley?

"It was boiling hot. The pitch felt like it had central heating. We were too negative in the first half and too spread out. When we pushed up in the second half, it looked as if we could score. It was a shame that we had so many efforts scrambled off the line because the Blackburn players had really gone. They were just hanging on. If we'd scored, we'd have won it."

What about the Speedie incident?

"There's no question that it was a dive but, to be honest, I would have done the same – although I'd probably have made it look better. The blame has to lie with the ref; but it goes on so much now, you have to do it to keep up with the rest. The refs get taken for a bit of a ride. A game with stakes that high has to be won any way it can, I'm afraid. I thought it was such an obvious dive that I turned to run upfield. By the time I turned round again, Speedie was arguing with a crowd of our players."

Surely not? David Speedie?

"But I wouldn't mind having him in my team, if I'm truthful."

There's been speculation about you...

"There have been a couple of bids but I can't shed much light on it. The 'For Sale' sign outside the house is not referring to me. We're moving because there are too many steps at this house for the kids. I'm quite happy at Leicester – if they can offer me security for my wife and kids. There doesn't seem to be much money around, though. Instead of Kitson leaving, they should have bought someone to play alongside him. City have got to take a

> **"There's no question that Speedie dived but, to be honest, I would have done the same."**

"Tony James was modelling the new all-blue kit, keeping the ball up. Five he got, his record. Well done, Jamesy!"

gamble some time."

When you finally conk out, would you like to stay in the game?

"I've never known anything but football. It's a bit frightening – no qualifications, and a wife and kids to keep. I'm 26, so I should have a few years left, but you never know. Your last game could be one tackle away – especially if you're playing Cambridge! But this is why you have to look after yourself when you play. Obviously, football fans like to see loyalty in a player but, if he had a bad patch, would the club be loyal? They'd get rid of him quick enough. It's a pretty cruel game at times. I don't know about being a manager – looking at Brian Little some mornings, it looks a bit strenuous!"

Ooh! Tommy Wri-ight 2

Tommy WRIGHT

In the boss's office at Nuneaton Town we met Tommy Wright, City's homegrown striker of the Bassett & Adams era. And he made former Forest star Steve Chettle make us a cup of tea.

You signed for City at the age of ten, and later rose through the ranks very rapidly...

"Well, I was scoring loads of goals, and they just seemed to propel me forward really quickly. I hadn't played for the reserves or even the Under-19s, and suddenly there I was on the first-team bench. Dave Bassett and Micky Adams didn't even know I hadn't played for the 19s, and I think Steve Beaglehole and Jon Rudkin got a ticking off over it. I had two unused sub appearances and then I came on against Leeds. The fans were brilliant to me. Obviously, off the back of the old Tommy Wright, they sang my name. It was the same song I used to chant on the terraces. That made me feel ten feet tall, with goosebumps down my spine."

Your full debut came against Forest in 2002/03. You scored the only goal of the game that virtually sealed promotion...

"Yes, Micky told me an hour before the game, and I absolutely shat myself! If he'd told me the previous night, it would have been playing on my mind. I didn't have time to think about it. The goal came from all those years of listening to experienced strikers saying, 'Always follow in on a shot in case the keeper doesn't deal with it.' Jordan Stewart shot from the edge of the area, the keeper blocked it, and there I was in the right place. I have a photo where I have a smile on my face before it's hit the net. It was everything I'd always wanted, and I jumped straight over the hoarding into the crowd. I can't remember if I got booked, and I don't care! I think Trevor Benjamin and Muzzy also jumped over, so he couldn't book all of us. It was something I'd always dreamed of. It was also nice for my dad, who'd been a mad keen Leicester fan all his life. My great-grandad was there, too, and he was crying. It felt great to make my family proud like that."

How did Micky manage you after that?

"Well, he left me out of the next game! And then the next season I was loaned out to Brentford. I was a bit unlucky with managers changing at the wrong time

for me, as Craig Levein came in then. I think, at one point, Mark DeVries had gone 20-odd games without a goal, and some of the crowd were shouting for me to get a chance. But he brought Nathan Blake on instead of me and the fans booed. He didn't like that. It seemed that the more the fans wanted it, the more he wasn't going to do it. It felt a bit like I was challenging him, but it wasn't coming from me. In the end, he sent me to Blackpool on loan. I scored eight goals in 13 games. I returned to Leicester feeling really up for it, and I walked into his office and he completely popped my balloon. He said, 'Barnsley have bid £60,000 for you, and I want you to go.' I was absolutely gutted, I really didn't want to leave. His assistant, Rob Kelly, who I got on very well with, took me outside and said, 'Look, I think you'll come back to haunt him. Make sure you do.' I was close to tears that day. Although I had 18 months left on my contract, I felt that I'd been bullied into leaving."

From Barnsley, via Darlington, you were soon up in the Scottish Premier League...

"Aberdeen is a big football club, and when they play Rangers and Celtic you realise just how big it is. Rangers at home was a full house and really hostile. Everywhere you went, the fans were all over you, getting you to sign their Panini albums and everything. For a lot of the players, though, all they could talk about was going down to England, for better money; but the level they were aiming at was League Two. I said, 'I've come

> **"It seemed the more the fans wanted him to give me a chance, the more he wasn't going to do it."**

from there and, compared to this, League Two is shit!' I told them they wouldn't be playing in front of 60,000 like they did at Parkhead. Even if it was 60,000 people who wanted to kill you!"

Which managers most influenced you?

"Micky Adams, definitely. Mark McGhee. He knew my Leicester connection, and we had a bit of a laugh about him failing and then jumping ship. I also learnt how not to do things from Martin Allen at Brentford. We were up in Hartlepool, training pre-match. He gave us a speech about all being in it together, and doing what we said we'd do – then stripped all his clothes off and swam across a river full of rubbish and shopping trolleys. He was really shivering, and making these noises because it was so cold. We didn't know whether to laugh or not. He then picked up his clothes and walked back across the main road and into reception, still naked. I haven't taken much from him into my managerial career!"

Tommy is currently boss at Darlington, following in the footsteps of Brian Little.

Alan YOUNG

Under Jock's influence

We met Youngy in the Little Chef on the Six Hills Road, sparking golden memories of a tough, wiry Scot with an eye for goal and a fierce sense of loyalty, of right and wrong. He first appeared on our radar in 1979, scoring a hat-trick for Oldham to knock City out of the Cup.

At what point after that did Leicester make an approach for you?

"Well, I suppose I can say it all now, though it was illegal then and Jock Wallace, God bless him, is no longer with us. Martin Henderson was a boyhood friend and best man at my wedding in Oldham. He said to me before the game, 'The Gaffer fancies you. Would you be interested?' It was double my wages, but I was a bit concerned. I said to Jock, 'But I'm still with Oldham, what happens there?' Jock said, 'Leave that to me.'"

You scored two goals on your debut at home to Watford, and got off to a great start in your relationship with the fans.

"It's crucial. But with the Leicester City fans I think they liked what they saw anyway, because I'm a trier. I hated getting beat. I hated the referee giving them a throw-in when I knew it was ours. Little things like that. I used to argue and argue with them and get booked over a throw-in. I used to get hammered by Jock, who'd tell me to shut up and leave the referee alone, but I couldn't help myself."

We won the Second Division title in 1980 with a win at Orient on the last day...

"Yes, Martin got stripped by the fans and went down the tunnel in just his pants."

But there was one embarrassing blip that season – the Cup defeat by Harlow Town...

"Away at Harlow... Christ Almighty. We threw everything at them. The kitchen sink, the Hoover, everything. But we couldn't score. It was an awful night. Probably the worst. And what did we do on the way back? Stopped the coach at a pub. 'Get in the pub you lot,' Jock growled."

The following season was a tough one which saw City relegated from the top flight with a very young side...

"I think part of the reason was that Eddie Kelly left. The Gaffer let him go to Notts County and I don't think he should have done. We missed his experience and his guiding hand. I think it was at Birmingham when we hadn't scored for a few games and then we went 2-0 up in the first ten minutes. We all piled into the corner to celebrate and Eddie was grabbing us saying, 'Stay here! F***ing stay here!' Clive Thomas came over and Eddie said, 'Come on, we haven't scored for ages!' Little things like that, making them wait to take the kick-off, he'd picked up at Arsenal – and it all helped."

The following season you were injured at QPR. Was the plastic pitch to blame?

"Oh, absolutely. If it had been grass,

Photo: Neville Chadwick Photography.

I would've taken a divot. Because it was Astroturf, my boot stayed and my whole leg twisted, damaging my knee. As I twisted I felt something go in my knee and I fell into a policewoman behind the goal. By Monday I was in the hospital on London Road having it operated on. To get me fit again Jock had me run up the steps of the Double Decker with a sack of cement on my back. This was just days after coming out of hospital."

The 1982 Cup run included the incredible quarter-final against Shrewsbury. What was it like playing as stand-in goalie that day?

"I went up and caught a cross but Bernard McNally got underneath me and rolled me. I landed on my head. I was out for a wee while and then I had three or four seconds of thinking, 'Where am I? Why am I lying down?' I felt sick and couldn't see properly. I went off to the treatment room for a few minutes, then I was back out and there's little Steve Lynex in goal! Why, I'll never know. I went up front, and then Jock told me to go back in goal again! Five-two. There's never been a game like it."

Unfortunately, the semi-final against Tottenham was a huge anti-climax. And then Jock chose to leave us for the chance to manage Motherwell...

"It was a total shock. My immediate thought was that I didn't want to stay

"There were good defenders, bad ones and nasty ones. They were all enemies on the day."

at Leicester if Jock wasn't there. At his funeral, his wife Daphne told me he thought of me as a son, which was a marvellous thing to hear, because he was like a surrogate father to me. I went to see him when he was at Colchester, but he seemed a bit bent over and shuffling. That night we went back to Jock's house after the game. He pulled out a bottle of malt whisky, saying, 'I've been keeping this for a special occasion.' I couldn't wait any longer. I said, 'What's up with you, Gaffer?' He replied, 'Alan, I'm going to tell you to shut the f*** up and don't ask me that question again tonight.' He had the first signs of Parkinson's Disease. We got halfway down the bottle talking about our time at Leicester City. The players, the games... I remember him laughing about young Paul Friar squaring up to Joe Jordan when we beat Manchester United 1-0 at Filbert Street. It was three o'clock in the morning when he took us down to the local Chinese restaurant and started banging on the windows. 'Ahh, Mr Jock!' They let us in, made us a lovely dinner and never took a penny. It just shows you the effect he had on people."

AUTHORS

Simon Kimber grew up in Lutterworth and has been a Leicester City fan since his first visit to Filbert Street in 1970 at the tender age of eight, when City drew 0-0 with QPR. Simon has contributed to *The FOX* as assistant editor since 1992. He is the author of *Youn9y: The Autobiography of Alan Young* and is an accredited Premier League photographer. Gary Silke was born in Leicester and nagged his parents into a first trip to Filbert Street in 1975. His first game was also a 0-0 draw, against Ipswich. He founded The FOX in 1987 and has written a weekly *Leicester Mercury* column since 1991. Along with Derek Hammond – who took on the huge task of editing this book – he is co-author of *Got, Not Got*, runner-up in the BSBA Football Book of the Year 2012, and the following series of books. Neither Simon, Gary nor Derek can still quite believe that Leicester City won the Premier League...

PICTURE CREDITS

ACKNOWLEDGEMENTS

To arrange and deliver the number of interviews that *The FOX* has achieved over almost 30 years requires a lot of help and many a favour. The odd phone number here, or introduction there, and before you know it another interview is scheduled.

We must pass on our thanks to a sizeable list of generous helpers, but one in particular – Clare Morris – deserves a commendation for helping us time and again to set up interviews with the great and the good.

Wright, Clive Bloomfield, Jon Holmes, Hayley Towse and Rachel Cluley.

And, of course, thanks are due to everyone

interviewed here, for so generously giving up their time to share their ideas and opinions on Leicester City, or else to relive their precious, personal stories with us all.

Without Clare, this book would only be half the size that it turned out to be, and we cannot thank her enough.

In addition, special mentions to the following: Alan Birchenall, Alan Bennett, Paul Robbins, John Bleby, Richard Gamble, James Johnson, Jenny Whitby, John Hutchinson, Lee Marlow, Dean Eldredge, Bill Gilmore, Maxine and George Goble, Rob Power, David May, Geoff Peters, Kevin

TEAMWORK

Grateful thanks to everyone who subscribed in advance to *Can't Buy That Feeling...*

Ann Holyoak, Queniborough.

Trevor Jolley, Fornham St Martin.

Richard Pole, Markfield.

Charles Middleton, Scaynes Hill.

Nigel Hill, Chessington.

Andrew Crookes, Leicester.

Mark Peachey, Heckington.

Nigel French, Syston.

Graham Marsden, Desborough.

Mick Mills, Leicester.

Ed Moore, Narborough.

Craig Airey, Derby.

Dave Hilton, Blaby.

Dylan Jellett, Garforth.

Mark Beasley, Rugby.

Christopher Barlow,
                Middleton Cheney.

Richard Storer, Dorking.

Steve, Tom & Matt, Dubai Foxes.

Jamie Deering, Leicester.

Paul & Sam Jackson, Clanfield.

Joe, Ceri, Elaine & Harry
                Greenfield, Bourne.

Simon Rainer, Blaydon-on-Tyne.

Chris Kerslake, Swindon.

Lee Baldwin, Wigston.

Richard Willcocks, Sileby.

David Bentley, Sutton Bonington.

Mr Stephen P Wain, Oadby.

Chris Mayes, Leicester.

Malc Mayes, Leicester.

Tim Harvey, Leicester Forest East.

Paul Marlow, Corby.

Darren King, Enderby.

Paula Barlow, Scunthorpe.

Jon Leigh, Birmingham.

Richard Martin, Enderby.

Henryk Cynkar, Leicester.

Chris Baker, Sheffield.

Andrew Buckingham, Whitwick.

Andrew Paulson, Tonbridge.

Ian Paulson, Tonbridge.

Andy Wells, Brockely.

Gavin Musson, Hackney.

Paul Marcus, Mytchett.

Luke & Tiggy Bevans,
                New South Wales.

Andy May, Hungarton.

Bill Shelton, Leicester.

Bob Scott, East Grinstead.

Barry Lowe, Long Whatton.

Chris Lymn, Oadby.

Nigel Wright, Stags Head, London.

Jo Hoare, Torquay.

Stewart, Noah & Max Henry,
                              Mistley.

Nick Bonser, Upper Longdon.

James Johnson, Teddington.

Chris Griffin, Goostrey.

JA Johnson, Burton-on-Trent.

Mike Gurr, Ashby-de-la-Zouch.

Geoff Wheelton, Blaby.

Peter & James Burrows, Burley.

Mark King, Deal.

Ian Clements, Isle of Man.

Martyn Knott, Chilwell.

Robert Howling.

David Joss Buckley, Eltham Park.

Chris Lewitt, Market Harborough.

Loz & Jeannie Farmer, Lewes.

Philip York, Stoke Golding.

Daryl Burrows.

Allan Gambles, Houghton.

Ian Mason, Newark.

Darren Hankey, Durham.

David Toone, West Haddon.

Miroslaw Olszewski, Leicester.

Richard J Sherriff, Yate.

Ian King, Stoney Stanton.

Ady Martin, Hull.

John Campbell, Redgrave.

Tony Duric, Wigston.

Dave Johnson, Oadby.

Ian Johnson, Oadby.

Wayne Barker, Winchester.

Ken Herts, Batley.

Michael Joseph, London.

Helen Boyall, Barlestone.

Ian Chester, Alcester.

Barrie Underwood, Bradley Stoke.

Jamie Martin, Ashby-de-la-Zouch.

Garry McCreadie, Corby.

Ian Middleton, Leytonstone.

Peter Sharp, Humberstone.

Alan Mayes,
                    Norton Juxta Twycross.

Ed Thomas, Glen Parva.

Michael Auton, Stockton-on-Tees.

Nigel Lewis, South Croxton.

Raj Lal, Rainham.

Steve Hitchcox, Banbury.

Steve Scott, Wigston.

Alan Herbert, Long Itchington.

Iain & Janet Smith, Glenfield.

Rob & Archie O'Donnell,
        Market Harborough.

Nigel Cook, Wigginton.

John Pasiecznik, Hadfield.

Tom Hartwell, Ashby-de-la-Zouch.

Sophie Brookes, St Albans.

Brian Lee, Market Harborough.

Nick & Ethan Sharpe, Winchester.

Jeff Smith, York.

Chris Wellman, Littlehampton.

John Chambers, Northampton.

Sarah Newsome, Bramhall.

James Smith, London.

Stephen Smith, Sydney.

John May, Stevenage.

Tony Owen, Whitwick.

Bruce Anderson, St Neots.

Steven Burgess, Sheffield.

Ian Wharton, Carnforth.

Geoff Peters, Glen Parva.

Gavin Jacklin, Lutterworth.

David Wainwright, Loughborough.

Eddie Criglington, Wigston.

Mike & Julia Plant, St Albans.

Karl Hesmondhalgh, Elland.

Rob Waterton, Leicester.

Jeremy Wakefield, Clipston.

Chris Hulbert, Leicester.

Andy Hulbert, Whetstone.

Steve Buckley, Sheringham.

Tom Buckley, Portsmouth.

John Sparks, Swadlincote.

Keith Booth, Leicester.

Peter Kinal, Oakham.

Pat Mannion, Hinckley.

Irving Roberts,
        Market Harborough.

Michael Roberts.

Gavriel Family, Ramsgate.

Chris Hinsley, Leicester.

Jonathan Hinsley, Leicester.

Mark Robins, Leicester.

Jez Richards, Lancaster.

Simon Pollard,
        Market Harborough.

Glen White, Tokyo.

Steve Swift, Whitwick.

Robert Neville, Ashby-de-la-Zouch.

Adrian Hill, Lady Bay.

Andy Price, Hinckley.

David Wallwork, Cossall.

Mike Barker, Tutbury.

Simon Gilroy, Leicester.

Patrick Bishop.

Graham Carruthers, Loughton.

Andy Carruthers.

Andy 'Wints' Winter, Coalville.

Jonny Smith, Stockport.

Lloyd Glasgow, Leicester.

Claire Stevens,
            Market Harborough.

AP Bennett – aka Grandad Dogs,
            Great Bowden.

Julie Bamford, Birstall.

Paul Harrington, Arborfield.

The Foxes Trust.

Paul Loftus, Portlaw.

Martin Spencer, Desborough.

John Hutchinson, Leicester.

Alex Gurr, Ashby-de-la-Zouch.

AH Tyler, London.

Andy Wilkinson, Wigston.

Sharon Matts, Wigston.

Andy Oldham, Glenfield.

Phil Passingham,
            Market Harborough.

Tony Passingham,
            Market Harborough.

Neil Miller, Leicester.

Andy East, Leicester.

Nick Loney, Richmond.

Ian Harrington, Syston.

Adrian Harris, Sileby.

Nick Mullins, London.

Reid Anderson, Halifax.

Andy Buswell, Syston.

Henry Hammond, Oadby.

Tom Harvey, Salford.

Nigel & Matthew Shier,
            Skellingthorpe.

Paul Manson, Long Eaton.

Phil Moore, Baldock.

Bobby Moore, Nuneaton.

Glenn Brooks, Stoney Stanton.

Mike Carr, Ringoes, New Jersey.

Mark Harris, Stoney Stanton.

Shaun Hubbard, LE4.

Andy Buckingham, Northampton.

Stephen Parker, Kirkcaldy.

Dean Redshaw, Anstey.

Maria Prime, Muswell Hill.

Colleen Cator, Tipton.

Helen Cator.

Paul Kirk, Syston.

Mark Osborne, Epsom.

John Lunson, Twickenham.

Mark Weaver, Atherstone.

Geoff Wilkinson, Hartlepool.

Trevor Ringrose, Swindon.

Micky ADAMS Martin ALLEN
BARACLOUGH Alan BENNETT
David BLOOMFIELD Paddy BYR
Stephen CLEMENCE Stan COLLY
Roger DAVIES Tim DAVIES Paul
Sven Goran ERIKSSON Tim FLO
Phil GEE Colin GIBSON Davie G
Bryan HAMILTON Ian HOLLOWA
HOWARD Muzzy IZZET Pontus
Andy KING Tony JAMES Neil LI
Brian LITTLE Andy LOCHHEAD
MAY Gary McALLISTER Padd
McLINTOCK Tom MEIGHAN Jim
Carl MUGGLETON Richie NORM/
Martin O'NEILL Nigel PEARSON
PLEAT Kevin POOLE Chris POW
Iwan ROBERTS Dennis ROFE J
SMITH Richard SMITH David SPE
Peter TAYLOR Mark WALLINGTO
WHITE Mike WHITLOW Steve W
WORTHINGTON Tommy WRIG